WATTEAU'S SOLDIERS

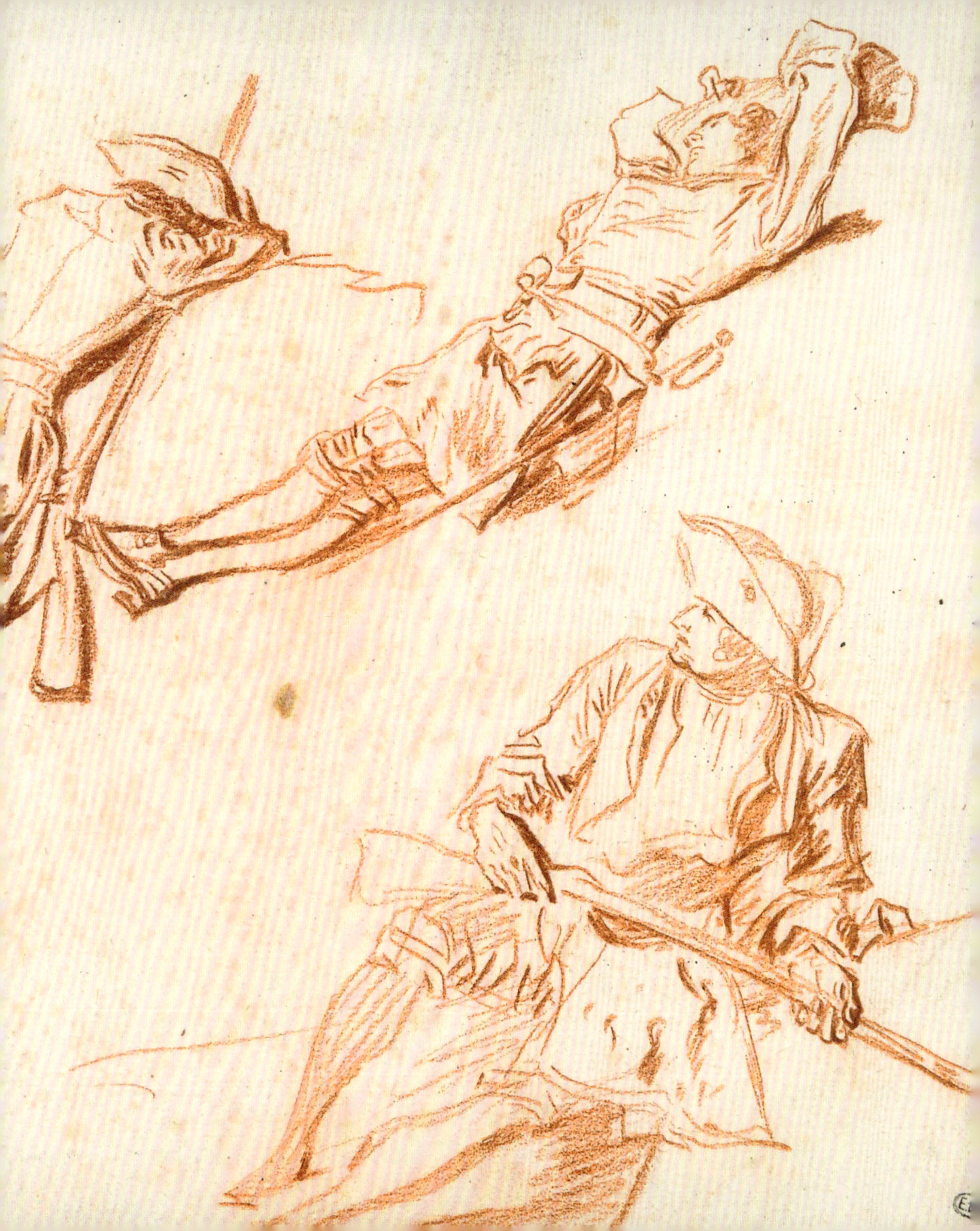

WATTEAU'S SOLDIERS

Scenes of Military Life in Eighteenth-Century France

Aaron Wile

The Frick Collection, New York
in association with D Giles Limited, London

This book is published in conjunction with the exhibition *Watteau's Soldiers: Scenes of Military Life in Eighteenth-Century France*, organized by The Frick Collection and on view from July 12, 2016, to October 2, 2016. The curator is Aaron Wile. Principal support for the exhibition has been provided by an anonymous gift in memory of Melvin R. Seiden, with major support from the David L. Klein, Jr. Foundation, Sally and Howard Lepow, The Andrew W. Mellon Foundation, and Aso O. Tavitian, with an additional contribution from Susannah Hunnewell Weiss.

Funding for the book has been provided by
THE VERSAILLES FOUNDATION, INC.

Published by The Frick Collection
Michaelyn Mitchell, Editor in Chief
Hilary Becker, Assistant Editor

In association with D Giles Limited

Designed by Alfonso Iacurci
Typeset in Garamond
Printed in China

The Frick Collection
1 East 70th Street
New York, NY 10021
www.frick.org

D Giles Limited
4 Crescent Stables
139 Upper Richmond Road
London SW15 2TN
www.gilesltd.com

Front cover and pages 70–71: Detail of *The Portal of Valenciennes*, ca. 1710–11 (cat. 46)
Back cover: Detail of *Three Studies of a Soldier, One from Behind*, ca. 1713–15 (cat. 27)
Frontispiece: Detail of *Three Studies of Resting Soldiers*, ca. 1713–14 (cat. 23)
At right: Detail of *Three Studies of a Soldier from Behind*, ca. 1713–15 (cat. 25)
Page 10: Detail of *The Halt*, ca. 1710 (cat. 43)
Pages 102–3: Detail of *Halt of a Detachment*, ca. 1715 (cat. 50)

Library of Congress Cataloging-in-Publication Data
Names: Wile, Aaron, 1986– author. | Watteau, Antoine, 1684–1721. Paintings. Selections. | Frick Collection, host institution.
Title: Watteau's soldiers : scenes of military life in eighteenth-century France / Aaron Wile.
Other titles: Scenes of military life in eighteenth-century France
Description: New York : The Frick Collection in association with D Giles Limited, London, 2016. | ?2016 | Published in conjunction with an exhibition organized by The Frick Collection, New York, and on view from July 12 to October 2, 2016. | Includes bibliographical references and index.
Identifiers: LCCN 2016001239| ISBN 9781907804793 (hardcover) | ISBN 9780912114668 (softcover)
Subjects: LCSH: Watteau, Antoine, 1684–1721—Themes, motives—Exhibitions. | Soldiers in art—Exhibitions. | Painting, French—18th century—Themes, motives—Exhibitions.
Classification: LCC ND553.W3 A4 2016 | DDC 759.4—dc23 LC record available at https://lccn.loc.gov/2016001239

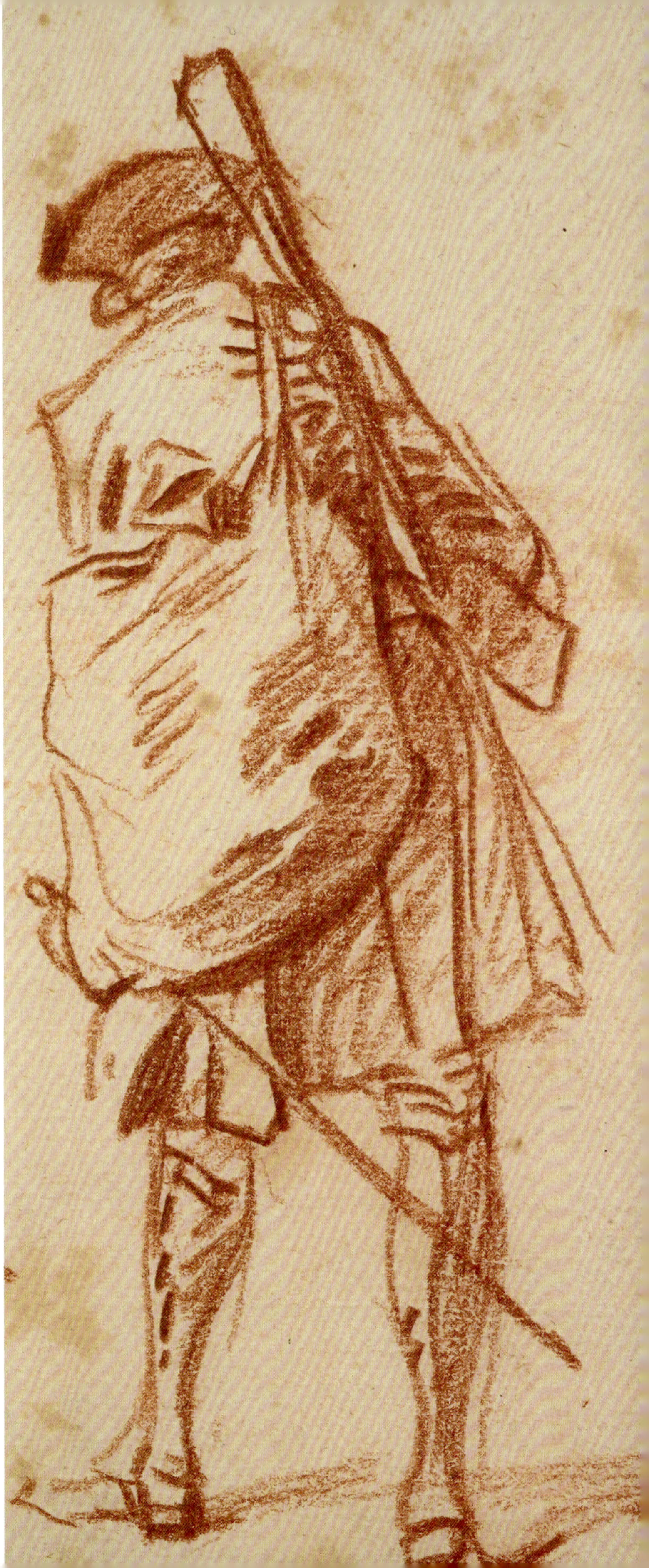

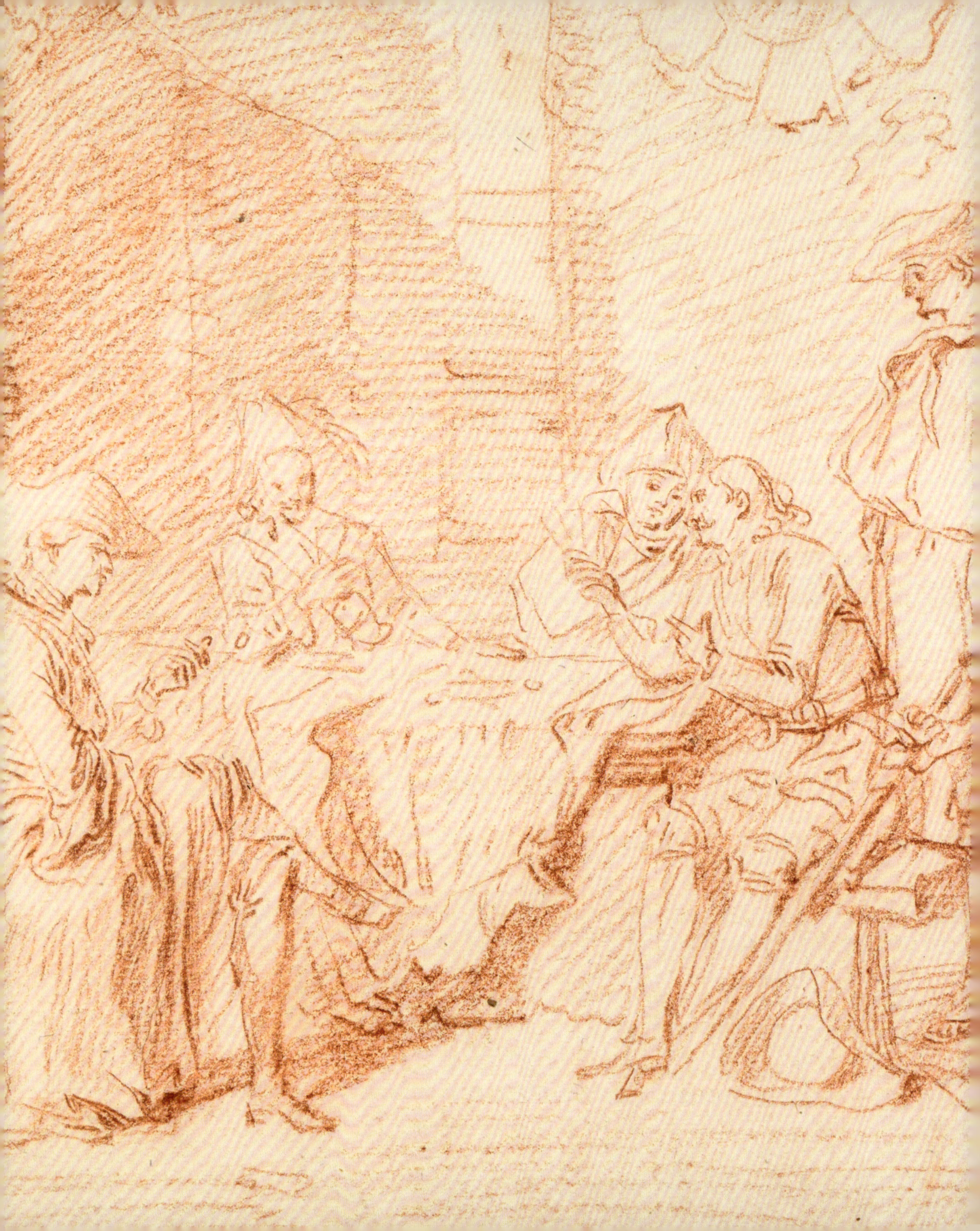

Director's Foreword

Jean-Antoine Watteau is most identified with the *fête galante*, a genre he invented that celebrates courtly love in dreamlike settings. To anyone familiar with this work, it should come as no surprise that the artist's earlier forays into the very different subject of military scenes also broke new ground. Rather than focus on battles, as his forerunners had, he looked to the noncombative aspects of the soldier's daily life. *Watteau's Soldiers* is the first exhibition devoted solely to these captivating paintings—many of which are lost and known today only through engravings—and has as its centerpiece the Frick's own *Portal of Valenciennes*.

First and foremost, I want to acknowledge the exhibition's curator Aaron Wile, the Frick's Anne L. Poulet Curatorial Fellow for 2014–16, for his intelligent organization of the show and for bringing new understanding to this body of work. I would also like to acknowledge the earlier work of our Chief Curator Emeritus, Edgar Munhall, on the Frick's *Portal of Valenciennes*, which offered key insights into the painting's history. Aaron offers a different view of Watteau's military works, one that places them in the context of contemporary artistic theory and philosophical notions about the self, showing that the scenes of military life and courtly love are not as dissimilar as one might think.

A number of Frick staff members have contributed to this project, most notably, Xavier F. Salomon, Peter Jay Sharp Chief Curator. Others include Adrian Anderson, Michael Bodycomb, Rebecca Brooke, Rika Burnham, Tia Chapman, Julia Day, Diane Farynyk, Allison Galea, Vivian Gill, Anita Jorgensen, Patrick King, Adrienne Lei, Alison Lonshein, David W. Martin, Heidi Rosenau, Stephen Saitas, Jeannette Sharpless, and Nick Stagliano. The editing and production of the catalogue were expertly overseen by Michaelyn Mitchell, Editor in Chief, with the assistance of Hilary Becker, Assistant Editor. It has been a pleasure to work with our publishing partner, D Giles Limited, London.

Public and private lenders from all over the world have generously lent their treasures, and we are extremely grateful to them for making this exhibition possible.

Finally, our profound gratitude goes to The Versailles Foundation, Inc., for their support of the catalogue. Our thanks also go to an anonymous donor whose generous support in memory of Melvin R. Seiden made the exhibition possible. Major support has also been provided by the David L. Klein, Jr. Foundation, Sally and Howard Lepow, The Andrew W. Mellon Foundation, and Aso O. Tavitian, with an additional contribution from Susannah Hunnewell Weiss.

Ian Wardropper
Director, The Frick Collection

Cat. 4 (detail)

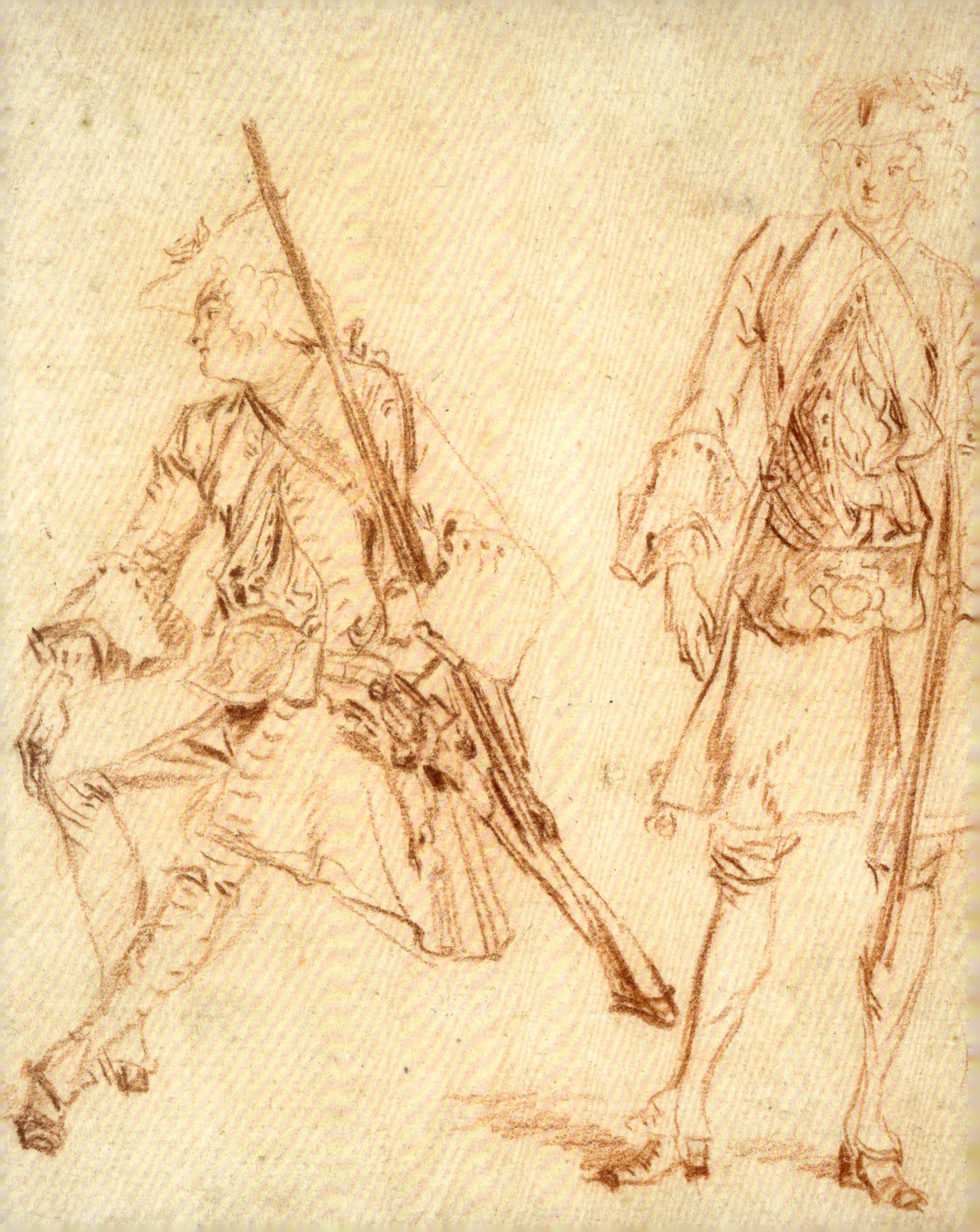

Acknowledgments

It gives me great pleasure to extend my gratitude to the many people who made this book and the exhibition it accompanies possible. First, I would like to thank Ian Wardropper, Director, and Xavier F. Salomon, Peter Jay Sharp Chief Curator at the Frick, for their unwavering support. I am particularly grateful to Xavier, who guided this project at every stage; I could not have asked for a more supportive and generous mentor.

Also at the Frick, curatorial colleagues Adam Eaker, Susan Grace Galassi, Margaret Iacono, Aimee Ng, Joanna Sheers Seidenstein, and especially Charlotte Vignon helped this project immensely, both practically and conceptually. In addition, I would like to thank Adrian Anderson, Michael Bodycomb, Rika Burnham, Tia Chapman, Diane Farynyk, Allison Galea, Lisa Goble, Robert Goldsmith, Caitlin Henningsen, Anita Jorgensen, George Koelle, Adrienne Lei, Alexis Light, Brittany Luberda, Jenna Nugent, Eloise Owens, Julie Rohou, Heidi Rosenau, Stephen Saitas, Jeannette Sharpless, Nick Stagliano, and Don Swanson, among many others at the Frick Collection and Library who were involved.

In preparing the exhibition, I have benefited from discussions with a number of eminent Watteau scholars and *dix-huitièmistes*: Martin Eidelberg, Margaret Morgan Grasselli, my advisor Ewa Lajer-Burcharth, Louis-Antoine Prat, Pierre Rosenberg, Perrin Stein, Jennifer Tonkovich, and Alan Wintermute. Martin Eidelberg and Alan Wintermute were particularly generous with their time and expertise. I am also indebted for their help in various ways with this project to Elizabeth Rudy, Edouard Kopp, and Mary Lister at the Harvard Art Museums; Ger Luijten at the Fondation Custodia in Paris and Ilona van Tuinen, then also at the Fondation Custodia; Mar Borobia and Maria Eugenia Alonso Asensio at the Thyssen-Bornemisza Museum in Madrid; Stephanie Buck, then at the Courtauld Gallery; Jennifer Alexander at the York Art Gallery; Emmanuelle Brugerolles at the École nationale supérieure des Beaux-Arts; Juliette Trey at the Musée du Louvre; Cristiana Romalli at Sotheby's; and Lionel Sauvage.

Susanna Caviglia, Adam Eaker, Caitlin Henningsen, Adam Jasienski, Ewa Lajer-Burcharth, Brittany Luberda, Meredith Martin, Elizabeth Petcu, David Pullins, Trevor Stark, Charlotte Vignon, Oliver Wunsch, and Daniel Zolli provided generous and insightful comments on my essay. Editor in Chief Michaelyn Mitchell and Assistant Editor Hilary Becker worked tirelessly to refine the text of the entire book.

Many thanks go to The Versailles Foundation, Inc., for their support of the catalogue, an anonymous donor whose generous support in memory of Melvin R. Seiden made the exhibition possible, as well as to the David L. Klein, Jr. Foundation, Sally and Howard Lepow, The Andrew W. Mellon Foundation, Aso O. Tavitian, and Susannah Hunnewell Weiss.

Finally, my family and friends, especially Nicholas Potts, provided much needed and much appreciated support, without which I could never have completed this project. I remain forever grateful to my parents, to whom this book is dedicated.

Aaron Wile

Cat. 16 (detail)

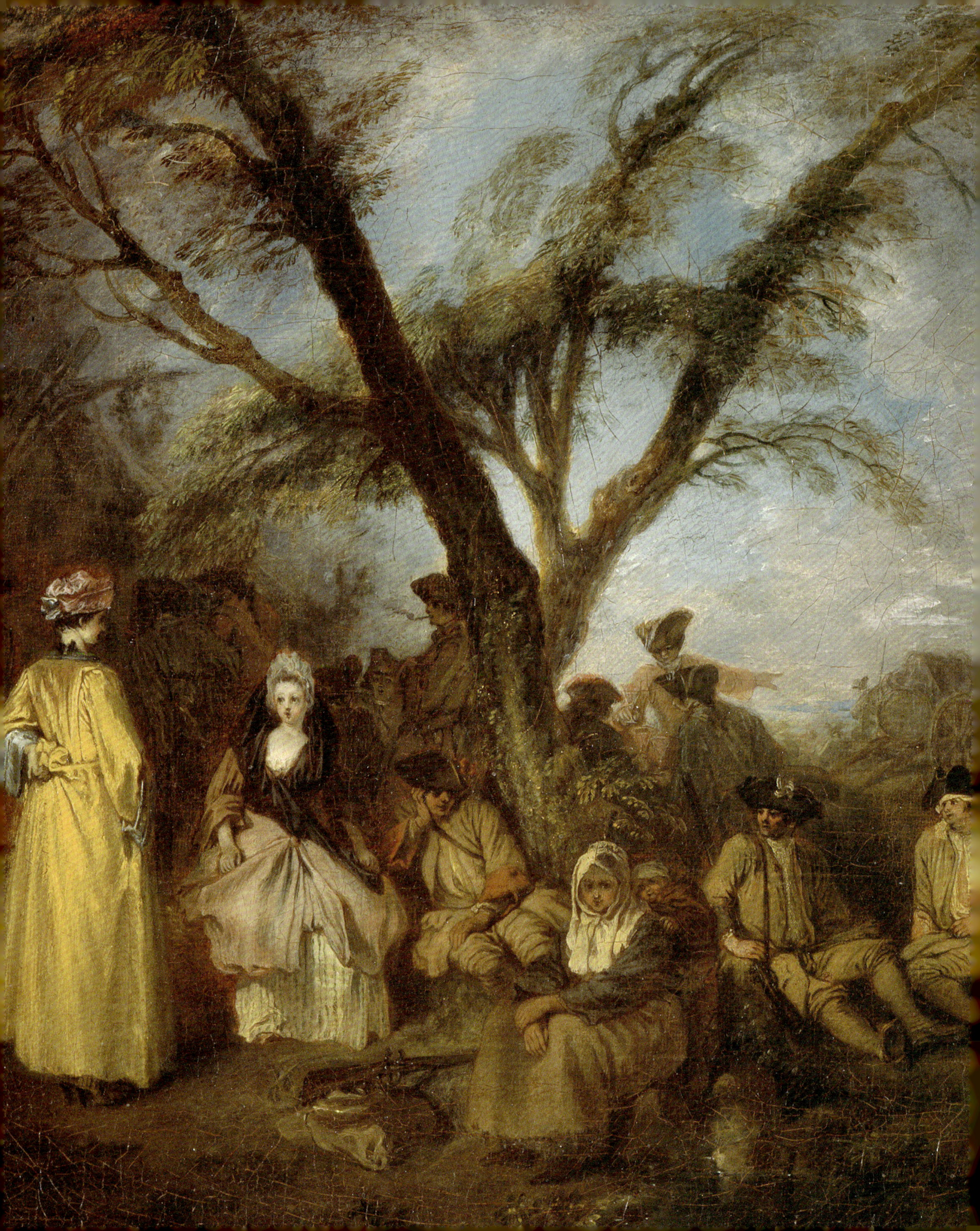

WATTEAU AND
THE INNER LIFE OF WAR

Figure 1

Jean-Antoine Watteau, *The Line of March* (*Défilé*), ca. 1710 (cat. 42)

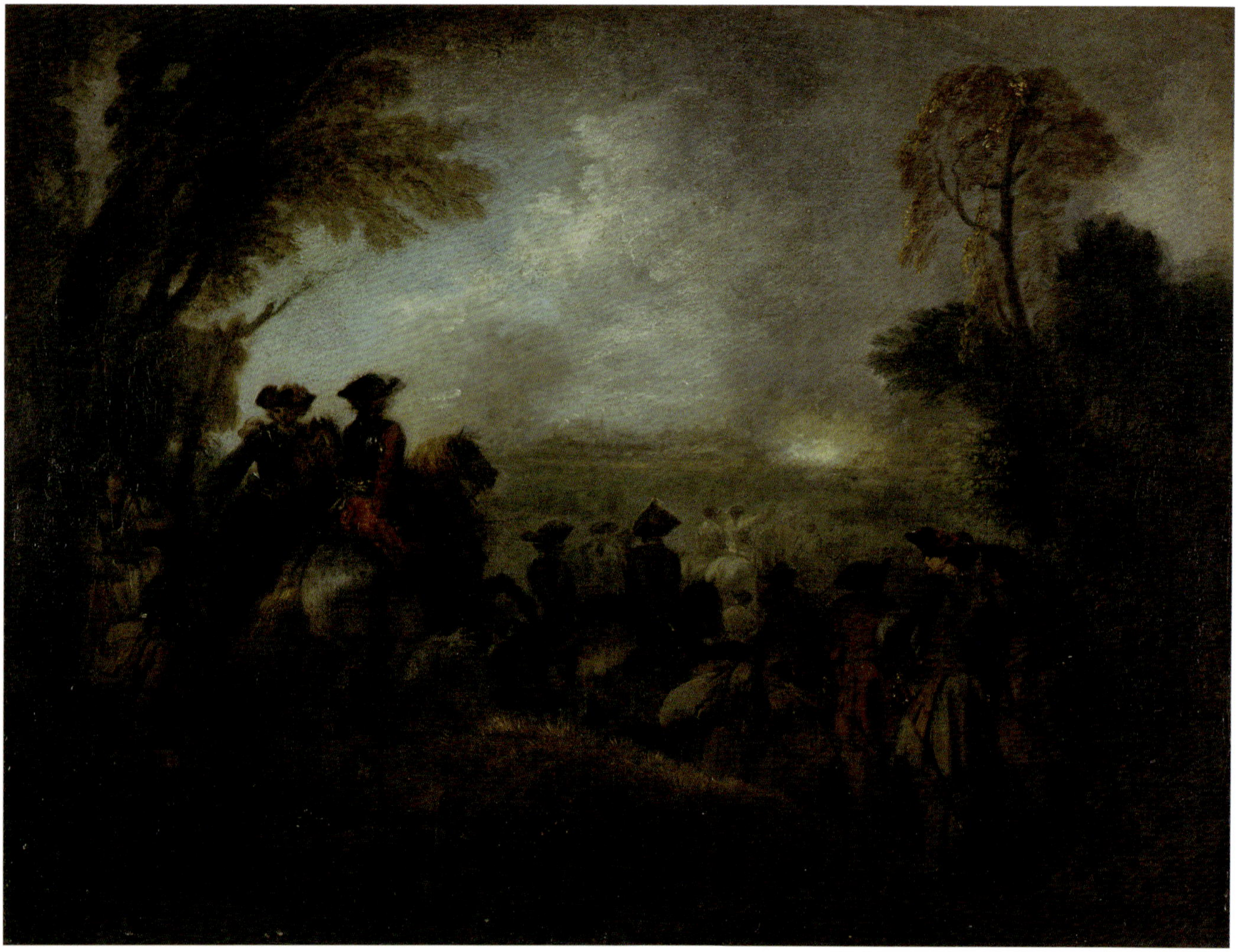

Watteau and war? We know Jean-Antoine Watteau as a painter of amorous aristocrats and melancholy actors, a dreamer of exquisite parklands and impossibly refined *fêtes*. It would be difficult to think of an artist further removed from the muck and misery of the battlefield. And yet, early in his career Watteau painted a number of military scenes. The panoply of martial glory on which most military painters of the time trained their gaze—the fearsome arms and snarling horses and splendid uniforms of generals glittering amid the smoke of cannon fire—held no interest for him. Instead, he focused on the prosaic aspects of war: the marches, halts, and encampments that defined the larger part of military life. Notable for their intimacy and deeply felt humanity, the resulting works show the quiet moments between the fighting, outside of the regimented discipline of drills and battle, when soldiers could rest and daydream, smoke pipes and play cards.

Watteau's friend and biographer Edme-François Gersaint (1694–1750) relates the origin of these paintings, a classic tale of success spurred by personal and creative frustration. Chafing under the supervision of his master, the decorative painter Claude III Audran, and homesick for his native Valenciennes in northeastern France, Watteau, Gersaint tells us, "ventured in his spare time to create a painting of genius that depicted a departure of troops." In order to raise funds for a trip home, he sold the painting to the art dealer Pierre Sirois, who "was so satisfied with the painting that he begged him to send a pendant to it from Valenciennes," a military halt, "all of it . . . painted from nature." In short order, the two paintings were "viewed by several collectors who wanted to acquire them, and soon his talent blossomed and was known to all connoisseurs."[1]

We do not know the extent to which Gersaint's tale is accurate or the product of mythmaking. What is fairly certain, however, is that Watteau left Paris for Valenciennes in September 1710[2] and produced about ten more military paintings and many more drawings—all executed between 1709 and 1715.[3] Today, four of the paintings are known only through engravings, and those that have survived are in relatively poor condition due in large part to Watteau's overreliance on oils to speed the drying process. As a result, the works have fallen into obscurity. Yet in their own day, they counted among his most admired productions. Even the comte de Caylus (1692–1765), a friend of the artist who was otherwise sharply critical of his work, admitted, "They are full of harmony and color, the heads are subtly and intelligently perceived, and the brushwork preserves the particular qualities of his drawing even in the extremities and the draperies and, generally, in his conception of the subject." He concluded that "these early works equaled the most beautiful works he did afterward."[4] By the end of the eighteenth century, they had entered into some of Europe's most prestigious collections, including those of Louis François Joseph de Bourbon, Prince of Conti, Cardinal Silvio Valenti Gonzaga, and Catherine the Great. Copies, in paint and print, proliferated.[5]

Watteau executed most of his military drawings and paintings during the War of the Spanish Succession (1701–14), which saw the French king, Louis XIV, battle against almost the whole of Europe in his bid to place his grandson, Philip, Duke of Anjou, on the Spanish throne. Louis ultimately succeeded in his quest, but the costs were staggering: hundreds of thousands of people died, and France was saddled with massive debts in the longest war of his reign. Watteau himself had close contact with the hardships caused by the war. He returned home to Valenciennes just months after the Battle of Malplaquet, the bloodiest battle of the eighteenth century, had been fought not far from the city.[6] Caylus himself served as an officer in the battle, and another friend of Watteau's, Antoine de La Roque, the owner of two of his military paintings, lost a leg in the battle.[7]

And yet, despite Watteau's exposure to the worst of the War of the Spanish Succession, there is no indication of fighting in his military works except for what is likely his first military painting, *The Line of March* (fig. 1). Nothing in them hints at a specific location or event, and, aside from signs of boredom and fatigue and the occasional arm in a sling, little suggests the suffering a soldier would experience in war. Even the Frick's *Portal of Valenciennes* (see fig. 22), though long assumed to depict the actual ramparts of Valenciennes, cannot be linked conclusively to the city.[8] Although marked in some ways by the War of the Spanish Succession, these are generalized images that give a mostly pleasant taste of a soldier's routine.

Anodyne images of war were the stock and trade of seventeenth-century Dutch and Flemish genre scenes by artists such as David Teniers the Younger (1610–1690) and especially Philips Wouwerman (1619–1668), whose work enjoyed a vogue among collectors in early eighteenth-century Paris and inspired Watteau's paintings.[9] But Watteau's work is set apart from these earlier examples by its focus on the *experience* of the soldier. More than his predecessors, Watteau offers an intimate vision of war, where the human element takes precedence. His soldiers seem to be endowed with an inner life, with subjectivity.

Watteau's distinctive approach has not gone unnoted. The historian Arlette Farge, for example, has written that Watteau paints "the private, interior space that emerges in human beings when they experience the misery of war."[10] But what does it mean to depict such a space? What does Watteau actually show us? In my view, what drives the artist's interest in military life is the way war, as an extreme circumstance outside the bounds of civil society, heightens and tests the primal relationship on which society itself is founded, the relationship between self and other.[11] At their core, his drawings and paintings wrestle with what it means to encounter other people in the world, to come face to face with the subjectivity of another. Far from making the experience of the soldier open for identification, they lay bare how alien that experience can be. An unbreachable and inviolable gap separates each self from every other self in Watteau's world, and the inner lives of his military subjects are revealed to be opaque, inscrutable, unknowable. This vision of selfhood penetrates Watteau's entire artistic process, structuring, in a fundamental way, how he went about making his art.

Figure 2

Jean-Antoine Watteau, *Four Studies of Soldiers at Rest and a Standing Woman*, ca. 1713–14 (cat. 22)

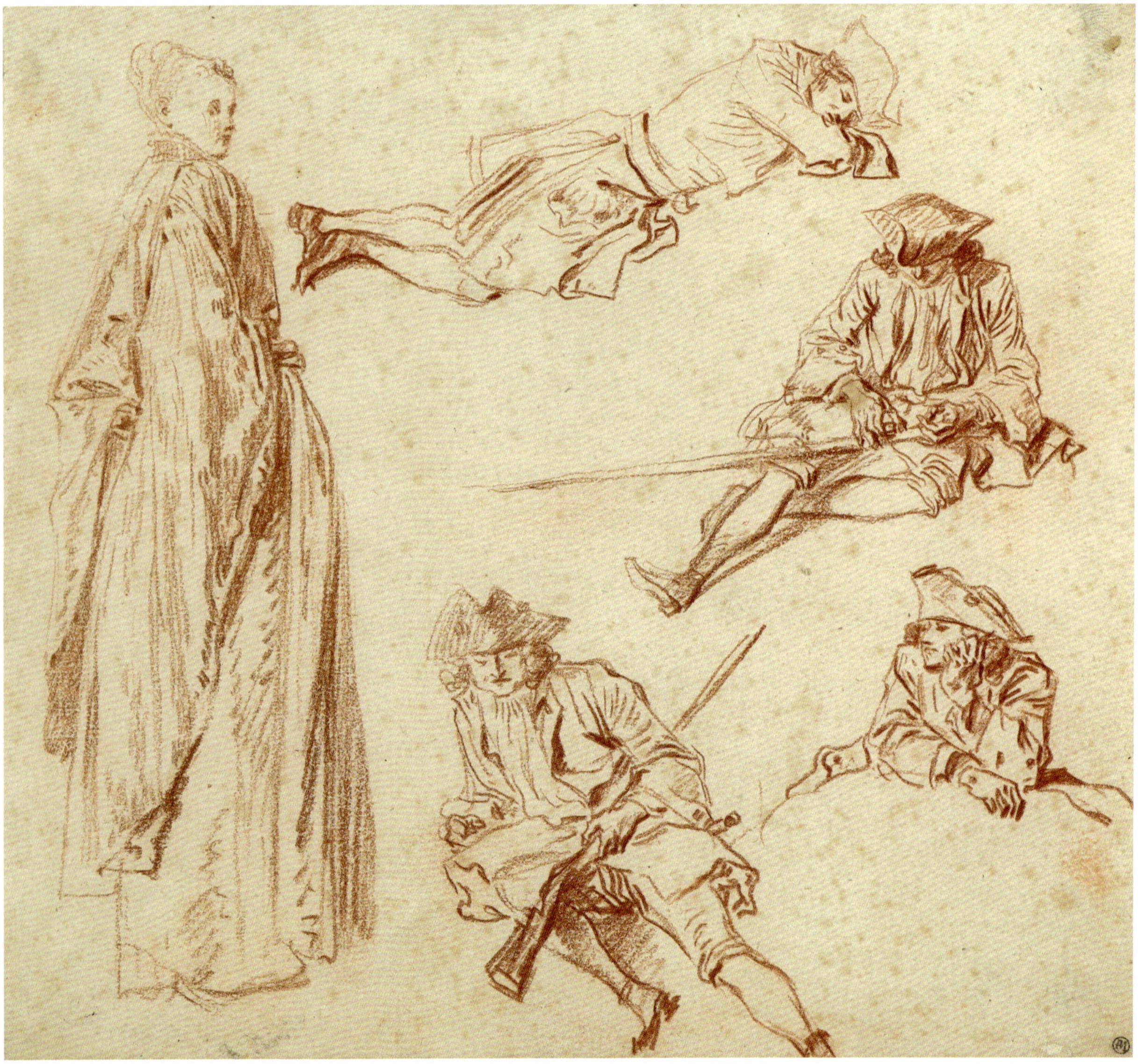

Drawing and Interiority

Before he conceived a painting, Watteau drew. He was, the connoisseur and art historian Dezallier d'Argenville (1680–1765) tells us, an inveterate draftsman, sketching "continually, even during his recreation and his walks."[12] He did not draw with a specific end in mind but rather found subjects that interested him and recorded his encounters in his notebooks.[13] Like most artists of the time, Watteau worked from live models. He departed from his contemporaries, however, in how he posed them. Eschewing the repertoire of poses borrowed from classical sculpture that formed the bedrock of academic practice, he depicted his models, as Caylus put it, "in attitudes that nature presented to him, preferring those that were the most simple."[14] Certainly, there was no shortage of soldiers to observe in such "natural" poses in Valenciennes. The military encampment of Le Quesnoy was not far from the city,[15] and it was here that his interest in military life seems to have blossomed. Although some studies were no doubt executed during his stay in Valenciennes, Watteau likely drew many more upon his return to Paris, posing models in ways inspired by what he had seen in his hometown.[16]

Watteau concentrated his attention on two kinds of studies: those exploring how soldiers rest and those exploring how they move. The persistence with which he probed these themes and the variety he managed to find within them are remarkable. In the first category, we find images of soldiers lying flat on their bellies, slumped over, leaning on their hands, burying their heads in their arms, or looking dreamily into the distance—no artist devoted so much attention to the various ways men position themselves in repose. *Four Studies of Soldiers at Rest and a Standing Woman* (fig. 2)—with its semicircle of soldiers shown sleeping, cleaning weapons, lost in reverie, or slouched as though in a stupor—and *Three Studies of Resting Soldiers* (fig. 3) are perhaps the most notable examples. But his explorations are also evident in such drawings as *Three Studies of a Soldier and a Kneeling Man* (fig. 4) and *Two Studies of a Soldier, One Kneeling, the Other Lying Down* (fig. 5).

Figure 3

Jean-Antoine Watteau, *Three Studies of Resting Soldiers*, ca. 1713–14 (cat. 23)

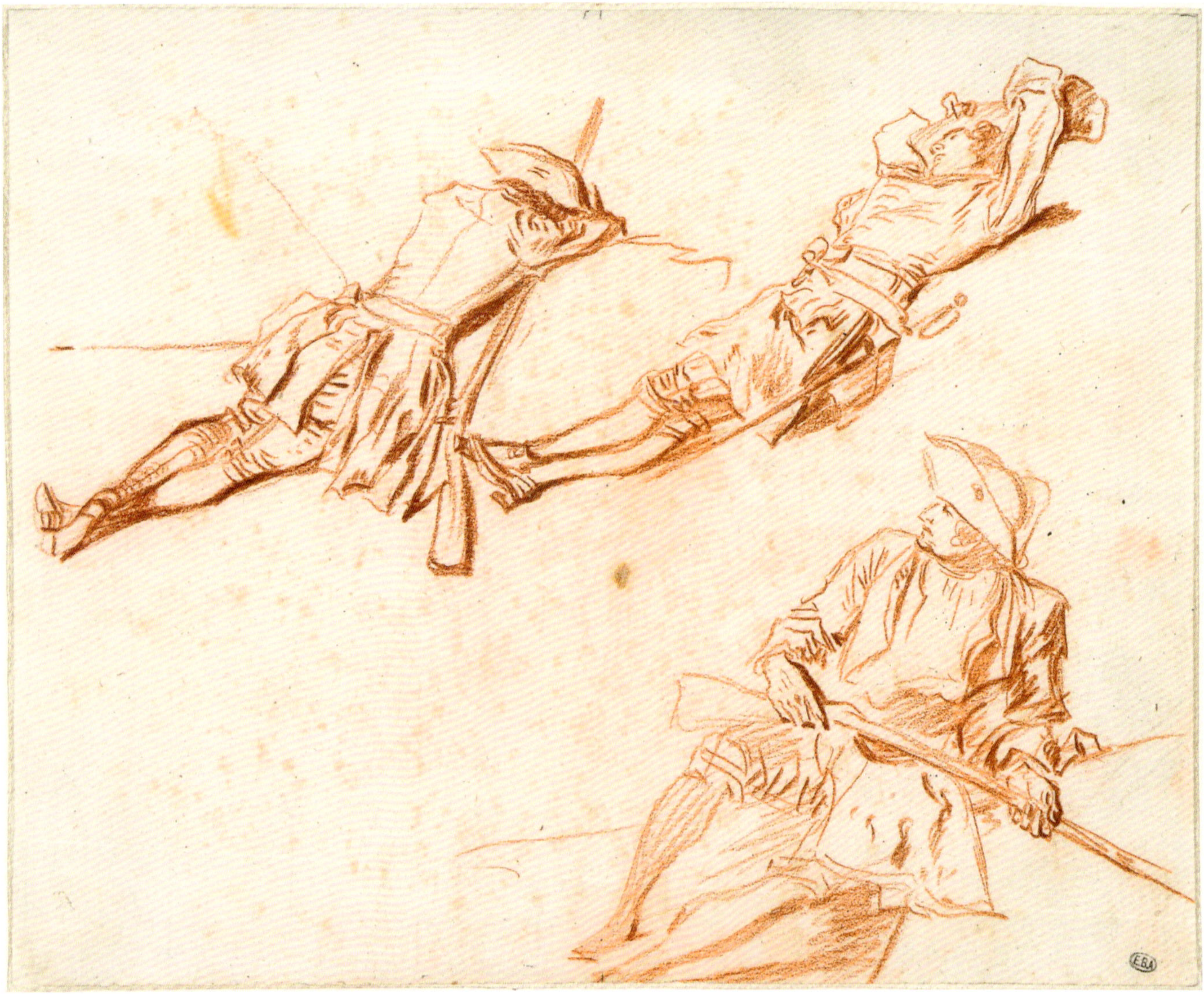

Figure 4

Jean-Antoine Watteau, *Three Studies of a Soldier and a Kneeling Man*, ca. 1710 (cat. 15)

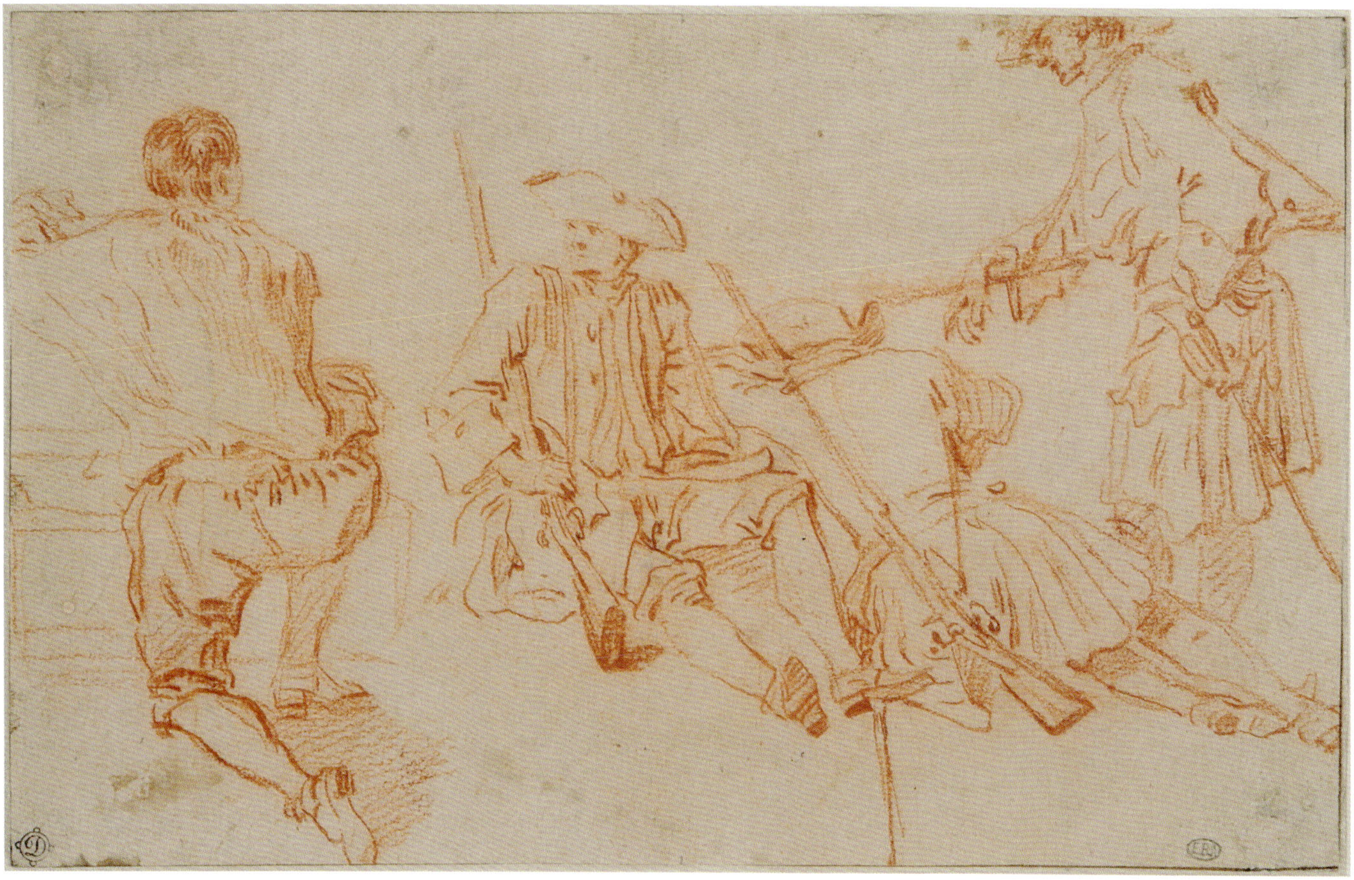

Figure 5

Jean-Antoine Watteau, *Two Studies of a Soldier, One Kneeling, the Other Lying Down*, ca. 1710 (cat. 14)

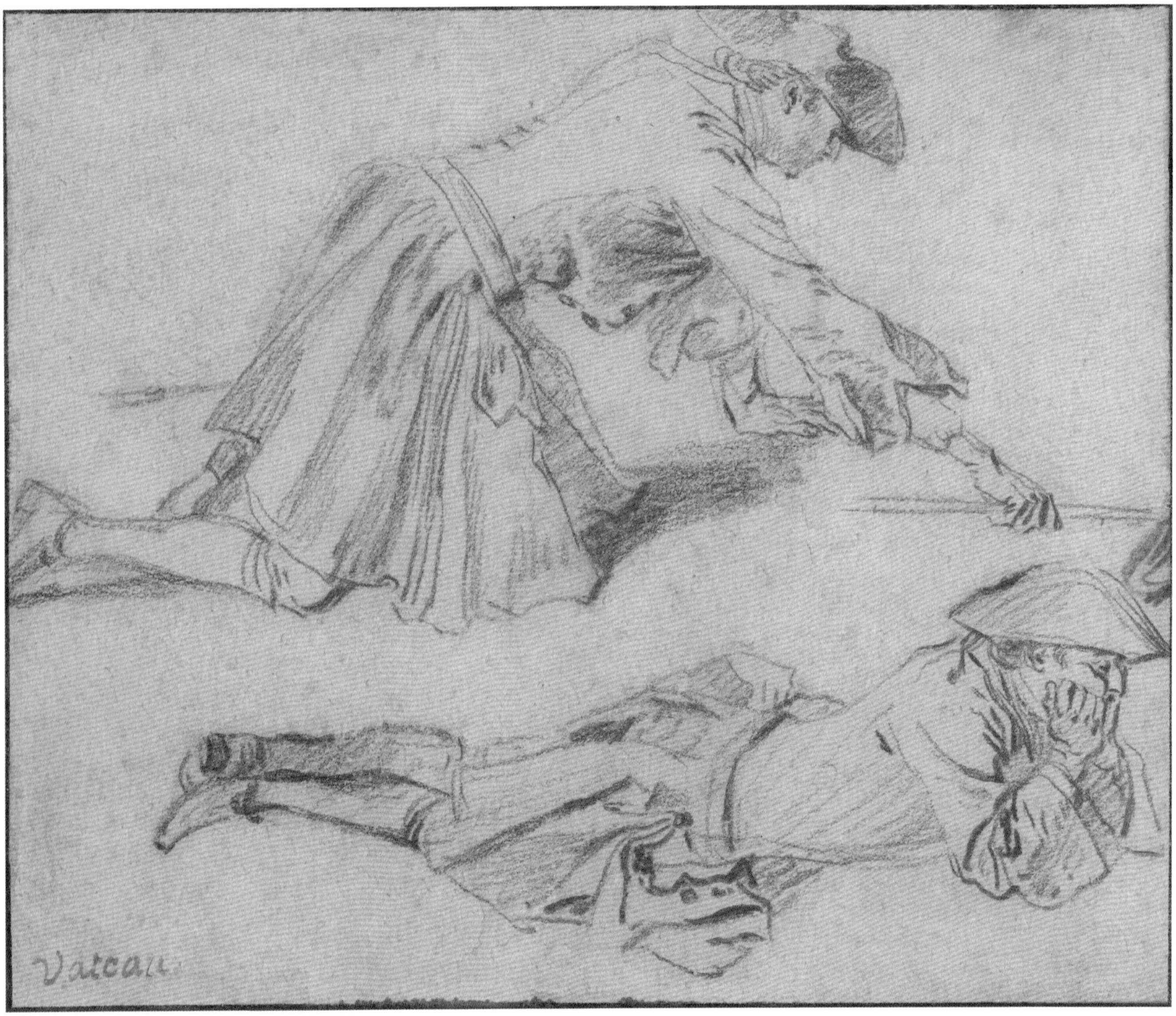

The drawings in the second category are no less attuned to the body's subtle changes in position and pose. The earliest examples, such as the sheets in Quimper (fig. 6) and Stockholm (cat. 1) showing a soldier performing military drills, are somewhat stiff, but the later examples—especially a group of five extraordinary drawings each showing a single soldier in three poses, including *Three Studies of a Soldier, One from Behind* (fig. 7)—are notable for their attention to the subtle variations of the movements of the body as it sways and shifts through space.

Although the two categories of drawing appear dissimilar—one concentrating on stasis, the other on movement—they are united in their focus on states of absorption and withdrawal. For what most attracts Watteau, as art historian Ewa Lajer-Burcharth puts it, are the "individual and private moments in his military subjects' existence . . . those thin slivers of time in which a soldier, in the dehumanizing context of war, may have personal experiences, and in which he is able to experience himself, if fleetingly, *as* a subject."[17] The artist's interest in his soldiers' inner lives is obvious in the studies of soldiers at rest. Their bodies show all the signs of a turn inward—of reflection, concentration, distraction, reverie, dreaming: moments when they could immerse themselves in their thoughts, feelings, and fantasies. Looking at these figures, who show little awareness either of the others on the page or of the beholder, we almost have the sense of intruding on a private moment.

Watteau's investment in interiority is perhaps less obvious in his studies of soldiers in movement, but here too their postures suggest retreat into the self. With the exception of the early sheets showing drills, the movements of these men have nothing to do with the disciplined, choreographed movements of a soldier in his official role. Rather, with their turned backs, they seem to be stealing themselves away, as though withdrawing from Watteau's gaze—the two figures in *Two Studies of a Soldier Viewed from Behind*, especially the man tying his shoe, are a case in point (fig. 8). The arrangement of bodies on the page often enhances this impression, creating an effect of turning away, of evading acknowledgment of the artist's presence, as in *Three Studies of a Military Drummer* (fig. 9). Even though they are on the move, the soldiers are absorbed within themselves.

Figure 6

Jean-Antoine Watteau, *Six Studies of a Soldier Charging His Musket*, ca. 1709 (cat. 2)

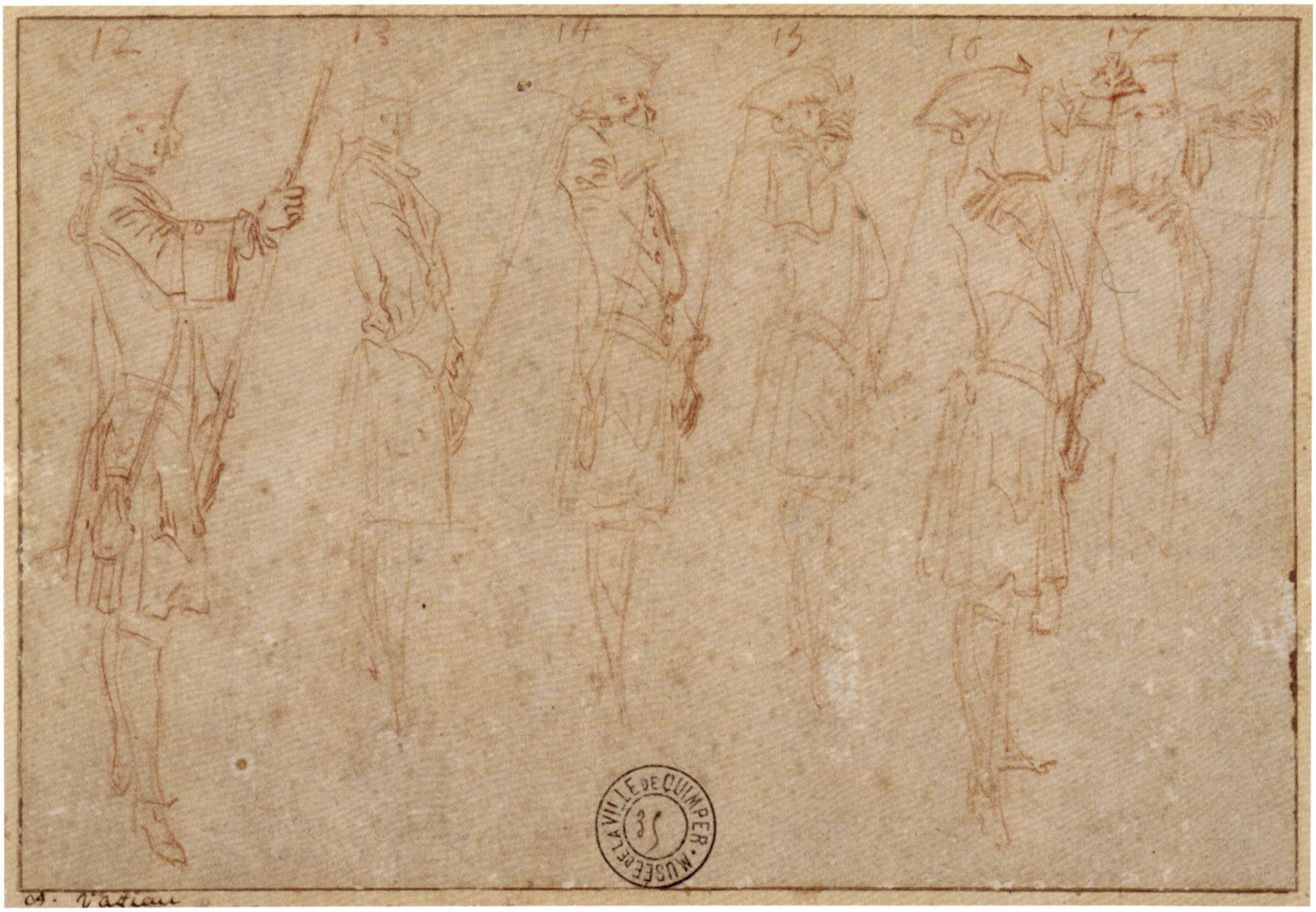

Figure 7

Jean-Antoine Watteau, *Three Studies of a Soldier, One from Behind*, ca. 1713–15 (cat. 27)

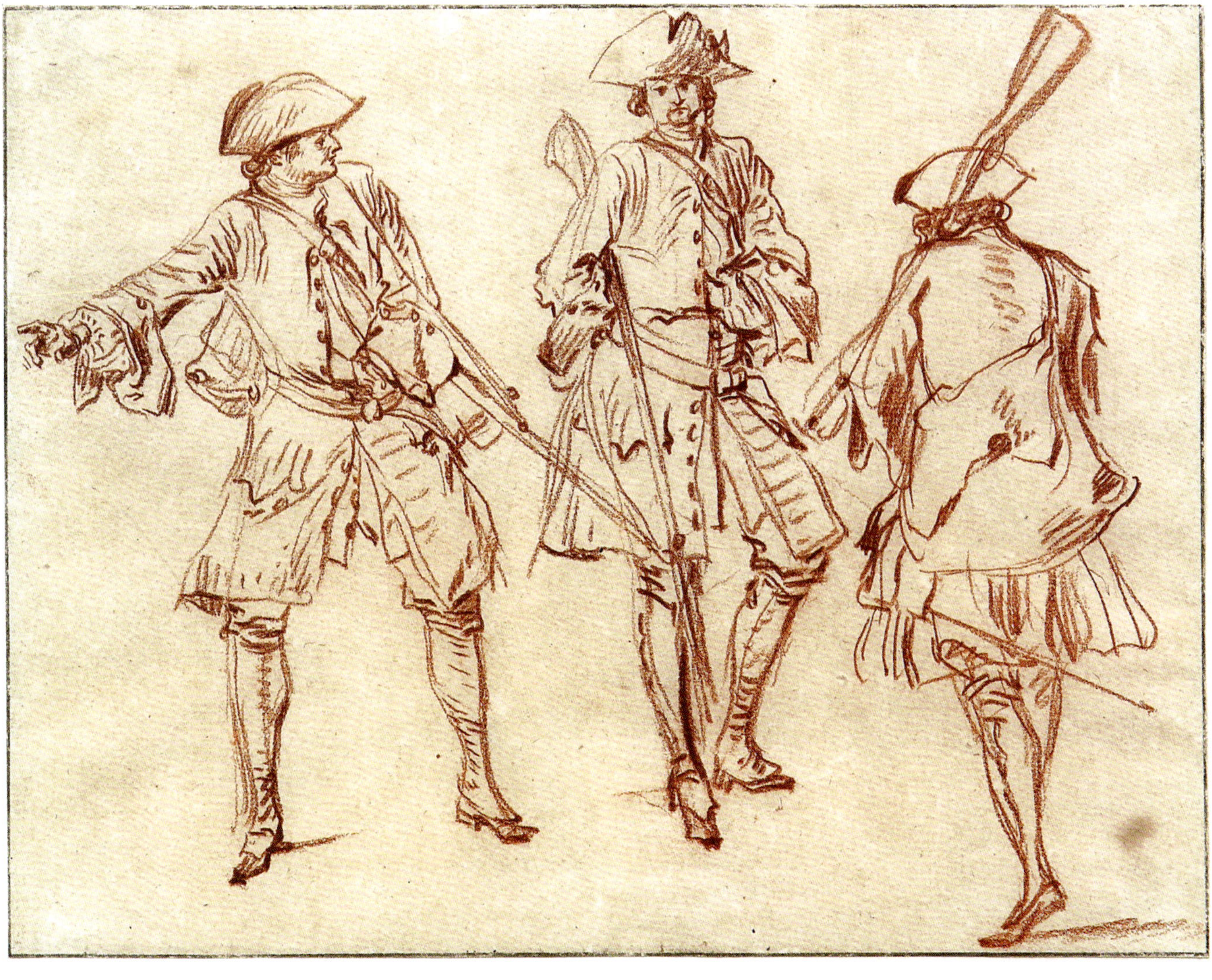

Figure 8

Jean-Antoine Watteau, *Two Studies of a Soldier Viewed from Behind*, ca. 1712 (cat. 18)

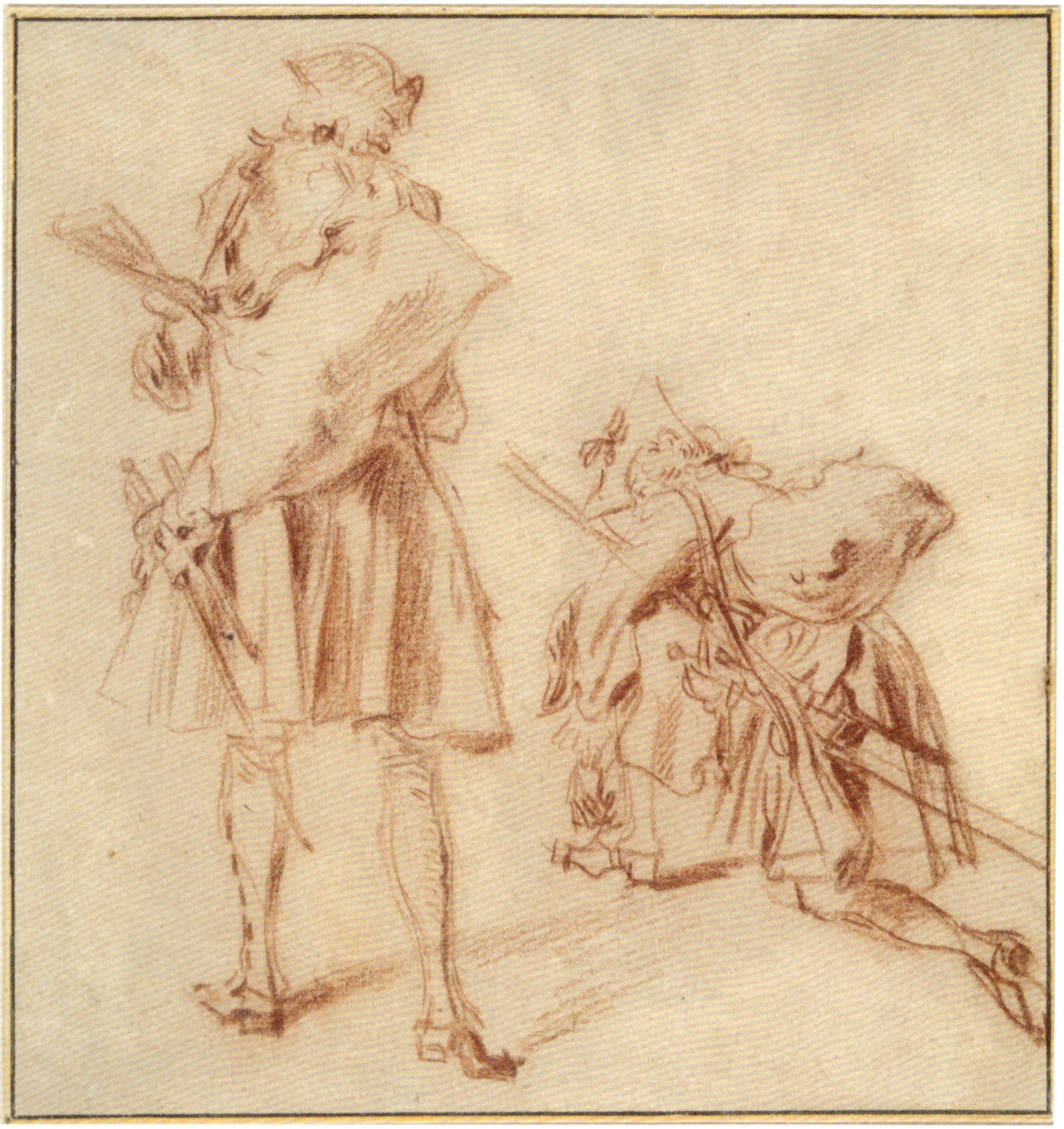

Watteau's focus on his soldiers' inner lives has its roots in momentous changes in the way the self was conceived around the end of the seventeenth century. As literary historian Joan DeJean has argued, the crucial years between 1660 and 1715, particularly in France, saw nothing short of a revolution in human subjectivity.[18] If the passions (as emotions were then called) had, since antiquity, been seen as external forces acting on a passive subject, now they were increasingly understood as the core of identity.[19] This was the period, for instance, that saw the publication of the first modern psychological novel, *The Princesse de Clèves* by Madame de Lafayette (1678), which put the emotions and thoughts of its characters under unprecedented scrutiny. Lafayette was far from alone in her investigations: a wide variety of philosophers, theologians, playwrights, and novelists developed a new vocabulary of affect and in the process charted psychological territory hitherto unexplored. Their efforts helped carve out, for the first time in a secular context, a conceptual space in which interiority could be examined, discussed, and understood.[20] For the writer Charles Perrault (1628–1703), it was precisely the emergence of such a space that marked the modernity of his age. "[J]ust as anatomy has discovered in the heart ducts, valves, fibers, movements, and symptoms of which the Ancients had no knowledge," he declared, "in the same manner moral philosophy has discovered attractions, aversions, desires, and repulsions which the Ancients never knew."[21]

This larger cultural shift helps explain Watteau's focus, but the object of his gaze—the infantryman, the common soldier—was nonetheless at odds with prevailing attitudes. For in the seventeenth and eighteenth centuries, the rank and file were largely anonymous, forgotten behind the ideal of aristocratic honor they were enlisted to serve; their individual experience held no interest.[22] The indifference to the common soldier was compounded by changes in the way warfare was conceived and conducted in the last years of Louis XIV's reign. Earlier, Louis XIV himself often led his troops into battle or else entrusted decisions to his generals on the field, but as he grew older he withdrew from the battlefield and managed every detail of war from behind his desk at Versailles. War became increasingly a science, a mechanized, rational

Figure 9

Jean-Antoine Watteau, *Three Studies of a Military Drummer*, ca. 1713 (cat. 21)

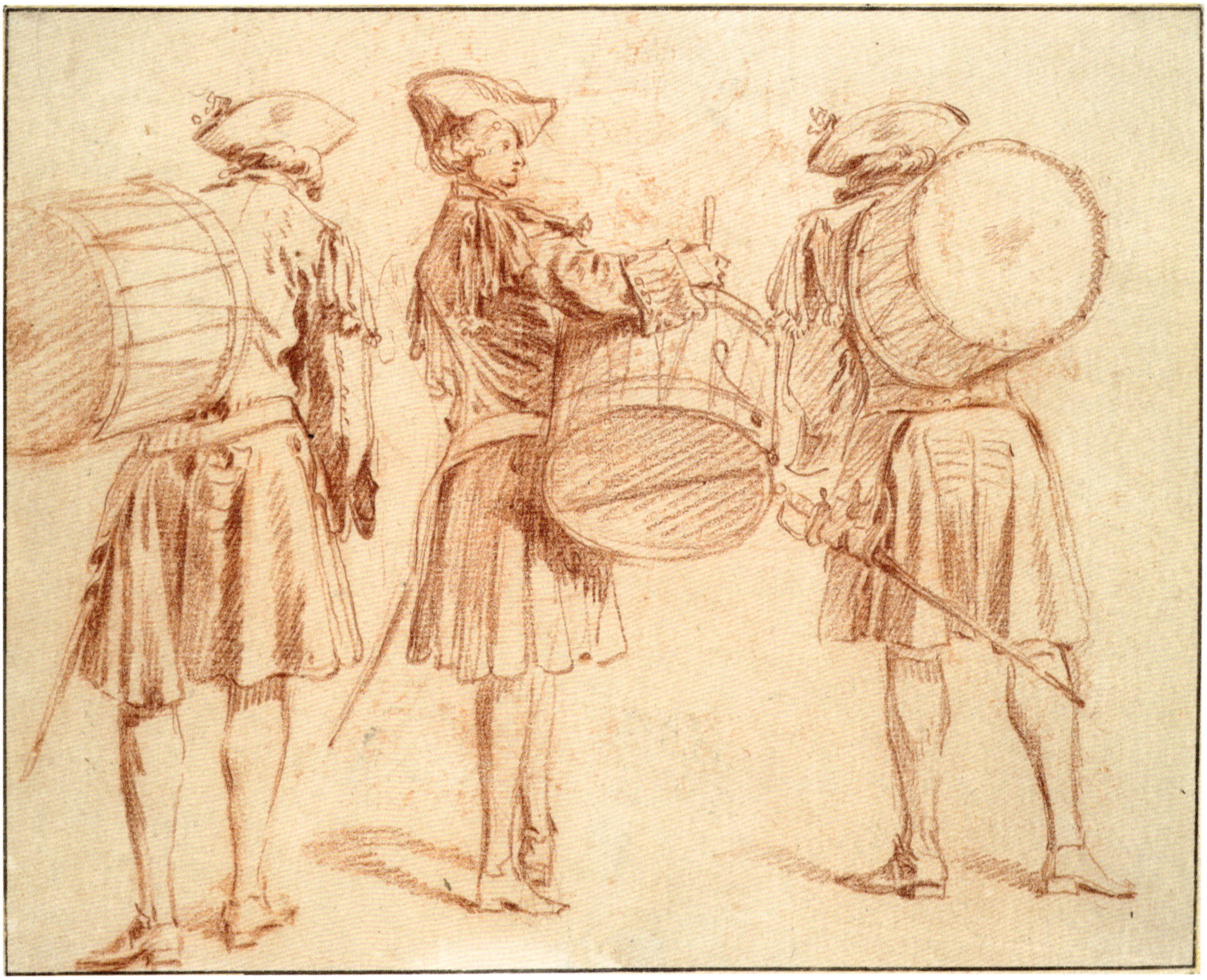

system that minimized the role of interpersonal relationships.[23] Exemplifying this approach was a treatise written by Jean-François de Chastenet de Puységur (1655–1743), an officer in Louis XIV's army at the beginning of the eighteenth century. In the foreword to the work, its publisher promised that it develops "in a sensible and concrete manner, a theory of war independent of practice and explains everything related to it in such a detailed and easy way that, just by studying it, and without leaving one's office, any attentive man, even if not very intelligent, could learn to apply these true principles to all the movements that it is necessary for troops to perform, whether for marches or for orders on the battlefield."[24] Sentiments like Puységur's meant that the common soldier, already faceless, was largely bypassed by the period's interest in subjectivity.

From this perspective, Watteau's military works broke new ground. If Louis XIV transformed war into an abstract system that operated according to rational rules, Watteau drew the remainder of this effort, the human, subjective element at the margins of the state's war machine. He pulled the common soldier from the oblivion to which he had been consigned, focusing precisely on the individual experiences that were otherwise discounted or neglected (even if his soldiers are not individualized portraits but generalized types). His efforts have a kinship with a nascent pacifist movement—led by the dauphin's former tutor François Fénelon (1651–1715)—that brought new attention to the plight of the common soldier, a connection already proposed in an influential reading of the military works.[25] They may even be linked to the subsequent push for reform in the middle of the eighteenth century that would transform prevailing views of the common soldier. The leaders of this campaign, influenced by Enlightenment ideas about human rights and autonomy, saw soldiers no longer as cogs in a machine but as what one scholar has called *soldats sensibles*, men whose physical and psychological suffering in the punishing conditions of military life demanded study and care. Even lowly infantrymen were now recognized as complex individuals with needs, desires, and rights.[26] Watteau's attempts to give visual form to his military subjects' inner experience were an early expression of this shift.

Drawing and the Impermeable Self

Watteau, however, was no Enlightenment reformer, confident that the psyche of the soldier would yield itself as an object of knowledge and improvement. While he acknowledges, in a way that no previous artist had, his soldiers' *sensibilité*, his drawings betray a more complex attitude about the intelligibility of the interior self. The late seventeenth century's investigation of the human heart fostered a dream of transparency between self and other, in which the contents of one's inner life could open for sympathetic identification.[27] A more or less direct line leads from this attitude to the emergence of the *soldat sensible* in the middle of the eighteenth century, when the "affective revolution" of the previous century finally caught up with the common soldier. But this was far from the only view on the matter. Just as the human heart was established as an object of knowledge, there emerged a new skepticism about its legibility. A closer examination of Watteau's chalk studies reveals that they in fact engaged this skeptical current far more than has previously been acknowledged: at their core, the drawings pivot on the intersubjective exchange between self and other that fired the "affective revolution" of the turn of the century. Yet, far from confirming the total accessibility of the human heart, they reveal that perfect knowledge of the other is impossible, that the dream of transparency is just that—a dream.

To flesh out how they do so, it would be instructive to revisit the well-worn comparison between Watteau and his predecessor Charles Le Brun (1619–1690), the most influential French painter of the second half of the seventeenth century.[28] Contrary to his reputation as a cold and inflexible rationalist, no artist better exemplifies his age's "discovery" of the interior self than Le Brun—indeed, for the painter's contemporaries, his commitment to reasoned principles was the source of his paintings' affective power. In his landmark lecture on expression given at the Royal Academy of Painting and Sculpture in 1668—and published for the first time in 1698 as *Méthode pour apprendre à dessiner les passions*—Le Brun proposed a revolutionary system of expression. Drawing on the work of Descartes, the artist argued that the movements of the face were the external manifestation of the internal movements of the

Figure 10

Charles Le Brun, *La Douleur corporelle et aiguë* (Bodily and Acute Pain). Pen, black ink, and black chalk on white paper, 7 ¾ × 10 in. (19.7 × 25.4 cm). Musée du Louvre, Paris (28306 recto)

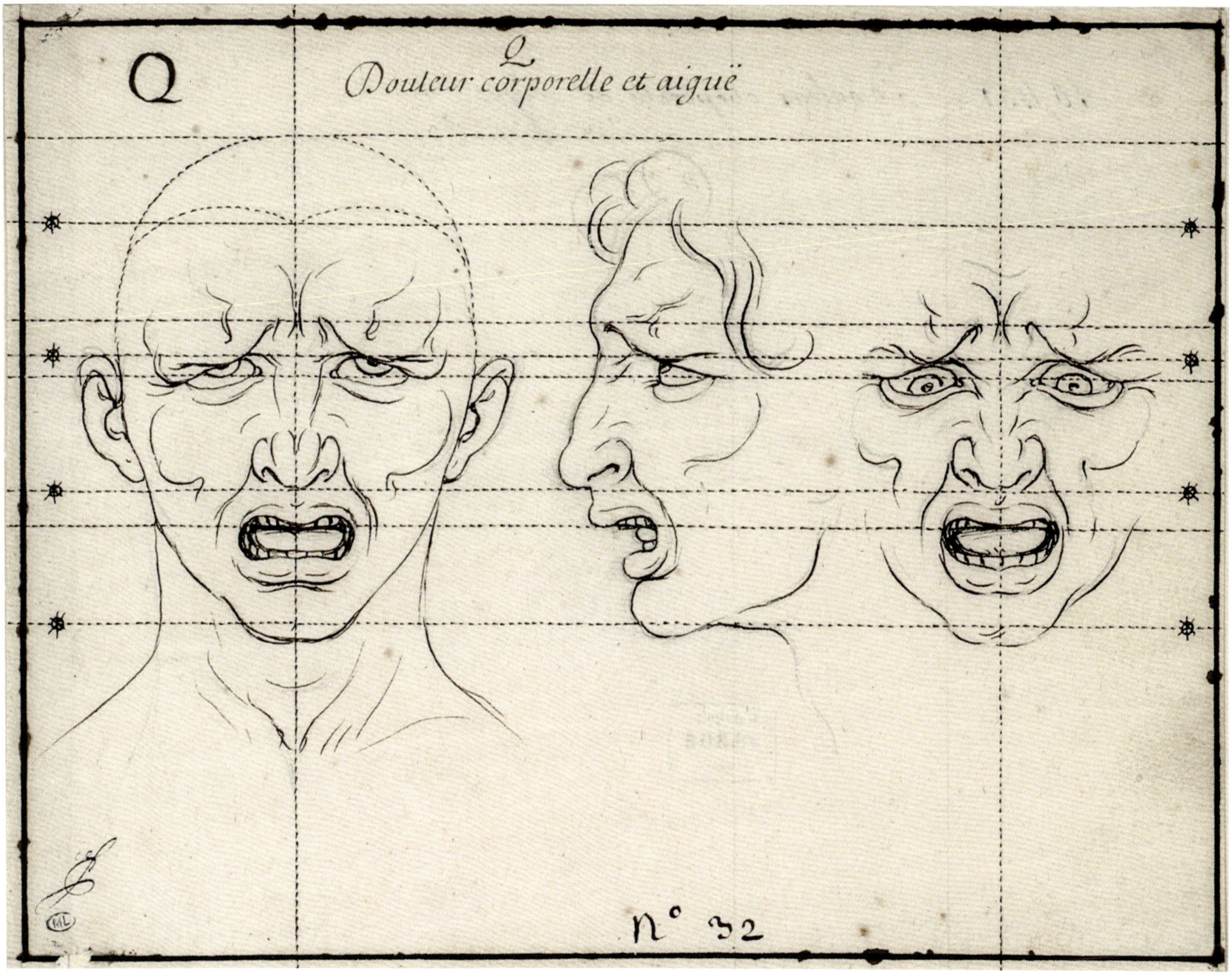

Figure 11

Charles Le Brun, *The Family of Darius at the Feet of Alexander*, also called *The Tent of Darius*, 1660–61. Oil on canvas, 117 ⅜ × 178 ⅜ in. (298 × 453 cm). Châteaux de Versailles et de Trianon (MV6165)

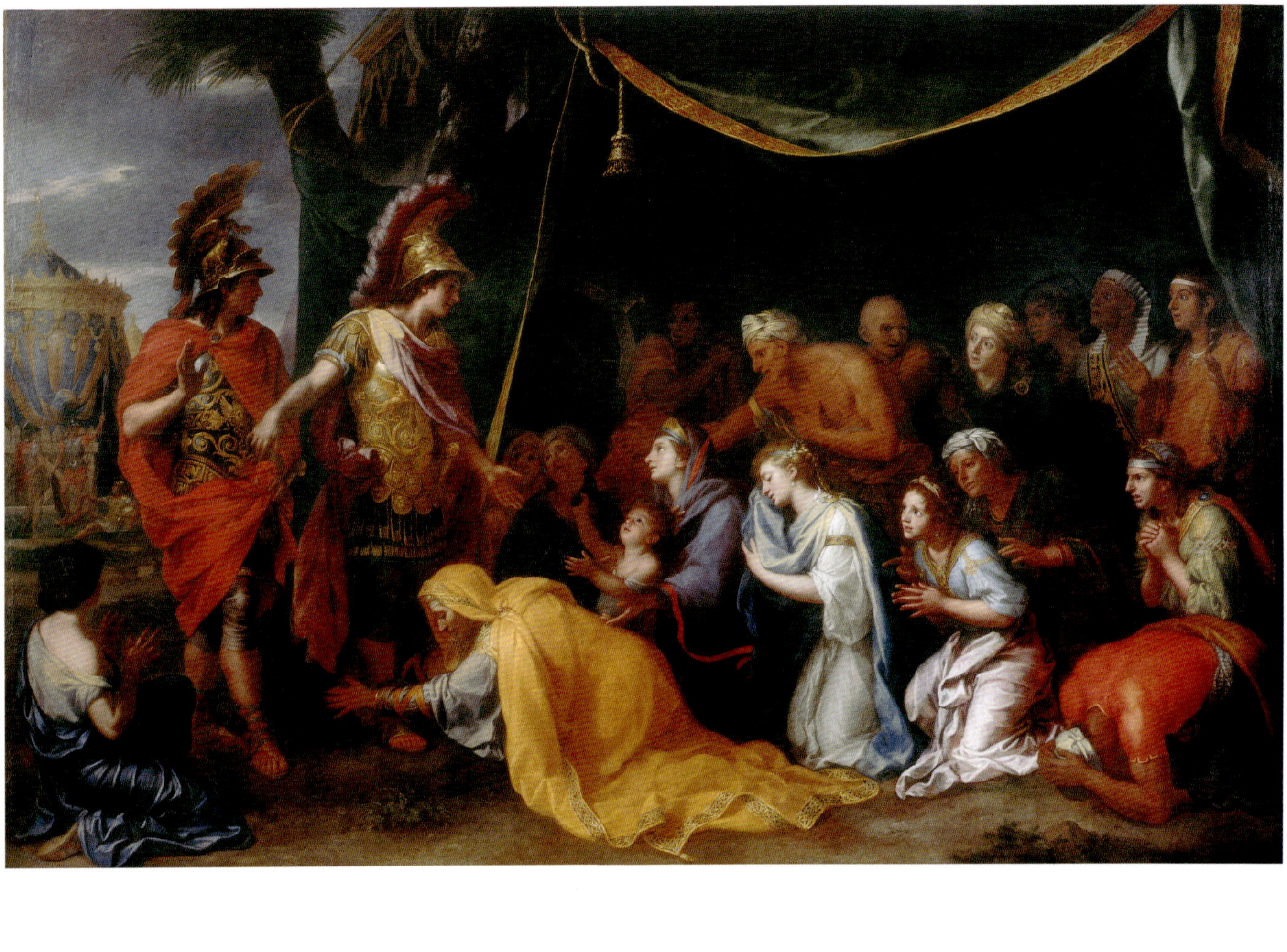

soul; once the mechanisms of the soul's movements and their resulting effects on the exterior were discovered, the face could become a legible, because universal, sign of emotion. To this end, he produced schematic renderings of the movements of the face that corresponded to various emotions: admiration, joy, sadness, anger, and more specific states like "bodily and acute pain" (fig. 10). Artists, he hoped, could use these facial types to endow their canvases with an emotional life immediately accessible to their audiences.[29]

Le Brun's own painting *The Family of Darius at the Feet of Alexander* (fig. 11), which he would later draw on in his lecture on the passions, exemplifies the potential of his system.[30] Here, Le Brun portrays the moment when Alexander, fresh from his triumph over the Persian emperor Darius at Issus, enters the encampment of the queens of Persia with his general, Hephaestion. Lying prostrate at Alexander's feet, the queens plead to him for clemency, even though some of the supplicants mistake Hephaestion for Alexander. Every face, every expression, is calibrated to reveal the emotions of the figures to the spectator, an intention borne out in a text by André Félibien (1610–1695)—published in 1663 to celebrate the painting—where the art theorist claims to read, with perfect clarity, the expression of each of the figures and the emotions they signify.[31] Of Darius's wife, the woman in blue holding her son, for example, he asserts, "One sees in her eyes and on her whole face the manifest unhappiness about the condition to which she has been reduced. . . . And one can even discover in her eyes and in all of her features the hope she has in the clemency of so generous a conqueror."[32] This was the dream of perfect affective legibility. With Le Brun's rational, universal rules, the inner states of any figure in a narrative painting could be rendered through the exterior, through the face.

If Le Brun embodied the normative approach to representing interiority, Watteau, working outside the confines of the grand genre of history painting, takes another tack. He eschews head studies of soldiers altogether, and what we see of their features yields little information.[33] More often than not the faces are obscured, turned to the side or buried in their arms, but even when he shows us one head on, as in *Three Studies of a Soldier, One from Behind* (see fig. 7), it appears almost affectless—eyes, eyebrows, and lips barely suggested by a few

Figure 12

Antoine Coypel, *Head of a Soldier*, ca. 1714–16.
Black and red chalk, heightened with white; on brown paper with grid, 5 ½ × 6 ⅜ in. (14 × 16.3 cm).
Musée du Louvre, Paris (25704 recto)

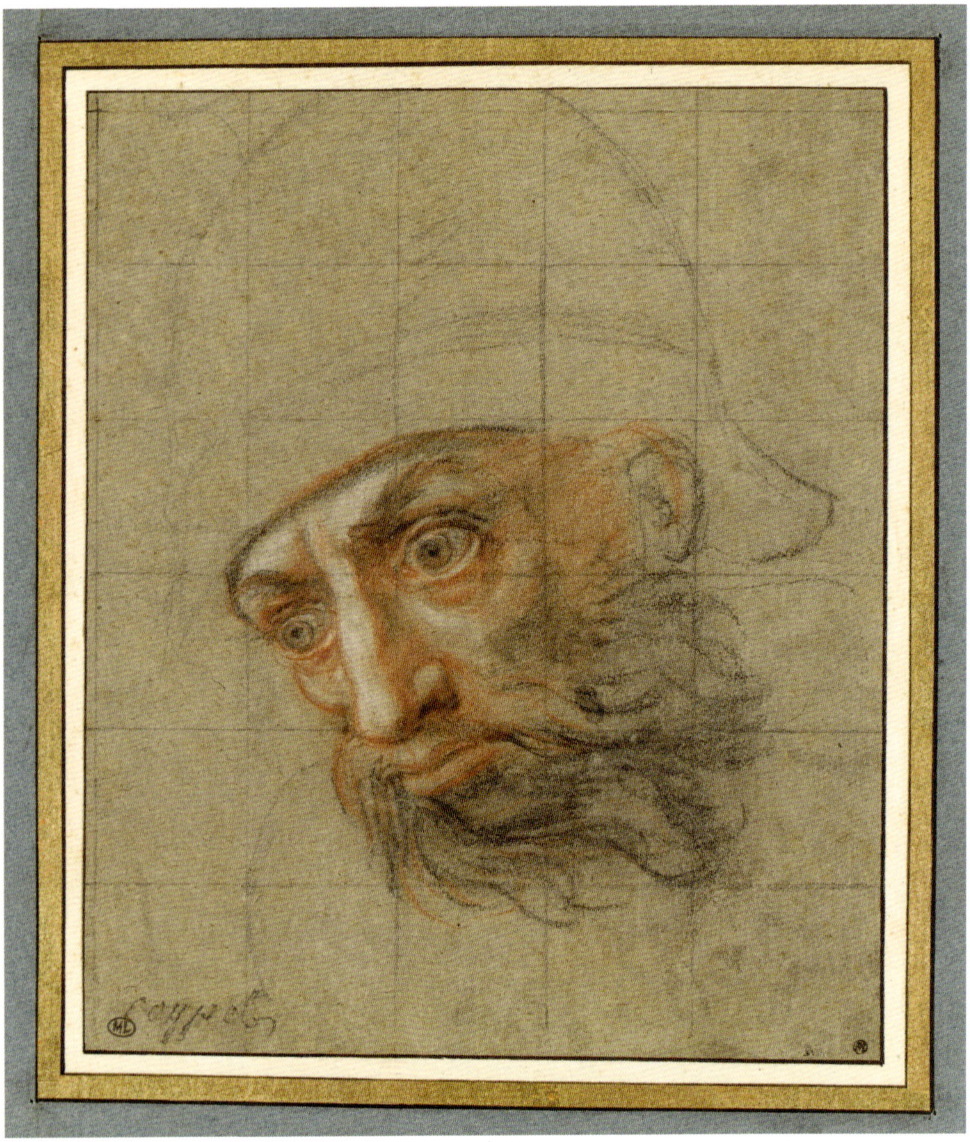

cursory lines. The contrast with a more traditional study of a classical soldier by Watteau's older contemporary Antoine Coypel (1661–1722), Le Brun's successor as director of the Royal Academy and First Painter to the King, is striking (fig. 12). Coypel's drawing, adapted from Le Brun's drawing of "anger" ("La Collere" in fig. 13) and destined for use in a scene from Virgil's *Aeneid*, depicts a rictus of rage, muscles tensed, eyebrows scowling, every movement carefully registered to distill the soldier's emotion. Proposing parity between interior and exterior, it illustrates Coypel's belief that art "must probe the deepest sentiments of the heart to render them visible to the eyes of men."[34] Watteau's soldiers, by contrast, are remarkable for their opacity; their faces reveal nothing about the contents of their minds, about their thoughts, emotions, or desires.

Clearly, Watteau is aiming at something fundamentally different from Le Brun and his followers. His studies of soldiers at rest, with their buried heads and prostrate bodies, and soldiers on the march, with their turned, hunched backs, represent not the contents of their subjects' interiority but rather the *condition* of self-reflexive withdrawal; not a single emotion distilled on the face but the subjects' immersion in the chaotic profusion of emotions that coexist in the interior. (It is no coincidence that the states associated with this withdrawal—reverie, dreaming, absorption, reflection—have no place in Le Brun's system.) The result is that, with Watteau, we are left with no access to that self, to the interior that defines individuality. The drawings betray a gulf that has opened up between the artist and the subjects he depicts.

The gap is symptomatic of a growing conviction at the turn of the eighteenth century about the essential disjunction between exterior and interior, appearance and reality. Le Brun's conception of art and selfhood is inextricable from the courtly ethos in which he worked; an ethos in which every gesture, every expression, every raised eyebrow or curl of the lips became a sign to be deciphered in a never-ending quest for visibility and favor.[35] According to this view, once one learned to read the face, the desires, emotions, and motivations behind it would reveal themselves. Thus Le Brun's successor, Coypel, could proclaim that the court was the "great theater of the world" where "you can study . . . the truth about customs, human nature,

Figure 13

Henri Testelin after Charles Le Brun, *The Expressions*, 1696. Etching (with later additions in ink), plate: 13 ¹⁄₁₆ × 17 ¾ in. (33.1 × 45.1 cm); sheet: 15 ⅜ × 21 ½ in. (39.1 × 54.6 cm). The Metropolitan Museum of Art; Rogers Fund, 1968 (68.513.6[6])

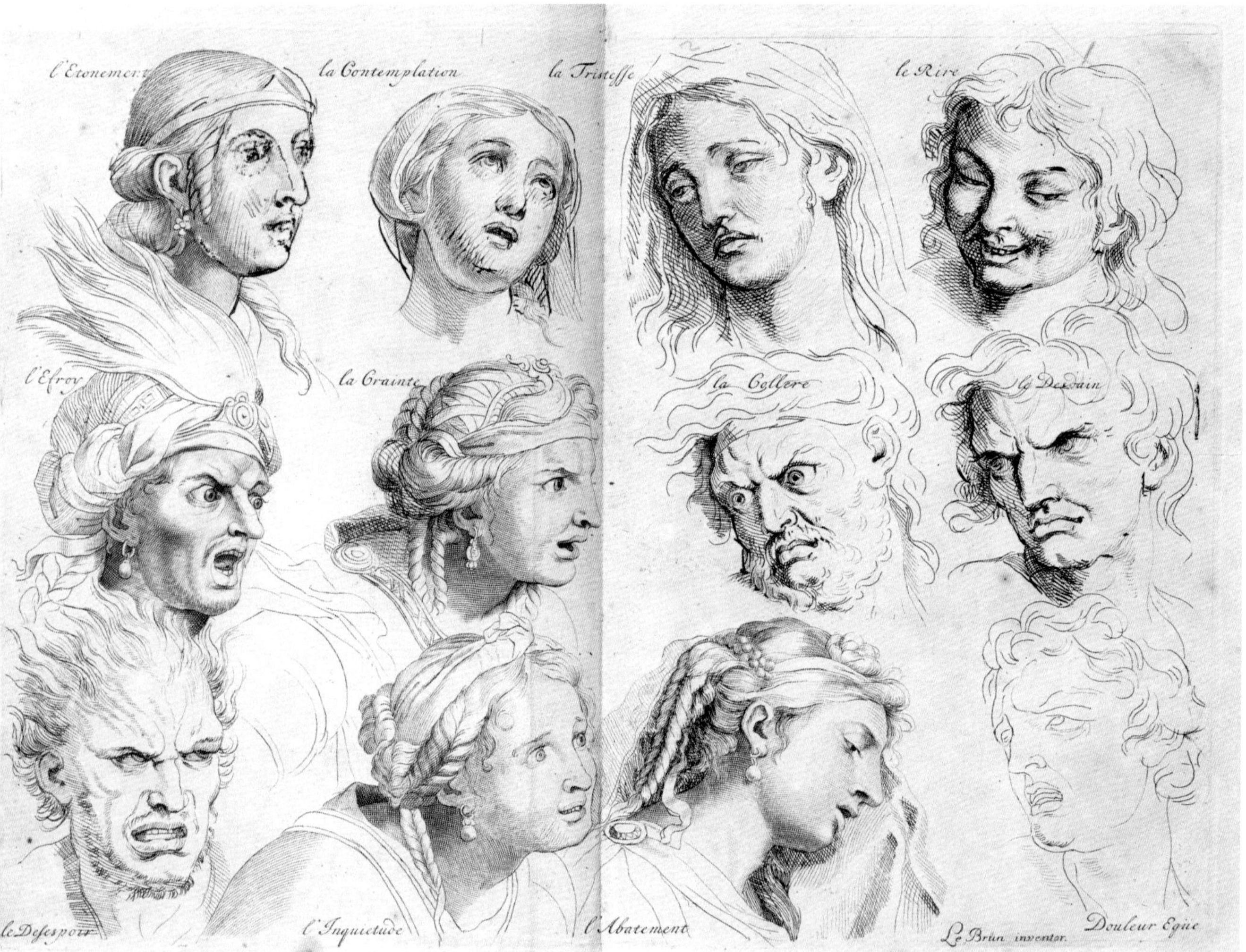

and the passions," about "all that agitates and troubles the heart and soul of all men."[36] Others, however, held a more critical stance toward the court, revisiting the view of it as a mire of deceit and falsehood. "A perfect courtier," the moralist Jean de La Bruyère (1645–1696) cautioned, "is master of his gestures, his eyes, and his countenance; he is profound, impenetrable; he seems to overlook every injury, smiles at his enemies, controls his temper, disguises his passions, belies his heart, speaks, acts against his sentiments."[37] The face was a mask, its expressions a lie, and the foundations on which a system like Le Brun's stood were revealed to be shaky indeed. The inner life of others was, writers like La Bruyère recognized, essentially inaccessible.

Watteau's drawings evince a similar awareness of the distance between a person's social facade and the inner life that it conceals.[38] The face is no longer a window through which we can peer into the core of others' identity but rather an opaque screen. Perhaps Watteau's immersion in the military camps—an alternate "theater of the world," where a rawer study of humanity, not only stripped of courtly artifice but also outside of the discipline required for drills and battle, was possible—paved the way for his refusal to make the face or the body a legible sign.[39] Certainly, it seems likely that the social conditions of the military camp prompted Watteau to think more deeply about how people relate to each other and to develop a technique to capture it. In any case, his refusal amounts to more than a simple rejection of Le Brun's grammar of the passions as so many artificial masks.[40] It points to a rejection of the whole notion of selfhood that undergirds Le Brun's theory of expression—the idea that our inner lives can be discovered and represented through rational, a priori methods.

What alternative vision of selfhood, then, do Watteau's drawings propose? Lajer-Burcharth has linked Watteau's drawing practice, and the understanding of the self on which it turns, to the philosophical current of empiricism, which holds that we acquire knowledge not through deduction from first principles but through the senses. This is a crucial insight.[41] Whether recording the body as it moves through space and time or observing the minute variations of its resting states, Watteau aimed to depict the body as it appeared to him in the moment he observed it. Unfiltered through the kind of assumptions that Le Brun's lessons implanted in other artists, his drawings aim to register his unmediated, sensible encounter with his subjects. With the quickness and vitality of their line, they exhibit an immediacy that preserves a sense of the moment, of the dynamic convergence between artist and model.[42]

Watteau's empiricism, however, raises a critical question about the artist's relation to the subjectivity of his subjects. According to John Locke (1632–1704), one of the founders of empiricism, when we speak of identity we must distinguish between two parts: *man* and *person*. *Man* is the material substance of a human being; a *man* remains the same *man* only when his body persists over time. By contrast, a *person* is "a thinking intelligent being, that has reason and reflection, and can consider itself as itself, the same thinking thing, in different times and places; which it does only by that consciousness which is inseparable from thinking"—a being defined, in other words, by its interiority.[43] It is, he concludes, in the *person* alone that identity resides, for "consciousness alone makes self."[44] To illustrate his theory and its implications, Locke introduces a parable about a prince and a cobbler. Suppose, he says, that the soul of a prince, with all its attendant memories, thoughts, and feelings, were one day to enter the body of a cobbler. Since consciousness alone makes a *person*, the *man* would remain the cobbler, but the *person* would now be the prince. The consequence of this, however, is that the prince would be a prince only to himself; all others, judging by external appearance, would continue to see him as the cobbler. The self, then, is knowable only to itself—others can perceive only the matter that makes *man*.[45]

We do not know whether Watteau read Locke, but it is certainly possible. A French translation of *An Essay Concerning Human Understanding*, where the philosopher developed his theory of identity, was published in 1700 and quickly took Paris by storm, particularly in the circles Watteau would later frequent.[46] Whatever the exact nature of their connection, Watteau's drawings should not be taken as "illustrations" of Locke's theories; their relationship is deeper, shaped by a similar vision of the subject's place in the world. Most importantly, Locke's ideas about identity are useful for the way they capture, in terms specific to the period, the central problem with which the drawings wrestle: by the nature of their work, artists deal in appearances, in the sensible world of matter. But this means that, when depicting human subjects, they have access only to the *man*; the core of identity—the *person*—is out of reach.

Seen from this Lockean perspective, Watteau's drawings register a kind of failure—though, as we shall see, a productive one. The poses and attitudes of the soldiers indicate their immersion in their inner lives, yet the contours and contents of that life are frustratingly inaccessible. The soldiers present to us only their withdrawn, affectless faces and their shell-like bodies, huddled against the intrusions of the world. Far from the dream of an encounter between two sympathetic selves, equal and open, the drawings capture the meeting of an artist and an opaque and unknowable other.

From Drawing to Painting

Of course, unlike his drawings, Watteau's military paintings depict not isolated individuals but social situations: soldiers (and sometimes their families, friends, and hangers-on) talking, smoking, drinking, playing cards. But the aporia we have observed at the heart of the drawings—the unknowability of the other—nonetheless persists. To understand how it does, we must look more closely at how Watteau went about making his paintings.

As taught by the Royal Academy of Painting and Sculpture at the beginning of the eighteenth century and practiced by nearly every artist of the time, the steps to a finished painting followed an established path. The painter began, in high platonic fashion, with an *idea*, a mental image of a composition appropriate to the subject he wished to depict.[47] From there, he would create compositional sketches, known as *ésquisses* or *pensées*, to work out the overall shape his work would take and the disposition of its various elements. Next, he would make studies of the individual figures and various details such as hands and faces—often working from live models whom he would pose, drawing on famous antique and Renaissance prototypes, according to their role in the composition. Finally, he would create a *modello* or cartoon, a finished model of the final composition from which he would work to create his painting.

Figure 14

François Boucher, after Jean-Antoine Watteau,
Scene under a Tent (cat. 39)

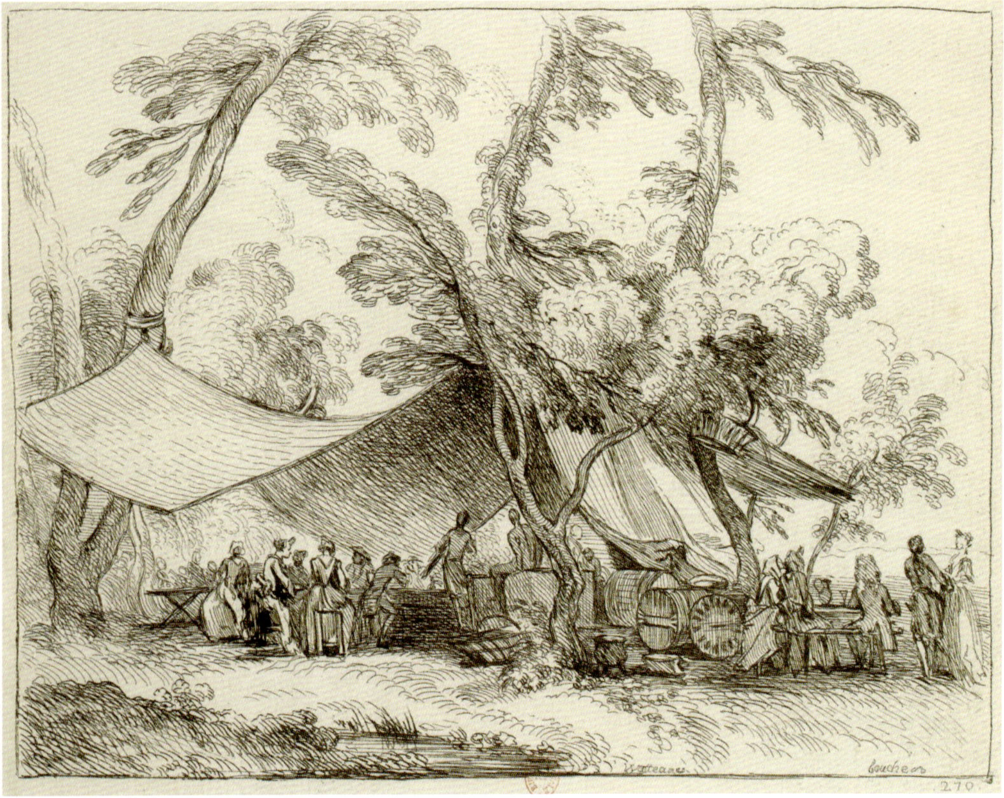

Figure 15

Jean-Antoine Watteau, *The Respite from War* (*Les délassements de la guerre*), ca. 1713–14 (cat. 47)

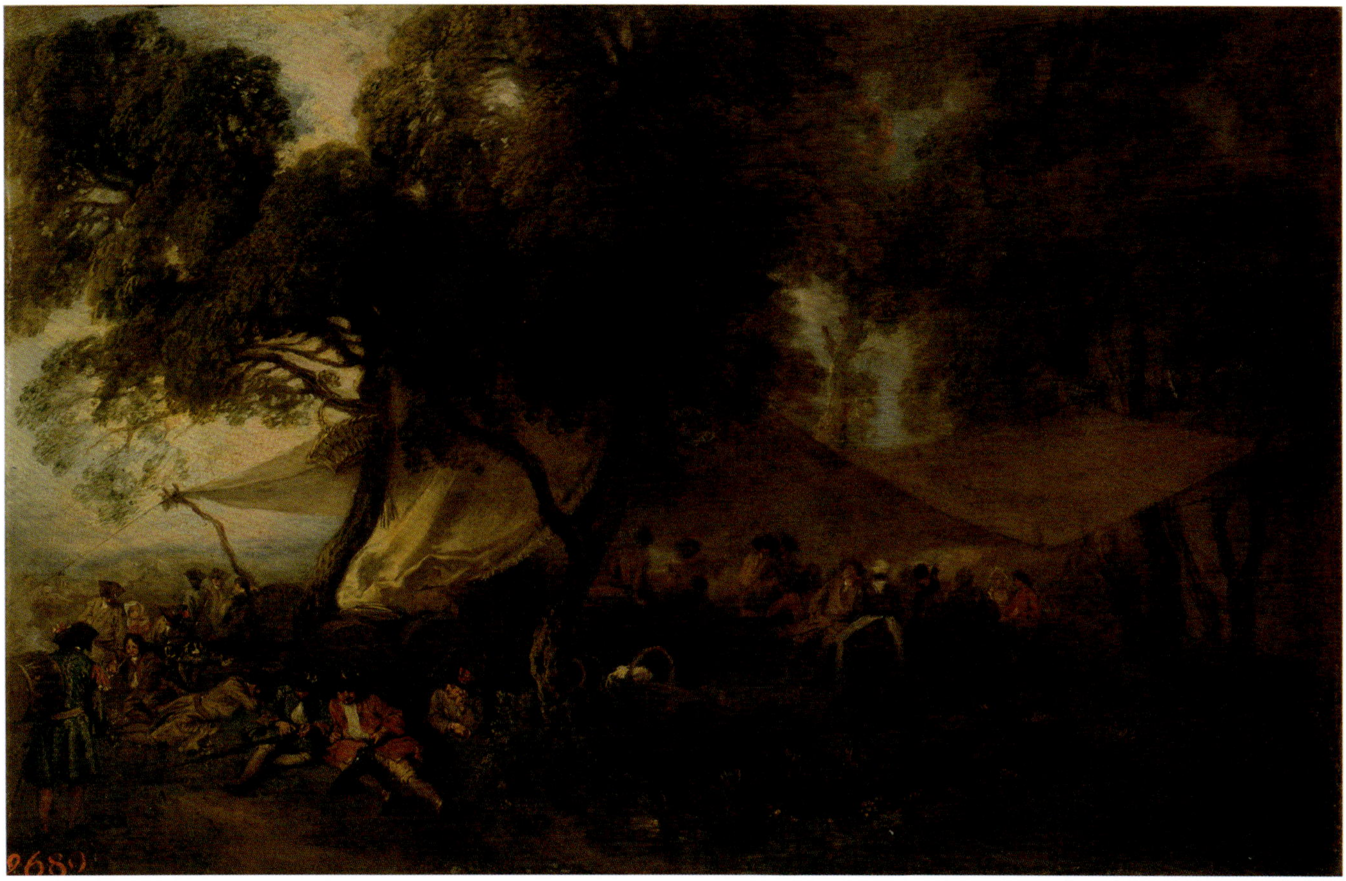

Figure 16

Jean-Antoine Watteau, *The Halt* (*Alte*), ca. 1710 (cat. 43)

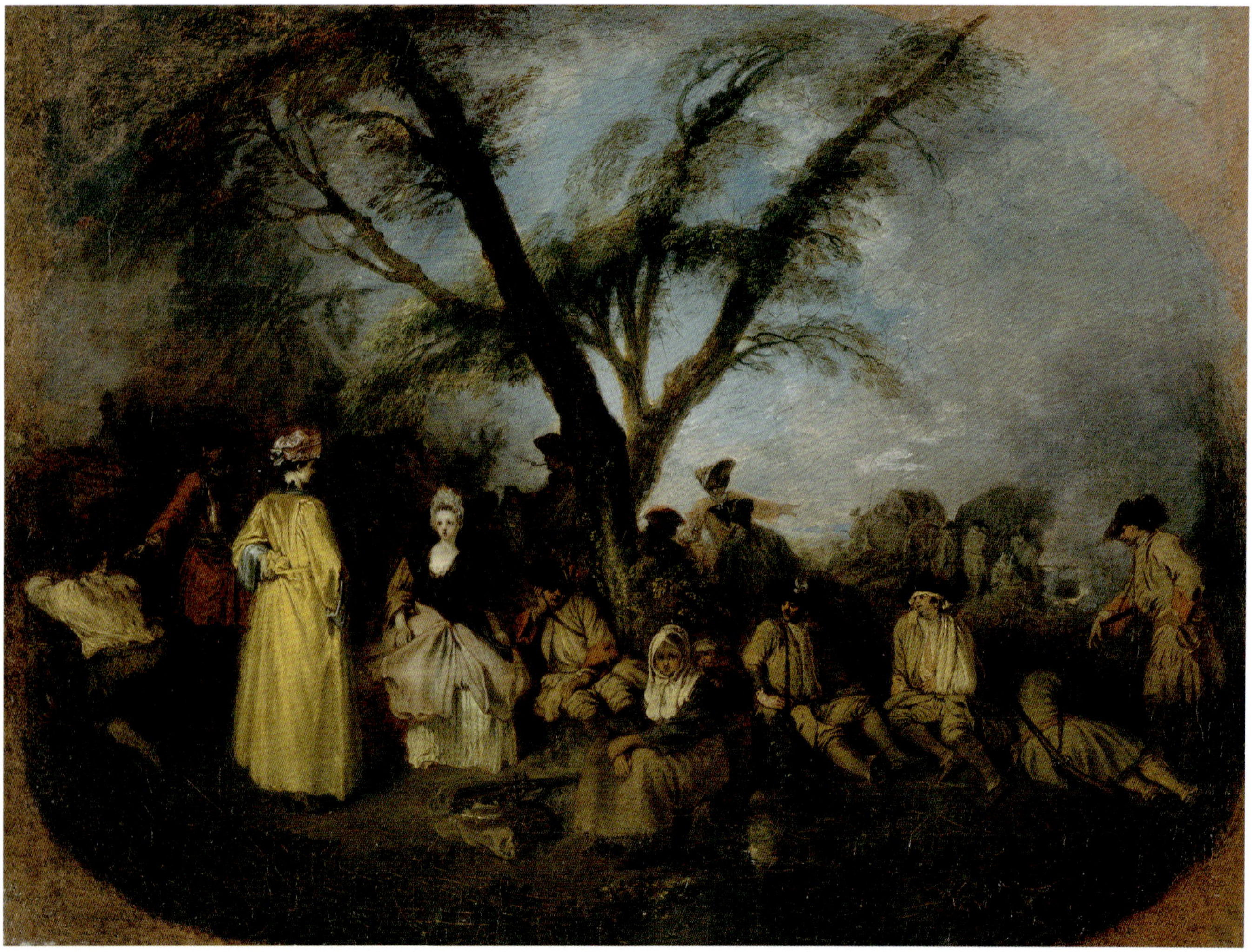

Watteau broke from this path entirely.[48] In the first place, he seldom made compositional drawings; in fact, we know of only one compositional drawing for the military paintings, a study that survives as an engraving (fig. 14) for *The Respite from War* (fig. 15).[49] Instead, he began with his studies from life. "He never made *ésquisses* or *pensées* for any of his paintings," Caylus recounts with some exaggeration. "His custom was to draw his studies in a bound book, so that he always had a large number at hand." As a result, the process of making a painting took on a spontaneous, almost aleatory logic, without appeal to a master idea. "When it took his fancy to paint a picture," Caylus says, "he turned to his collection of studies, from which he chose figures that suited him best at the moment," effectively cutting and pasting them onto the canvas.[50] "From these he made groups, most often to accord with a background that he had already conceived or prepared. He rarely made use of them in any other way."[51]

The sheet from the Museum Boijmans Van Beuningen (see fig. 2) and the paintings for which it was employed show the artist's process in action. On the right of the drawing, Watteau has drawn four studies of soldiers, each in different positions of repose—the top figure lies flat on his belly, his head resting on his arms; below him, a second soldier is shown tending to his musket; further down, we see a man propping himself up on his arm, lost in thought; and at the bottom of the page, another soldier with a musket is shown leaning on his right arm, looking on the verge of falling asleep. On the left, an elegantly dressed woman, probably drawn later than the soldiers, stands regally as she looks out at the viewer.[52] Though she has been related to the similarly positioned woman in *The Halt* (fig. 16), she matches no figure in any known painting exactly. We can, however, relate the other figures on this sheet to two of the military paintings: the four soldiers appear in *The Respite from War* (fig. 17); and the dreamy soldier resting his head on his hand reappears in *The Supply Train* (fig. 18). (As Caylus informs us, "Without realizing it, he repeated very often the same figure, either because it pleased him or because it was the first he saw when searching for one."[53])

Drawn as independent studies on the page, the figures have no obvious relationship to each other, but on the canvas the situation has changed. In the process of composing *The Respite from War*, Watteau brought the four soldiers

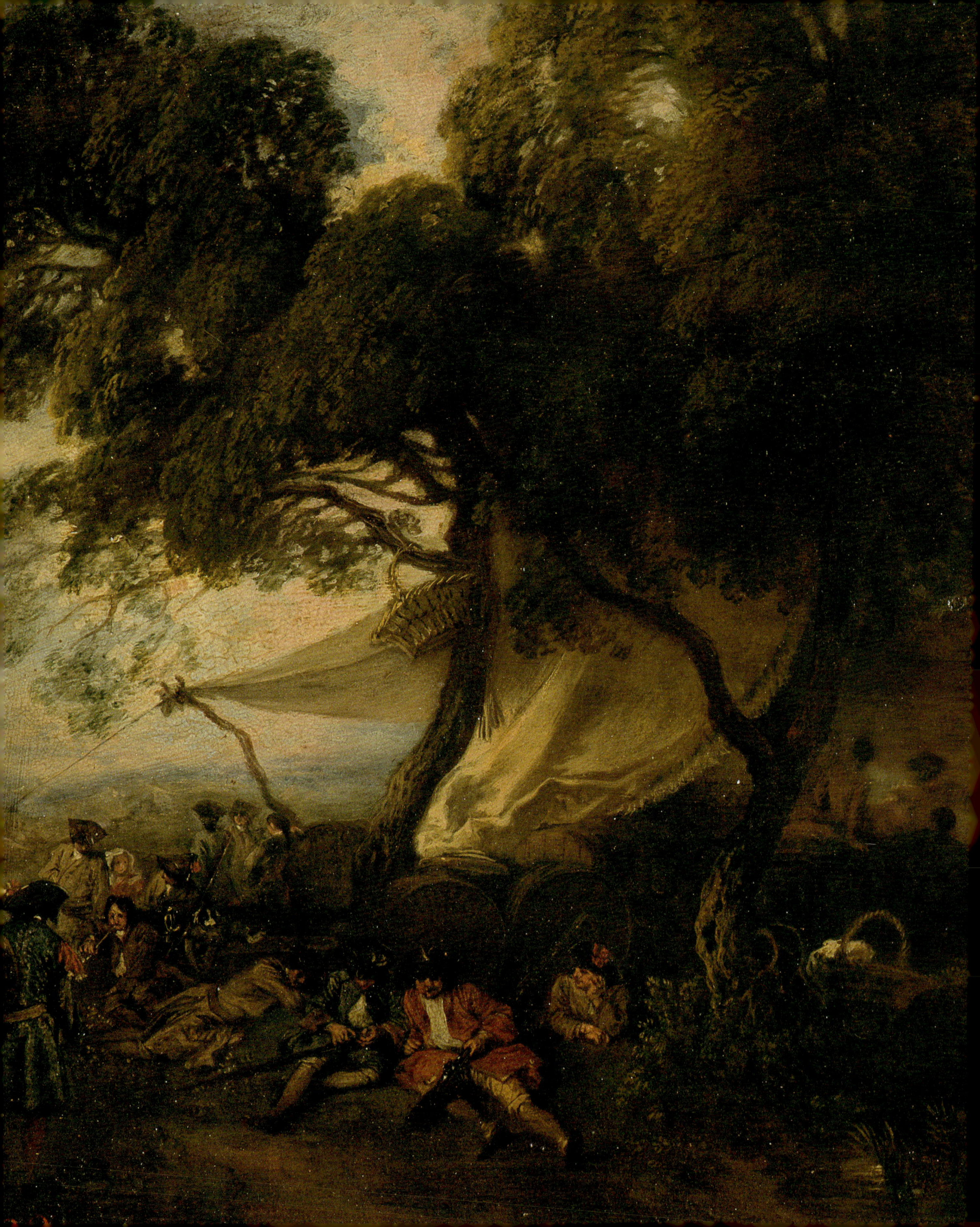

Figure 17

Jean-Antoine Watteau, *The Respite from War* (*Les délassements de la guerre*), ca. 1713–14 (detail of cat. 47)

together in a way he had presumably not foreseen when he first sketched them: the two men with the muskets now sit leaning into each other; the sleeping man lies to their right, just behind them; and the man resting his face on his hand is shown to their left. As the soldiers migrate from sketchbook to canvas, their new proximity generates relationships not present in the sketch. The soldier resting his head on his hand, for example, appears lost in reverie in the drawing, yet in *The Respite from War* the same figure now seems to be gazing at the sleeping soldier on the other side.

What is the nature of these relationships? One art historian has argued that the military scenes evince "a strong sense of social cohesiveness" and that "warm companionship and revitalizing conversation always dominate Watteau's sympathetic, refined views of the soldier's life."[54] While sociability in the midst of war is a central theme of Watteau's scenes, even our cursory look at the figures in *The Respite from War* reveals a more complex social landscape. Is the man leaning on his hand actually gazing at the sleeping soldier or is he merely facing in his direction, lost in reverie as he appears to be in the original sketch? Even though Watteau shows us the trappings of communion, the exact nature of their relationship is far from clear.

Ambiguous relationships like this proliferate in Watteau's military paintings. *The Halt* (see fig. 16) is a case in point. The figures in the canvas are connected by a network of gazes: the officer in red, on the left, glares at the man tending to his horse while an elegantly dressed woman in yellow, perhaps his wife (wives were a common sight in early modern military camps, though Louis XIV discouraged soldiers from marrying[55]), looks toward the woman next to her. Meanwhile, a soldier with his arm in a sling on the other side of the tree seems to be staring across the canvas to the pair of women, as soldiers on either side of the tree look down at nowhere in particular, and, on the far right, another soldier gazes down at a man sleeping next to him. Various groups of conversing soldiers populate the background, rounding out a scene brimming with social life. Yet a closer look shows this is perhaps not the scene of social cohesion and warm companionship it first appears to be. Many of the figures, such as the man resting his head on his hand to the left of the tree, seem lost in their own world, and even

Figure 18

Jean-Antoine Watteau, *The Supply Train* (*Escorte d'équipages*), ca. 1715 (cat. 52)

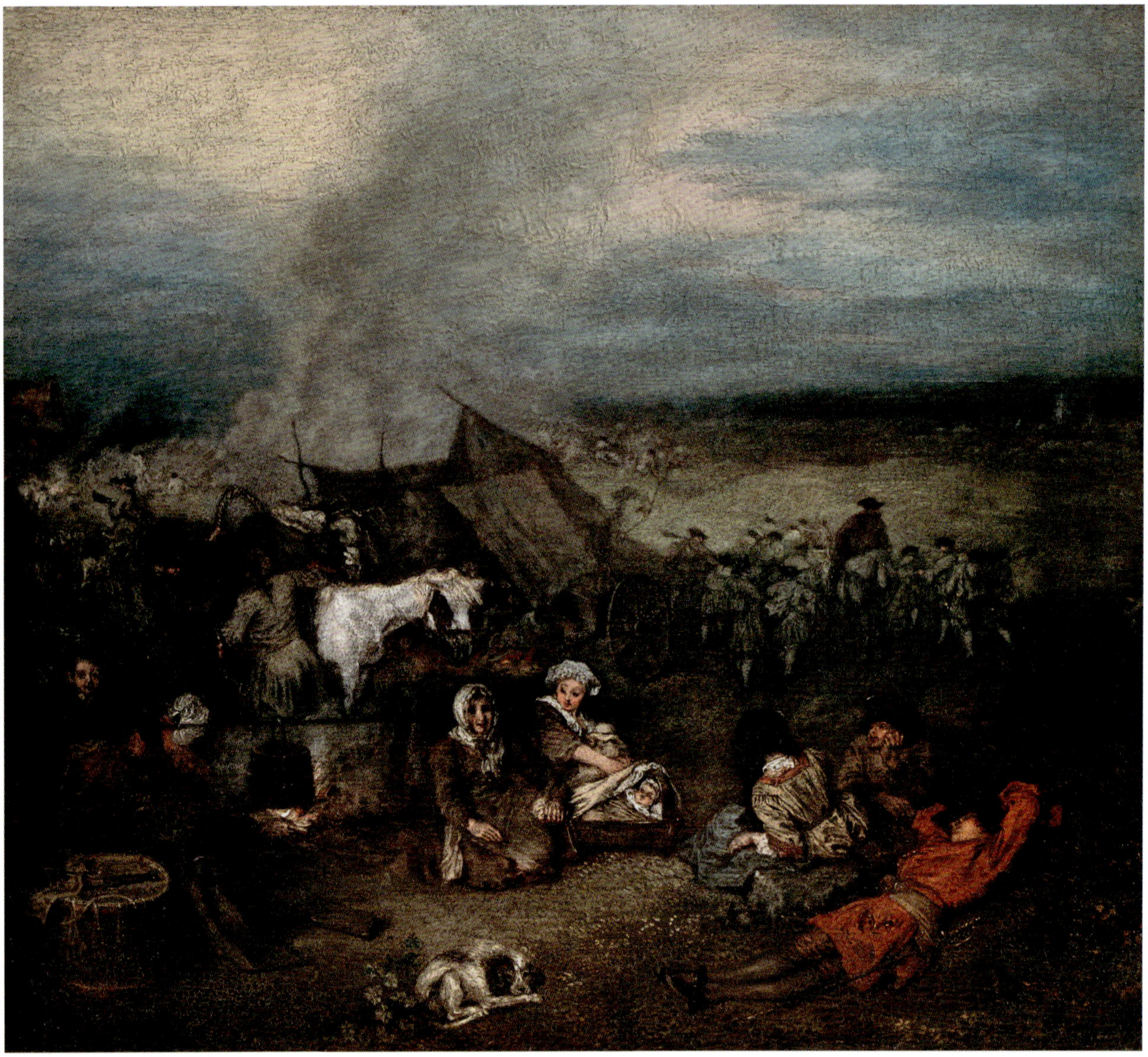

when one figure looks toward another, it is not clear that the gaze is returned or that a real connection has been made. An extreme case is the soldier on the far right looking down at the man sleeping with his head in his arms, but one could say the same for the soldier with the sling looking toward the women. Even the gazes of the women themselves do not seem to match up.

The lack of connection here is the direct result of Watteau's working method. Rather than being conceived as parts of a pre-determined whole, as elements of a coherent composition that Watteau had already begun to work out, the figures in the painting were executed first as independent and unrelated studies—four sheets of which we can relate directly to the work: *Three Studies of a Soldier and a Kneeling Man* (see fig. 4), *Three Studies of Women* (fig. 19), *Four Studies of Women, Alternately Standing and Seated* (fig. 20), and *Two Studies of a Seated Soldier* (fig. 21). Watteau likely executed these studies at different times, and only later did he return to them to create his painting, choosing various figures and drawing them into different relations.

Consider, for example, the five soldiers in the foreground—the four to the right of the tree and the one just to the left of it. The men here are taken from two sheets—the man with the sling and the man resting his head on his hand to the left of the tree from *Two Studies of a Seated Soldier* (fig. 21), the three other soldiers from *Three Studies of a Soldier and a Kneeling Man* (see fig. 4).[56] In the drawings, the figures have no narrative or affective relationship; they are wholly withdrawn into themselves. In fact, the two soldiers in the missing drawings are likely the same man in different positions, as are the three soldiers in tricorn hats in figure 4. But out of these fragments Watteau has built a whole social world on the canvas. With the exception of the standing and sleeping soldiers, he has shuffled all of the figures, breaking some apart and placing others together in new relationships. (The two central middle figures in the drawing, the seated and sleeping soldiers, also appear in *Halt of a Detachment* (see fig. 30), but their positions are reversed, generating yet another relation.)

The result is a marked tension between the soldiers' absorbed, solitary state in the drawings and their interplay in the paintings.[57] Far from

Figure 19

Jean-Antoine Watteau, *Three Studies of Women*, ca. 1710 (cat. 13)

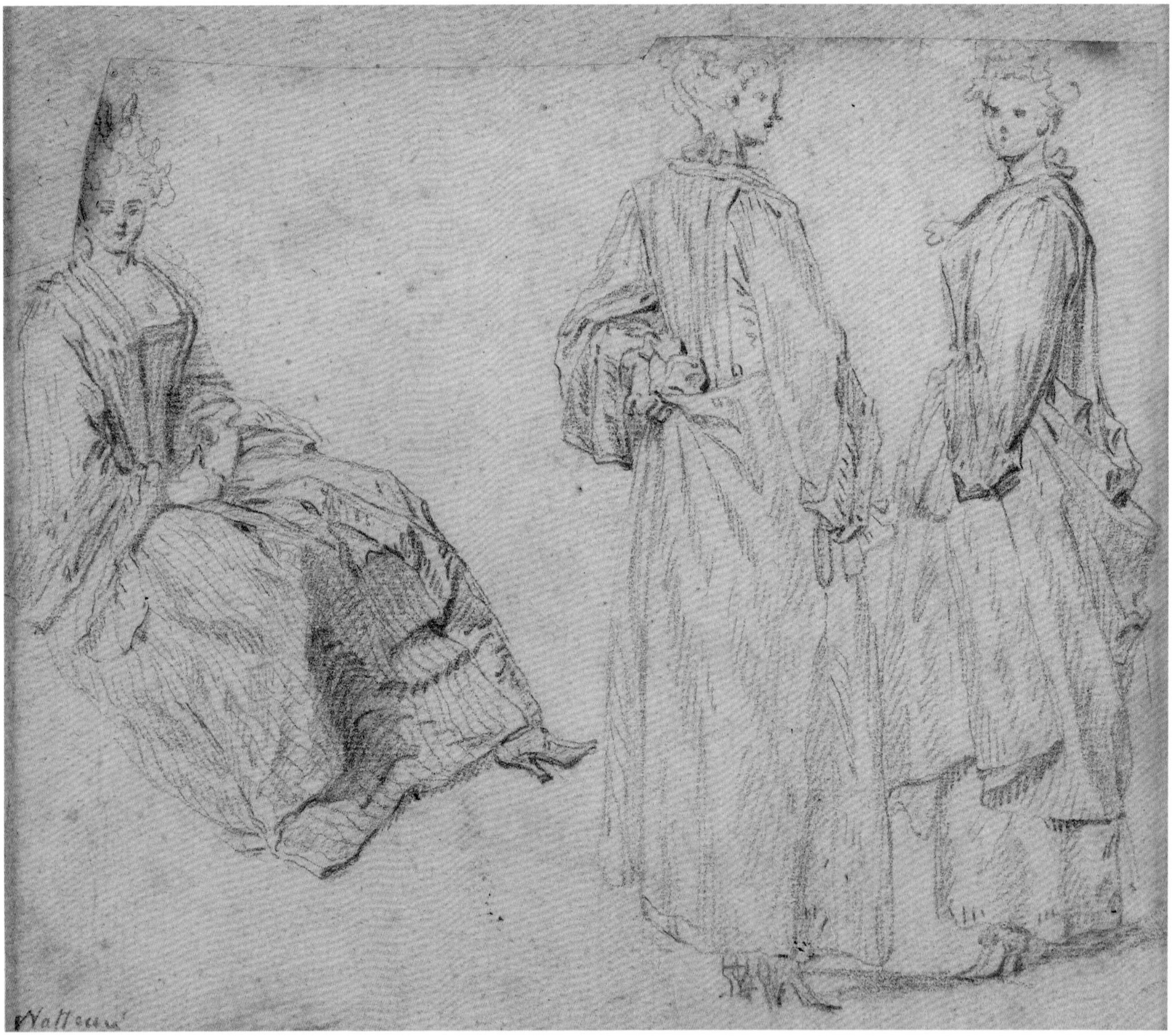

Figure 20

Jean-Antoine Watteau, *Four Studies of Women, Alternately Standing and Seated*, ca. 1710 (cat. 12)

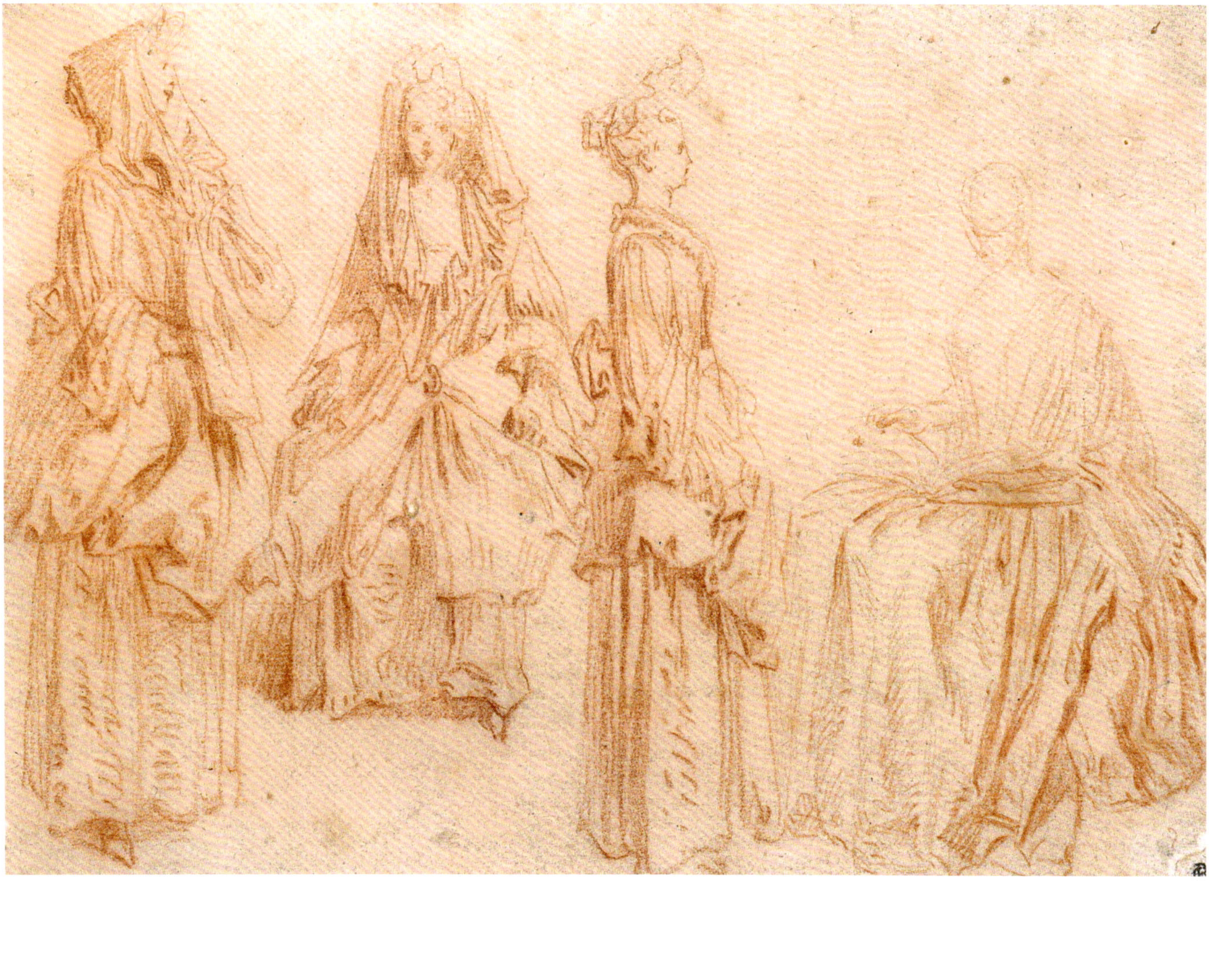

preserving the naturalism of his drawings, Watteau's working method undoes it, introducing a somewhat surreal disjunction among the figures he brings together. The soldiers stand in proximity to one another and many times even interact, but, disposed in almost arbitrary groupings, they rarely appear to connect. Each man in the military paintings remains an island unto himself, his encounters with his fellow soldiers stilted and disjointed.

A sense of communion forestalled is particularly pronounced in *The Portal of Valenciennes* (fig. 22). We know of three drawings related to the work: two from which Watteau has taken the figure of the seated soldier with a pipe (fig. 23) and the soldier on the far right of the painting leaning against the wall (fig. 24); and another whose central figure the artist has used for the standing soldier with the cape at the far left (fig. 25). The other figures—the two soldiers standing with their backs to each other, the man sleeping with his head buried in the crux of his arm, and the sallow-faced man slumped against the wall—derive, presumably, from studies that have been lost.[58] In constructing his painting out of these studies, Watteau establishes connections among the figures—or at least the implication of them—by putting four of his studies into dialogue, placing the two soldiers near the middle with their backs to each other so they face the two other standing soldiers at either end of the composition.

Here again, though, the remnants of the soldiers' previous isolation on the page persist. Because they were not originally drawn or conceived as engaging with each other, their gazes never quite meet. They look *toward* each other, certainly, but it is not at all clear that they look *at* each other. Perhaps the faint smiles of two men in the center, barely hinted at by a few strokes of Watteau's brush, suggest a desire for connection—conversation? camaraderie?—but the obscured faces of the other standing men offer no indication about whether this desire is reciprocated and a connection has been made. Meanwhile, the three other figures—one sleeping, another facing away from us, and the last casting his eyes downward—have withdrawn completely into themselves, oblivious to the people around them. What appears on first inspection to be a scene of conviviality (if not quite esprit de corps) gives way to a series of failed connections, a vision of uneasy and troubled social commerce.

Figure 21

Jean-Antoine Watteau, *Two Studies of a Seated Soldier*, ca. 1710 (cat. 8)

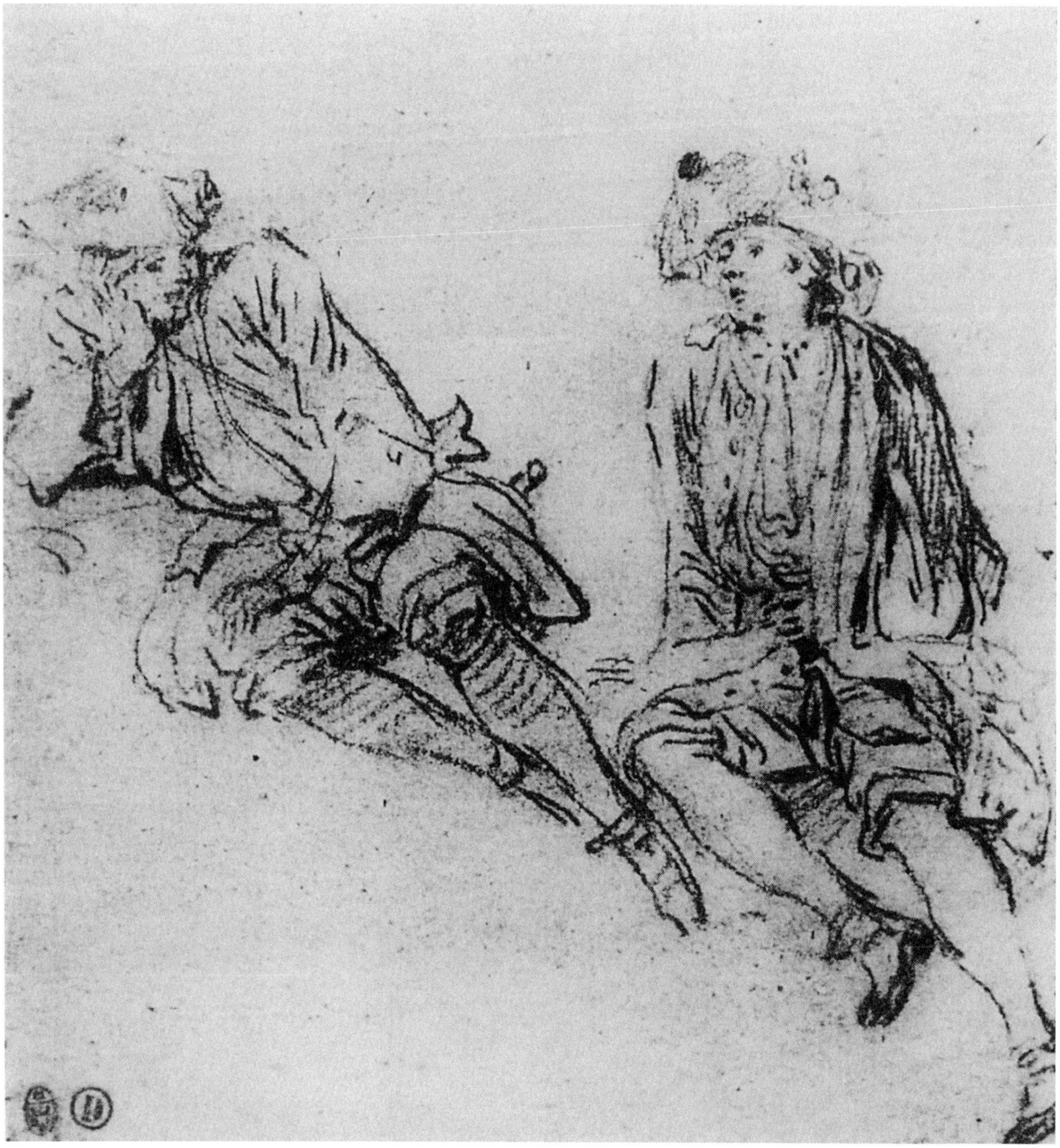

Figure 22

Jean-Antoine Watteau, *The Portal of Valenciennes* (*La Porte de Valenciennes*), ca. 1710–11 (cat. 46)

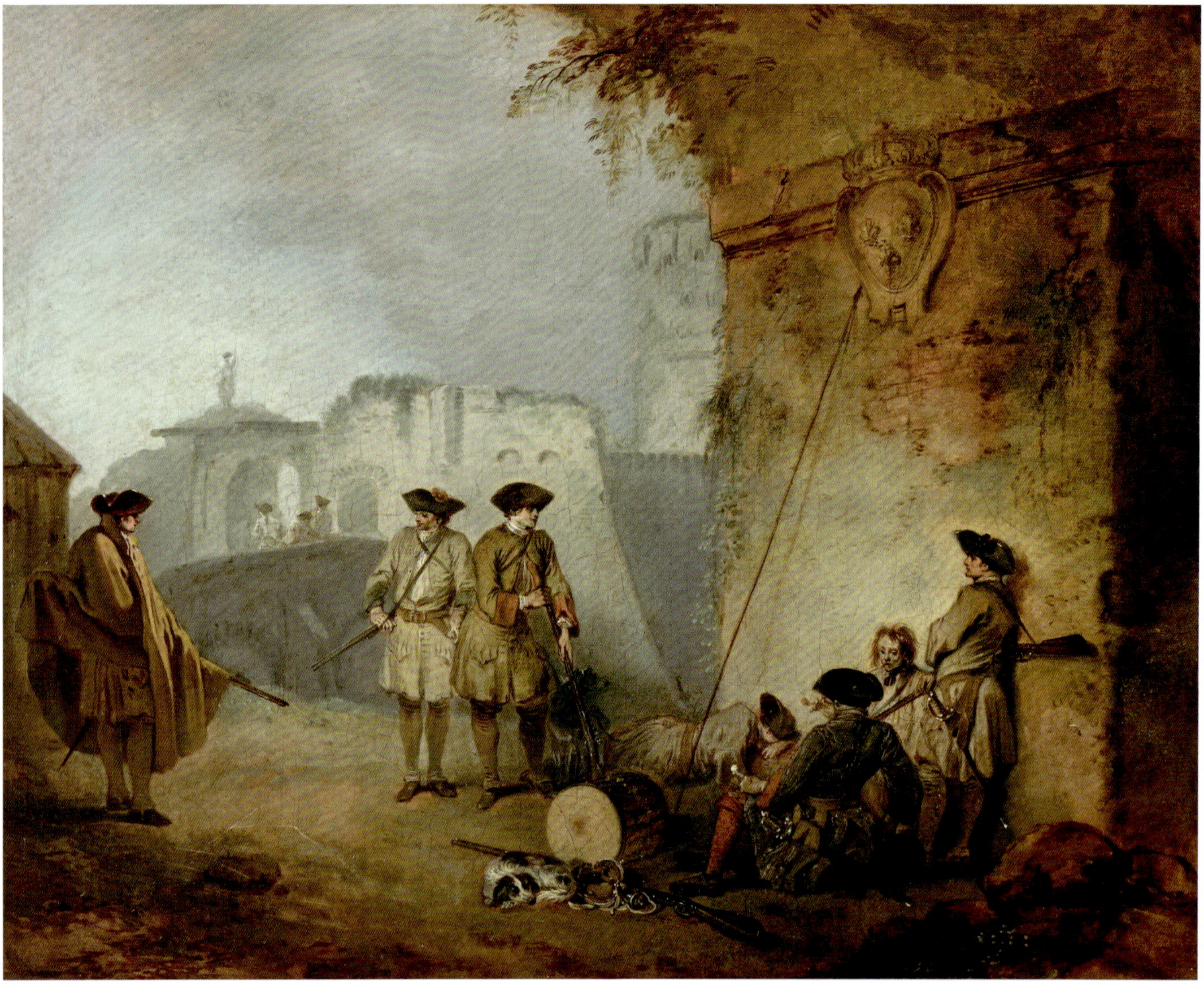

Figure 23

Jean-Antoine Watteau, *Two Studies of a Soldier, One Standing, the Other Seated and Holding a Pipe*, ca. 1710 (cat. 7)

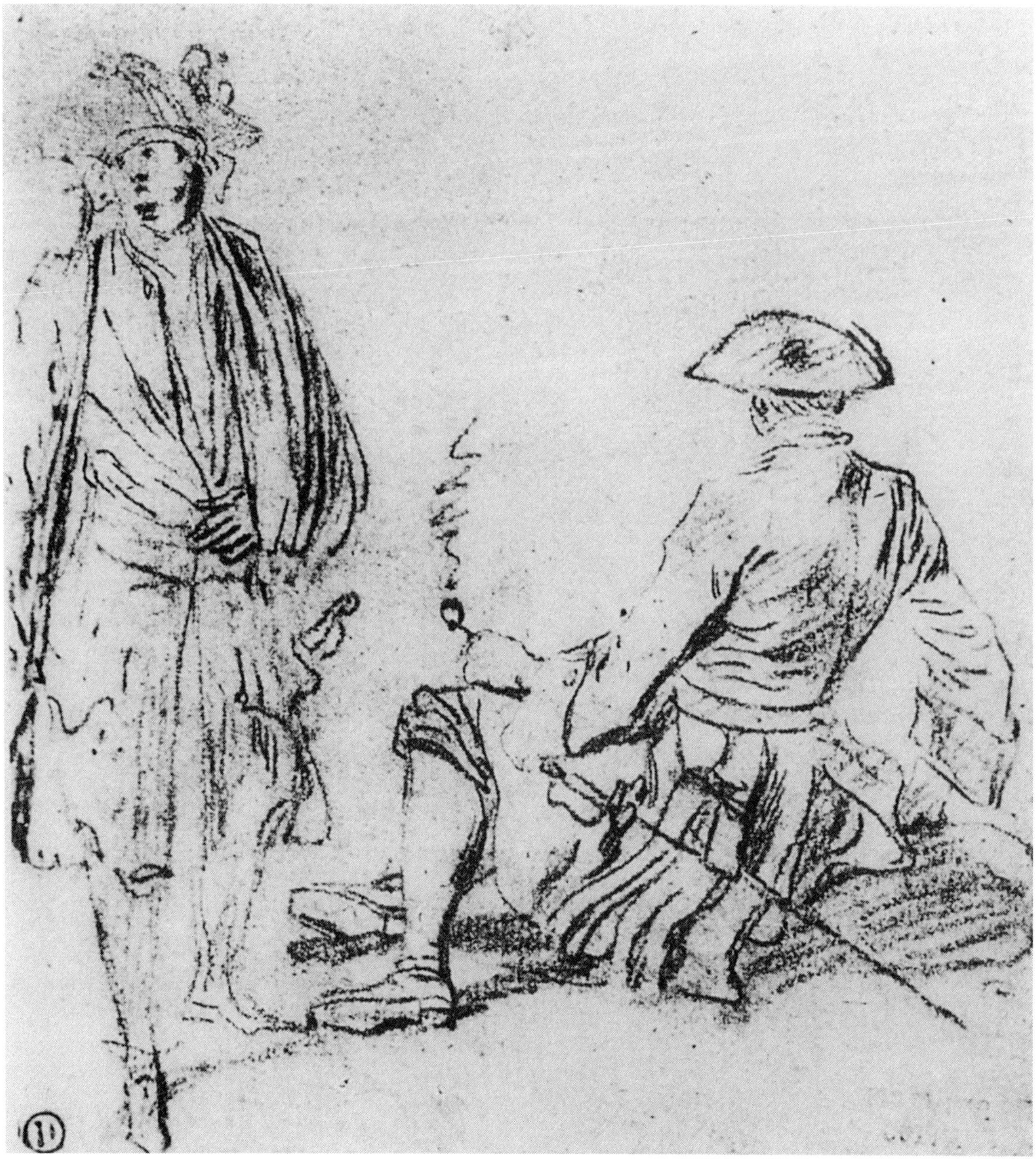

Figure 24

Jean-Antoine Watteau, *Two Studies of a Soldier Holding a Musket*, ca. 1710 (cat. 5)

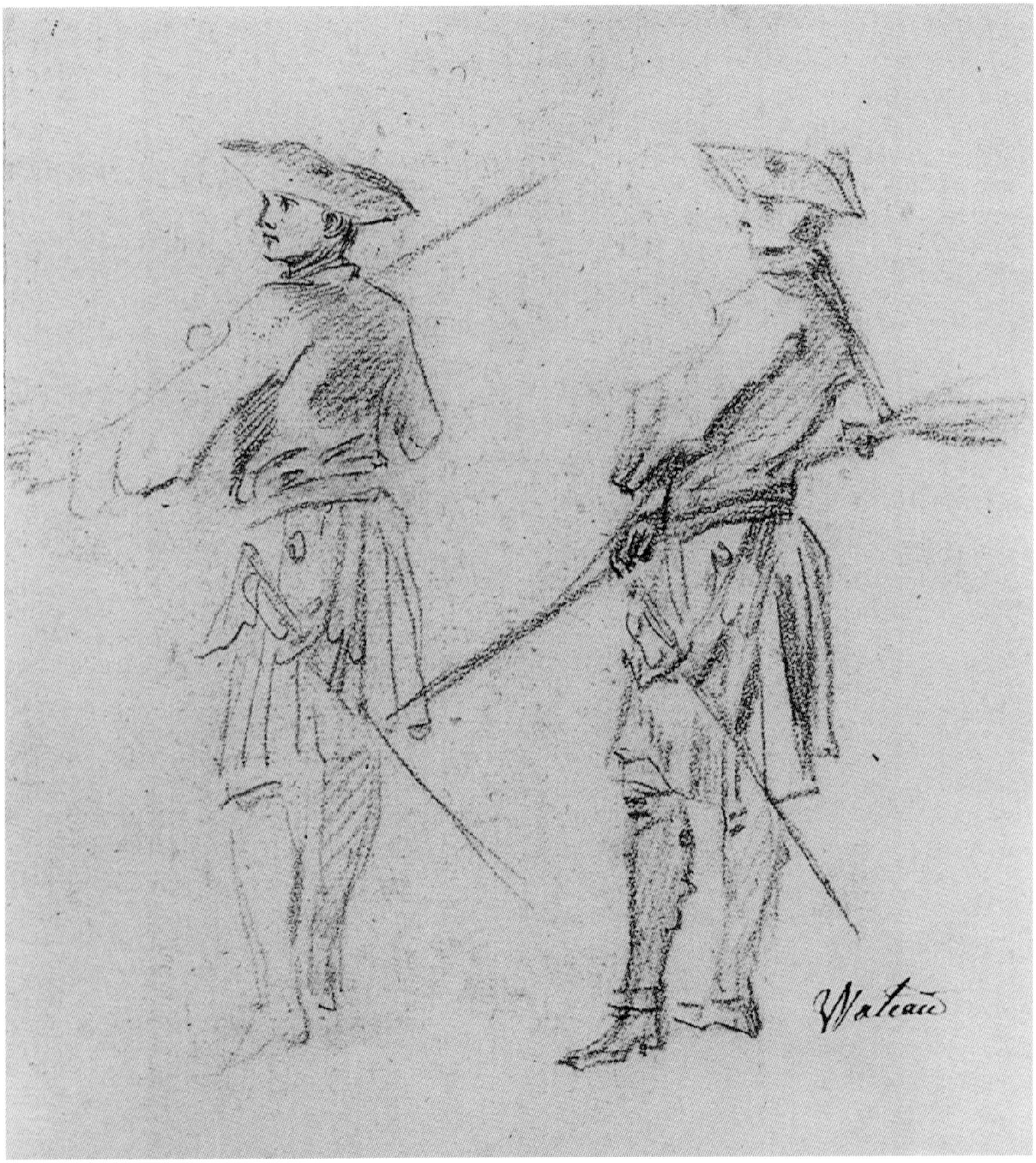

Failed connections like this are evident even in Watteau's paintings of soldiers on the march, where the figures' psychic isolation is at odds with their collective movement forward. *Recruits Going to Join the Regiment*, which survives as an etching after the now lost painting—in a rare first state by Watteau's hand alone (fig. 26), as well as in a second state retouched by Henri-Simon Thomassin (fig. 27)—is a particularly dramatic example. The work boasts a large number of related studies, the most remarkable of which is the series of five that shows a soldier disposed in three poses around a semicircle (not all of the figures, it should be noted, appear in the *Recruits*). Drawn as studies of a single soldier in motion and deployed to represent several different men, the men seem, in the new context of the etching, to be pulling away from each other rather than moving together. As a depiction of a march, the work makes little sense—with the soldiers' counterposed balletic movements, their procession would soon break apart—but as an evocation of a psychic break between two uncomprehending selves, it takes on new significance. Despite their proximity and probable shared destination, their experiences remain theirs alone, closed off within the swaying shells of their bodies.

The effect of *Recruits Going to Join the Regiment* and the others we have examined stands in sharp contrast to a painting like Le Brun's *Family of Darius at the Feet of Alexander* (see fig. 11). Here, Le Brun's figures are linked by an affective chain that endows the canvas with an emotional unity absent in Watteau. As Félibien writes in his description of the painting, "One . . . clearly sees that, in looking at Alexander in the way she does, she [the queen] attempts with her looks, which are the interpreters of her sadness, to make the soul of this prince capable of compassion."[59] Conceived as part of a unified pictorial composition, Le Brun's expressive faces facilitated (in theory, at least) this kind of sympathetic bond—the meeting of two sensitive hearts dreamed of by his contemporaries—between the figures in the canvas. Of course, like Watteau's studies, these were originally independent motifs, but unlike Watteau's stock of motifs, they corresponded to fixed passions and functioned almost like syntactic units: when brought together, they generated narrative and connected the figures at an emotional level.[60] The repertoire of poses employed

Figure 25

Jean-Antoine Watteau, *Three Studies of Soldiers Holding Muskets and Wearing Capes*, ca. 1710 (cat. 6)

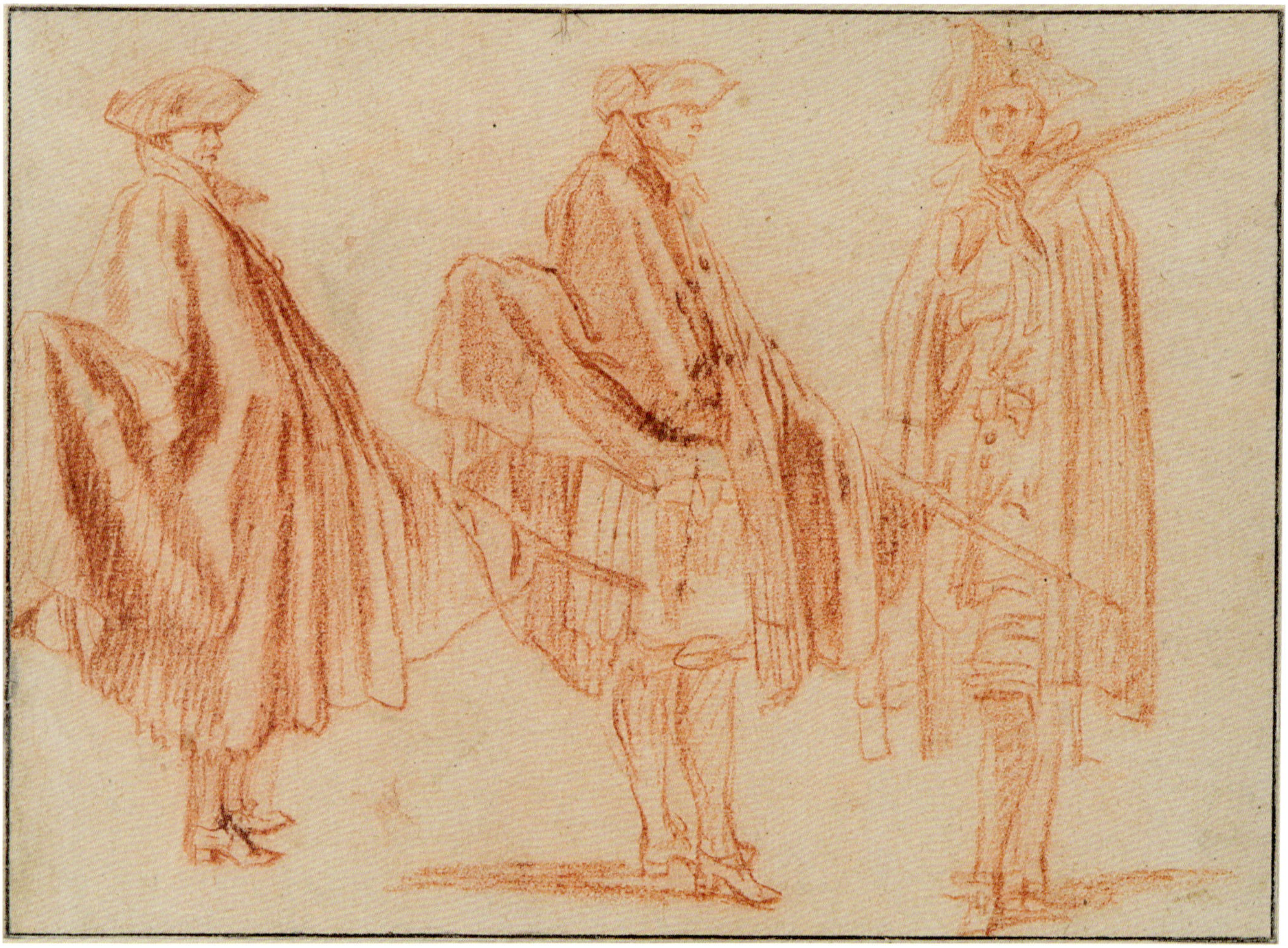

by academic artists functioned similarly, for they were associated with specific affective states. “Just as the twenty-four letters of the alphabet serve to form our speech and express our thoughts, in the same way the lineaments of the human body serve to express the various passions of the soul in order to make visible what one has within the spirit,” as Félibien reports Poussin, the most admired French painter of the seventeenth century, as saying.[61]

By contrast, since Watteau’s studies express only an empirical reality of his soldiers—their appearance in time and space—that is dissociated from their inner lives, their faces and bodies *mean* nothing. They are independent figures, not narrative units like Le Brun’s heads. They do not, as Jean de Jullienne (1686–1766) wrote, “need to be supported by the composition of a larger subject.”[62] As a result, the kind of emotional connection that Félibien sees as the driving force behind Le Brun’s painting (whether or not we find it convincing) is nearly impossible to imagine in Watteau’s scenes, crude, rustic worlds far removed from the martial glamour of Darius’s tent. Thus in *The Portal of Valenciennes* (see fig. 22), the soldiers stand near each other, half acknowledging their companions or else completely withdrawn, but they all remain, to one degree or another, enclosed in their own worlds. Ripped from their isolation in his sketchbook, they are forced into uneasy contact, as unknowable to each other as they appear to be to Watteau’s observing gaze in the original studies; in Lockean terms, we see *man* encountering *man*, rather than *person* encountering *person*.

In this way, the artist’s vision of the self, with its stress on the autonomy and opacity of the other’s interiority, persists through each stage of creation. This was no accident: Watteau’s unconventional technique provided him with the means not only to represent the gap between self and other but to introduce that gap into the organization of the image. The drawings served as the building blocks for a whole architecture of irresolution and ambiguity in the paintings, where the ideal of social cohesion they appear to depict teeters always on the edge of collapse.

Figure 26

Jean-Antoine Watteau, *Recruits Going to Join the Regiment* (*Recrue allant joindre le régiment*), ca. 1715 (cat. 51)

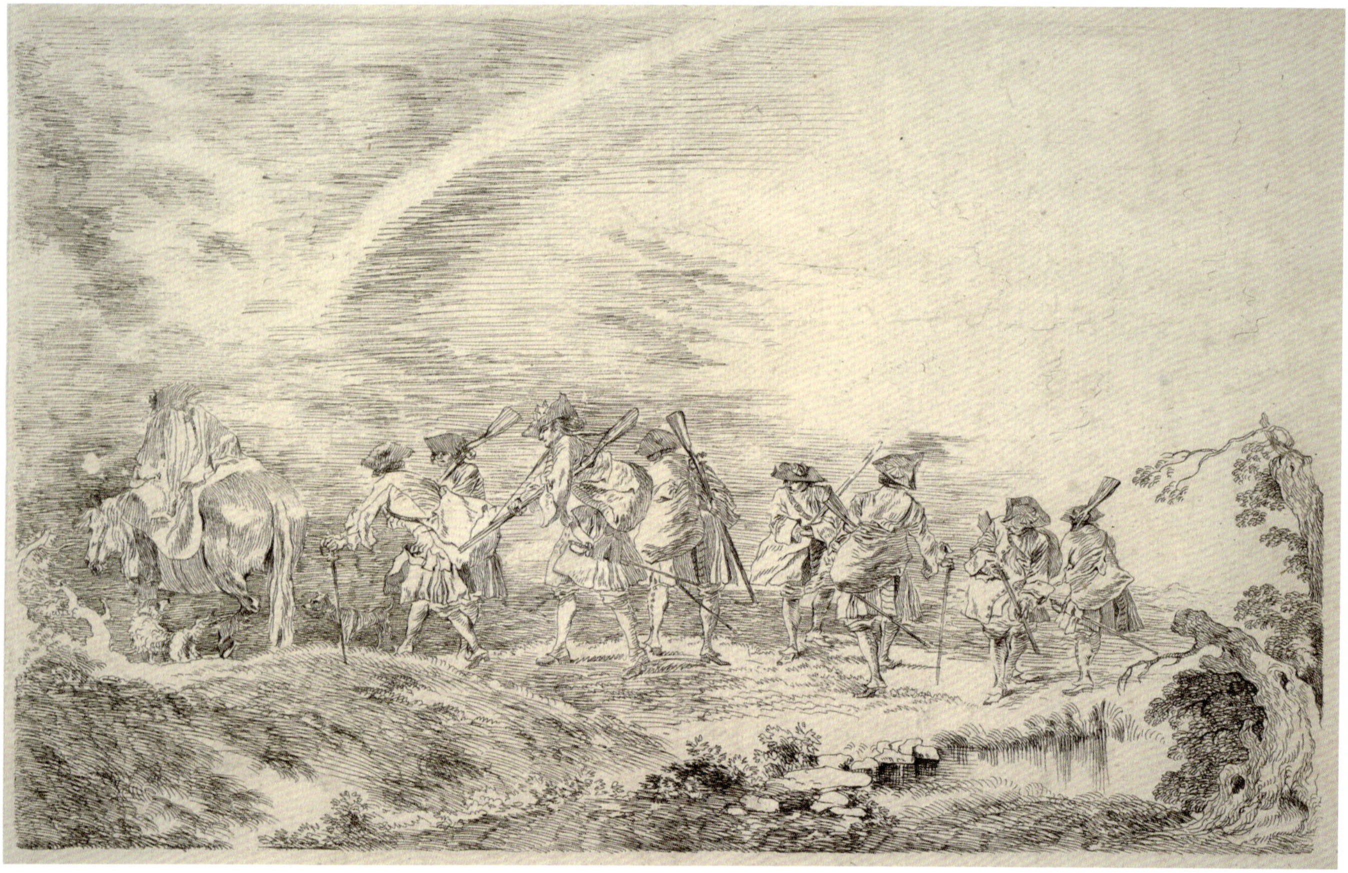

Figure 27

Jean-Antoine Watteau and Henri-Simon Thomassin, *Recruits Going to Join the Regiment*. Etching, dry point, and engraving. Musée du Louvre, Paris (N2486 folio 35)

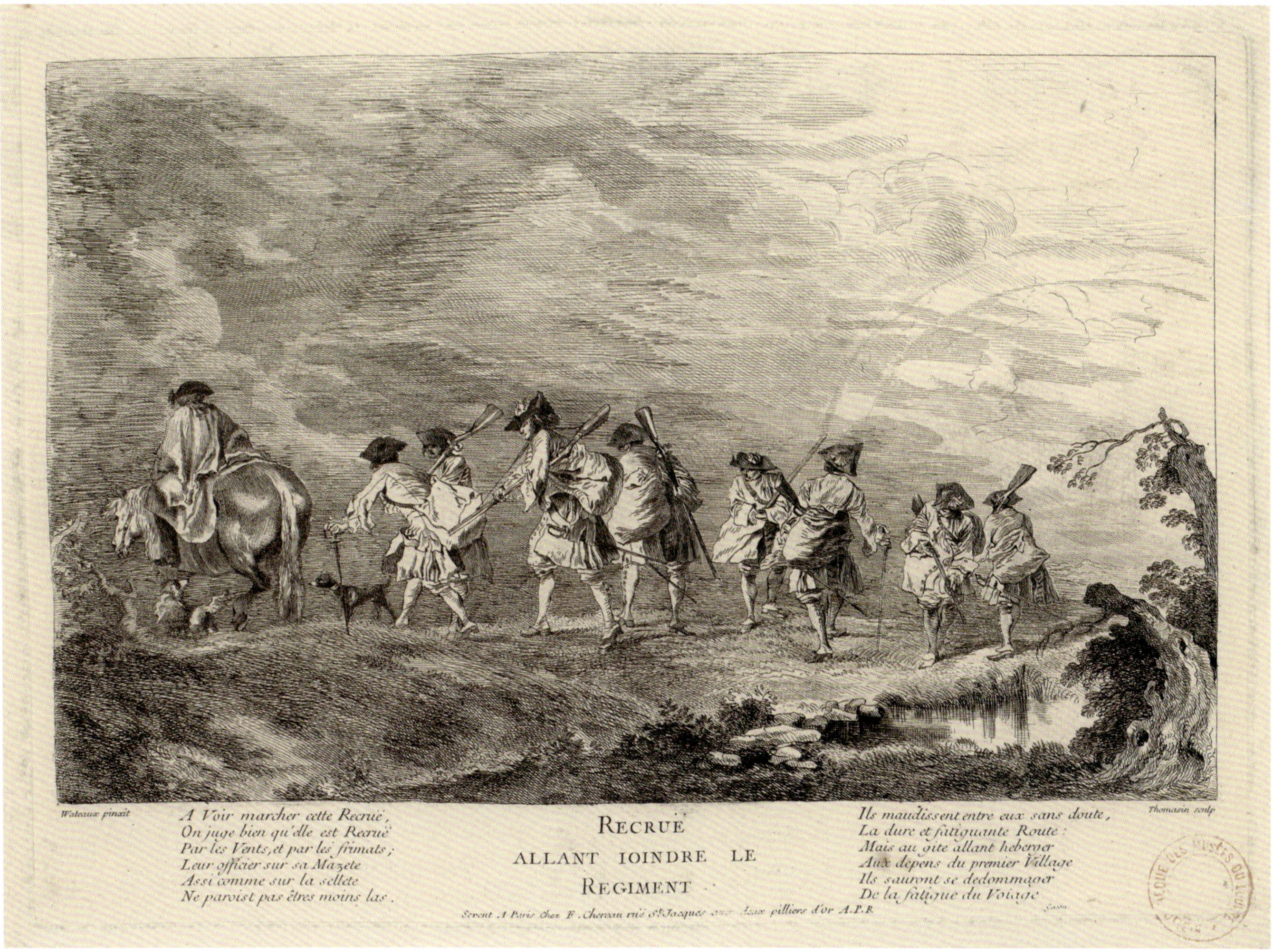

Painting and Beholder

The organization of this architecture deserves a closer look, for Watteau's paintings fail to resolve not only at the level of the individual encounters they depict but also as compositions. Scholars have noted the military paintings' "picturesque disorder" and their "charming disarray," but the significance of Watteau's compositional choices goes beyond the creation of picturesque or charming effects.[63] Inscribing the artist's vision of the self into the very structure of the image, they implicate the spectator in that vision.

Watteau, as we have seen, did not typically work out his compositions before creating his paintings but rather arranged his figures more spontaneously. This method went against the teaching not only of an old-guard academic artist like Le Brun but also of a more modish figure like Roger de Piles (1635–1709), the most influential art theorist in early eighteenth-century France. Contrary to Le Brun, de Piles argued that painting derived its power from visual and pictorial effects rather than its capacity to relate a narrative. Painting, he claimed, made its strongest impact when its forms were disposed in a unified and hierarchically ordered composition.[64] This he called the *tout ensemble*, a "general subordination of objects, one to another, which makes them converge all together to make but one."[65] To achieve the *tout ensemble*, a painting's composition had to be rigorously thought out, with the principal figures grouped in the center of the painting and accentuated with the proper distribution of light and shade, brightest in the center and progressively darker toward the periphery—an effect de Piles illustrated with a cluster of grapes, an analogy made famous by Titian (fig. 28, top).

Philips Wouwerman's *Cavalry Camp* (fig. 29), painted between 1638 and 1668 and a clear predecessor to Watteau's military works, exemplifies the *tout ensemble*[66]—hardly surprising given that de Piles derived many of his theories from the scores of seventeenth-century Flemish and Dutch works that were then entering Parisian collections. Here, the cavalrymen and horses are compressed in the center of the composition and bathed in light, much like Titian's bunch of grapes, while the few figures at the peripheries are cast in shadow. The upward thrust of the cavalryman's standard, augmented by

Figure 28

Roger de Piles and Pierre de Rochefort, cluster of grapes (above) and dispersed grapes (below), figs. 3 and 4 from *Cours de peinture par principe* (Paris, 1708). Etching and engraving. Houghton Library, Harvard University (Typ 715.08.693)

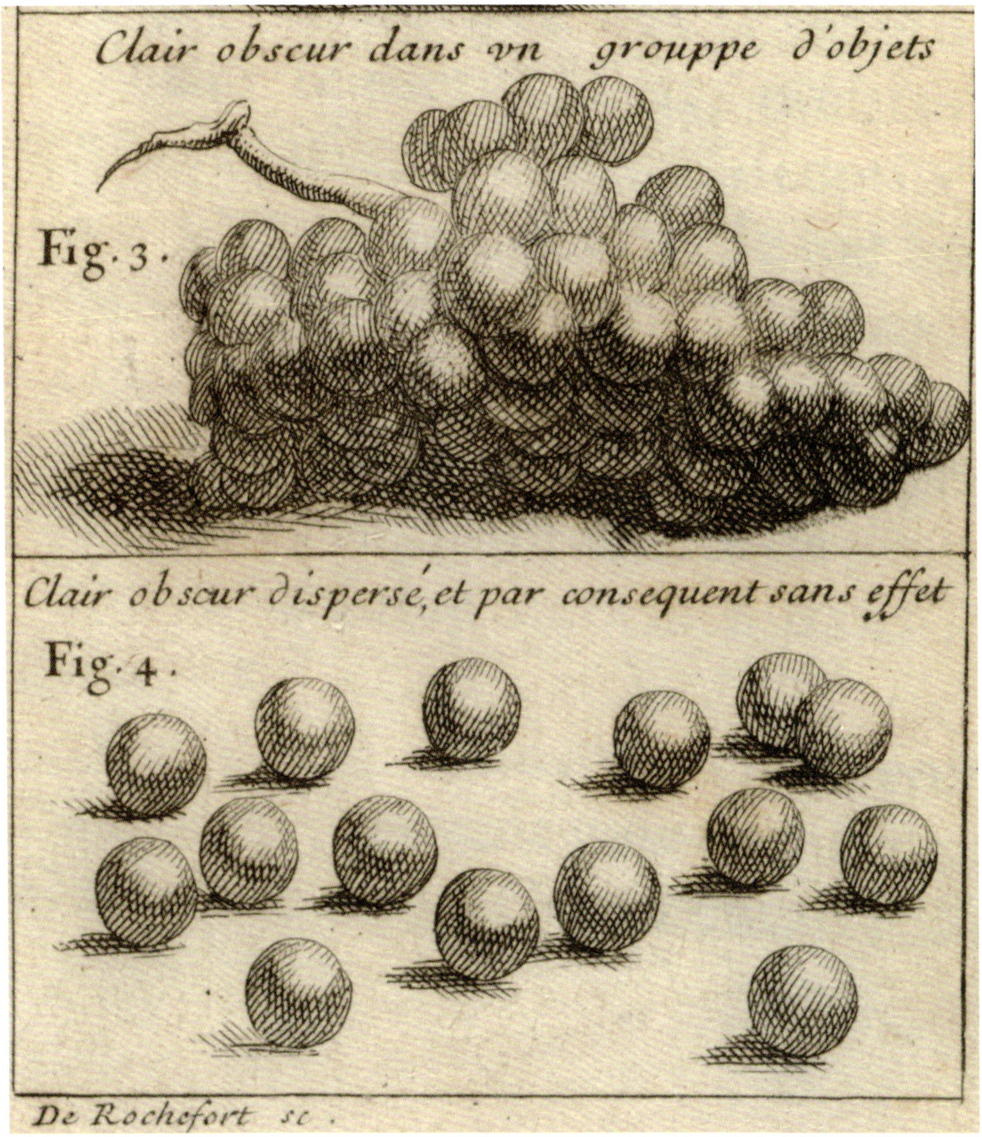

the jutting tents in the background and the sturdy column of clouds rising in the sky, reinforces this pull toward the center. The whole scene rises up with the quiet dignity of a mountain, harmonious and serene; the figures seem an almost natural part of the landscape, as though they have always been there.

The effect of a painting like Watteau's *Halt* (see fig. 16) is entirely different. Here, the soldiers and the women who accompany them are spread out almost haphazardly across a stage-like terrain, gathered into various, vaguely connected groups. No figure or group of figures dominates, and no hierarchical pictorial structure prevails (reflecting, in part, Watteau's focus on the common soldier, outside of the hierarchy of rank that structured the army). Where the unity of Wouwerman's painting deflects attention from the individual soldiers, subordinating them to the impression they create together in the overall pictorial structure, here the composition's *dis*unity makes each figure stand out individually, creating competing centers of interest.

The impression of disunity in the painting is enhanced by the effects of light and shade generated by the way Watteau deploys his drawings. Because he transposed his figures directly from his sketchbook, he copied the distribution of light as he first observed them onto the canvas as well.[67] This kind of light de Piles calls the "incidence of particular lights and shadows," the objective qualities of light, the way it actually falls on individual objects,[68] but for him a second kind of light took precedence: *clair-obscur*, which refers to the overall distribution of light across the painting and contributes to the unity of the *tout ensemble* by highlighting the figures and objects massed in the center.[69] In Watteau's canvas, the *tout ensemble* thus falters both in the distribution of objects in space and in the distribution of light on those objects. The effect is much like de Piles's counterexample to his bunch of grapes—a collection of grapes scattered about, with no concentration of form or light in the center (see fig. 28, bottom).

The compositional strategies of *The Halt* can be found, to one degree or another, in all of the military paintings—in the similarly frieze-like disposition of *Halt of a Detachment* (fig. 30); in the even more random distribution of figures in *The Supply Train* (see fig. 18), *The Burdens of War* (fig. 31), and *The*

Figure 29

Philips Wouwerman, *The Cavalry Camp*, 1638–68.
Oil on oak panel, 16 ¾ × 20 ¾ in. (42.5 × 52.7 cm).
The Frick Collection; Henry Clay Frick Bequest
(1901.1.136)

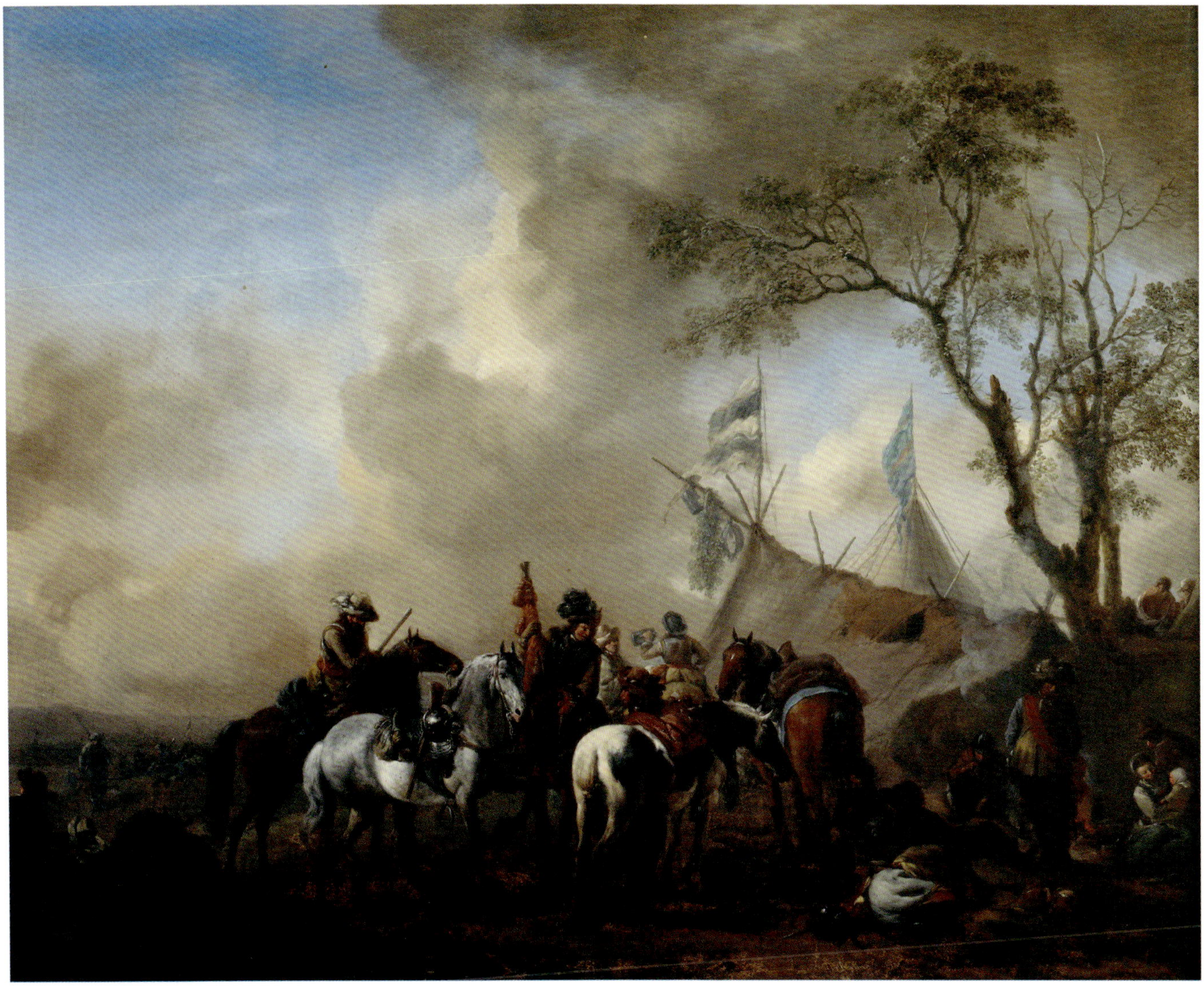

Respite from War (see fig. 15); and in the chaotic profusion of bodies strewn about in *Bivouac* (fig. 32). Not even Watteau's follower Nicolas Lancret went so far. In his *Military Camp* (fig. 33), for instance, he seems to have adopted Watteau's cut-and-paste method—in fact, many of the figures are borrowed directly from his master—but he could not resist the temptation to order the composition into a pyramid, and the result is a somewhat awkward stack of resting soldiers on the hill to the right. Watteau, on the contrary, never let the exigencies of a preconceived pictorial hierarchy determine the shape of his paintings. If the purpose of de Piles's *tout ensemble* was to impose order on the chaos of the world, Watteau embraced disorder as the wellspring of his art.[70]

On the one hand, Watteau's violation of the *tout ensemble* reinforces the psychologically fraught encounters among his soldiers. In *The Portal of Valenciennes* (see fig. 22) or *The Halt* (see fig. 16), for example, the disjunction among the figures not only results from their being forced from their isolation in the sketchbook into a social relation; it also derives from the physical distance between them. Instead of standing together at the center of the composition, many of the figures gaze toward each other from opposite ends of the canvas, their spatial detachment reinforcing the lack of convincing connection among them. In addition, their competing sources of light enclose each in his or her own luminary world, reinforcing the isolation and self-sufficiency of their interior worlds.

On the other hand, and perhaps more importantly, the compositional disorder of the military paintings draws the viewer into the vision of selfhood at their core: formal disjunction evokes psychological disjunction, and the disconnectedness among the figures finds an analog in the disconnectedness between painting and beholder. The purpose of de Piles's prescriptions was, above all, to concentrate the spectator's attention and give pleasure to the eyes, enthralling with illusion. The *tout ensemble*, he declared, "prevent[s] the eyes from wandering, and fix[es] them agreeably" in the center of the composition, seizing the attention of the spectator at first glance and "mak[ing] the painted objects more true . . . than the actual [*véritables*] ones."[71] The result was a kind of total absorption in the painted world—

Figure 30

Charles-Nicolas Cochin, after Jean-Antoine Watteau, *Halt of a Detachment* (*Détachement faisant halte*), ca. 1715 (cat. 50)

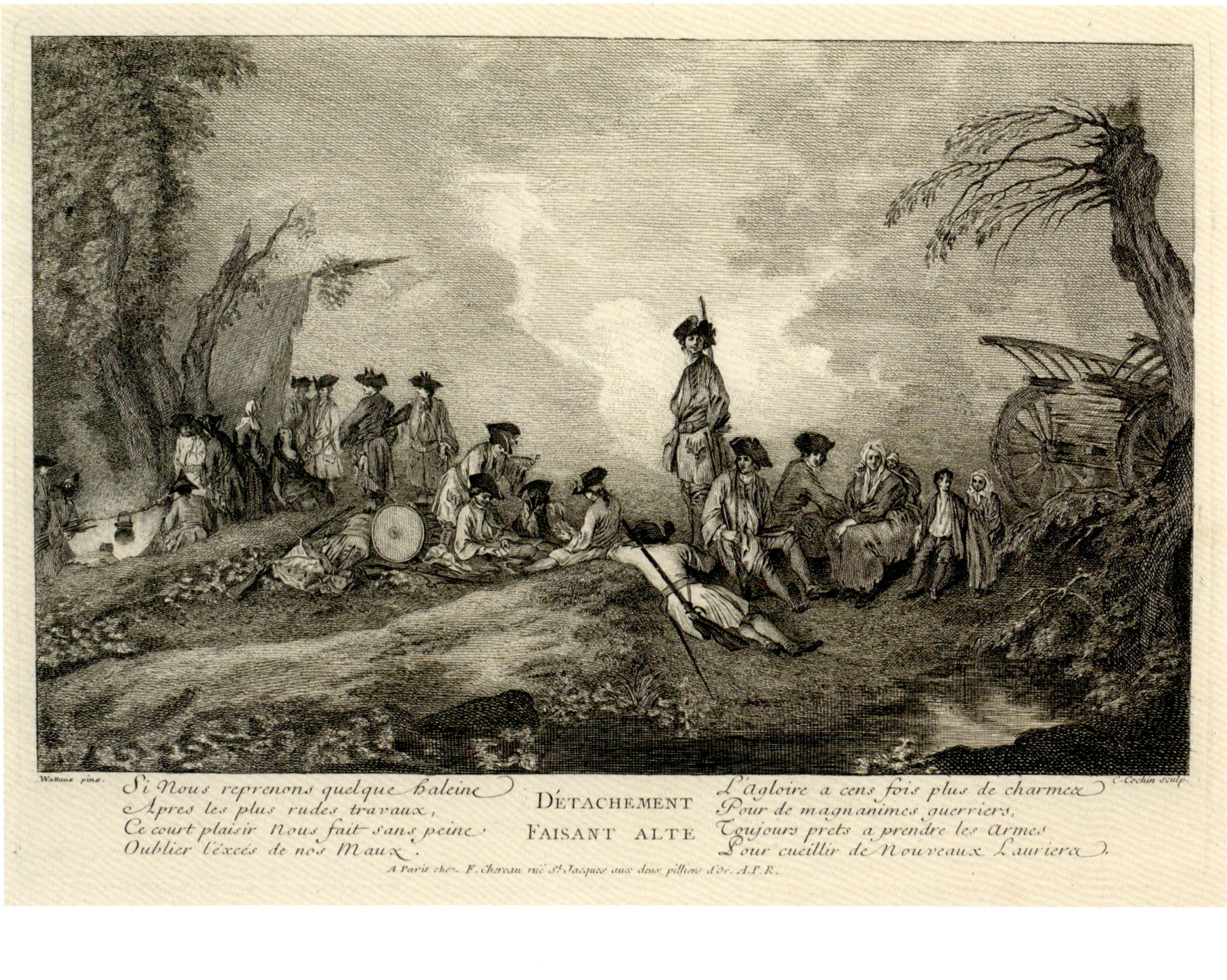

Figure 31

Jean-Antoine Watteau, *The Burdens of War* (*Les fatigues de la guerre*), ca. 1713–14 (cat. 48)

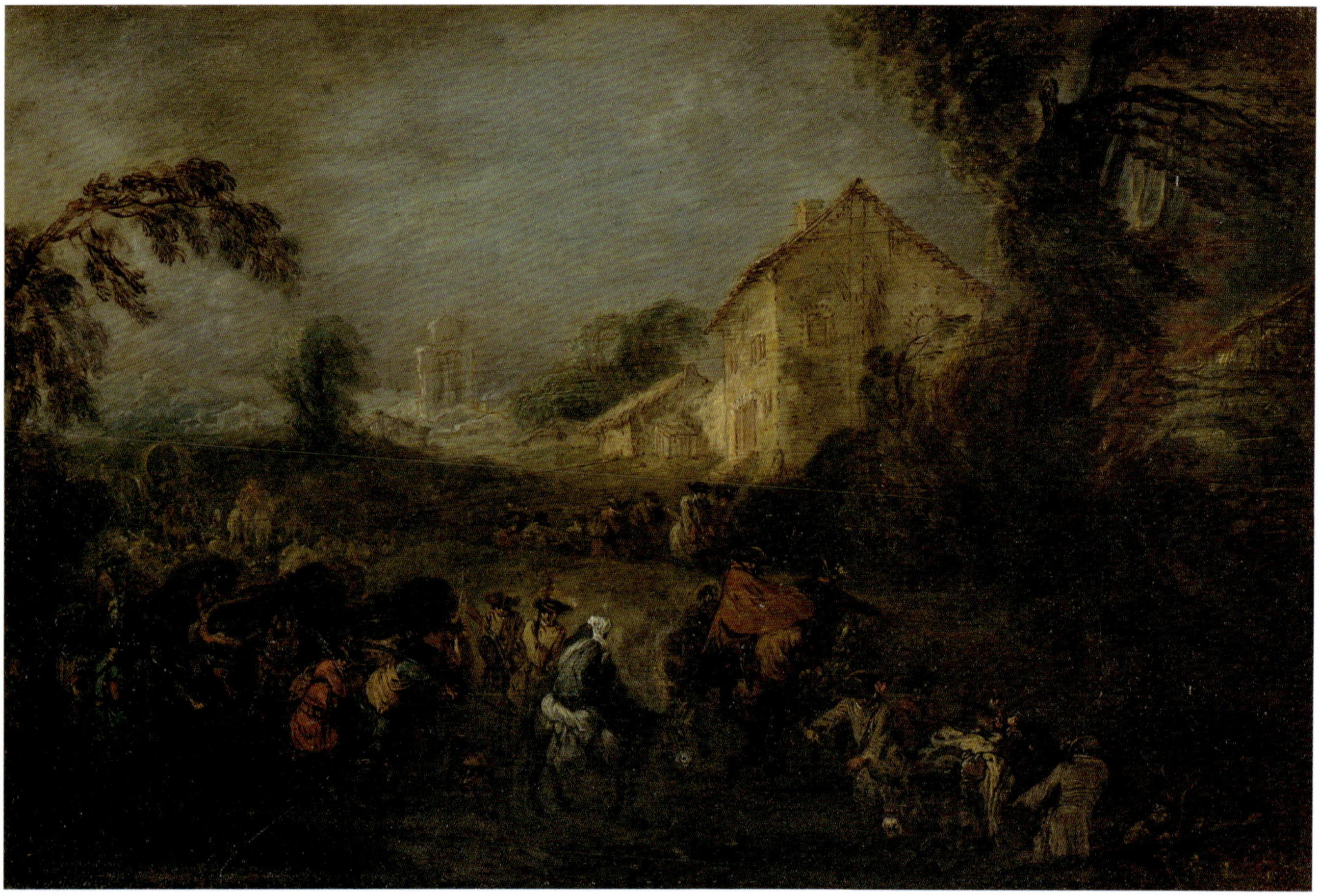

Figure 32

Jean-Antoine Watteau, *Bivouac* (*Camp volant*), ca. 1710 (cat. 44)

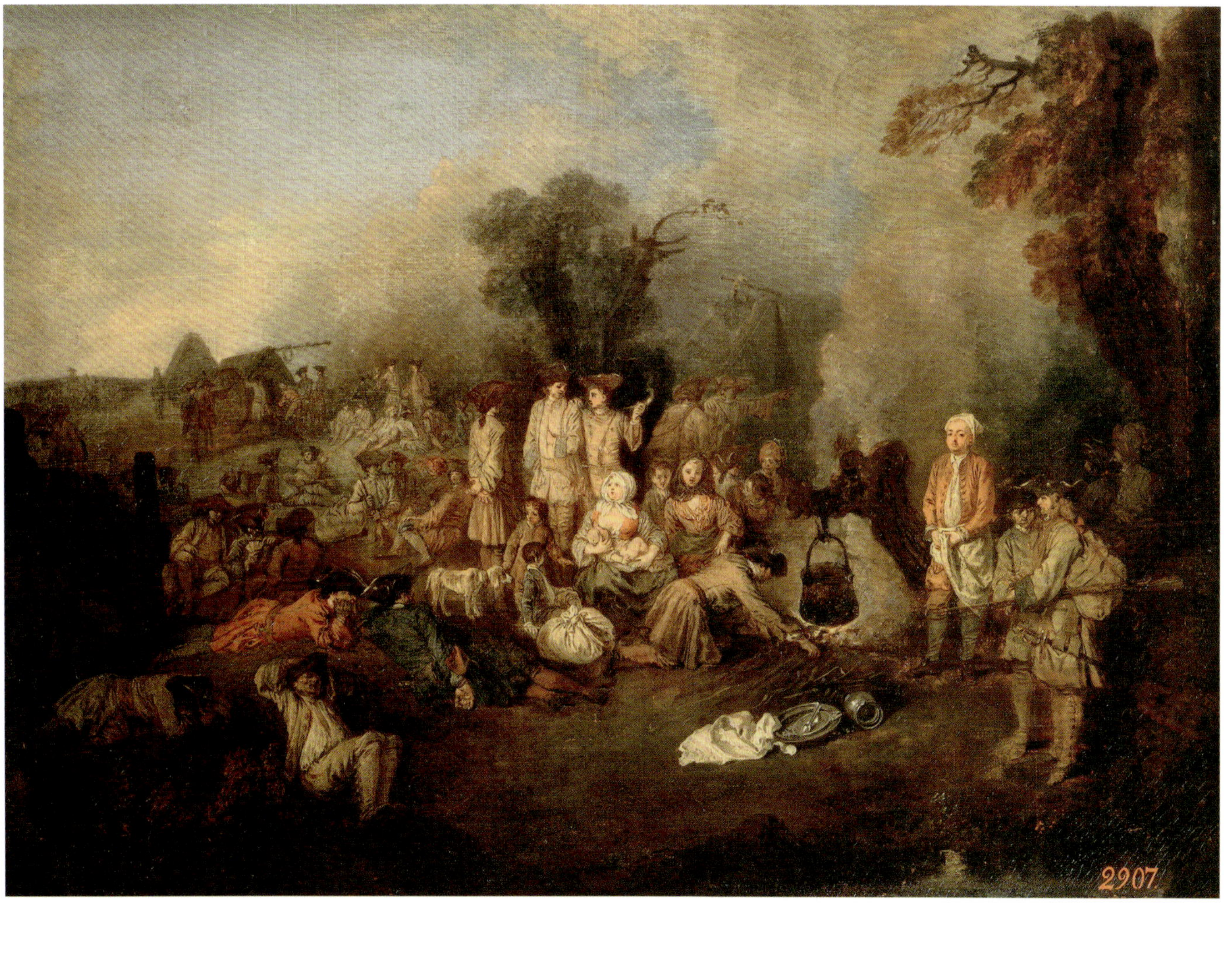

Figure 33

Nicolas Lancret, *Military Camp*, ca. 1722.
Oil on panel, 6 ⅞ × 8 ⅝ in. (17.5 × 22 cm).
Collection Dr. Mary Tavener Holmes

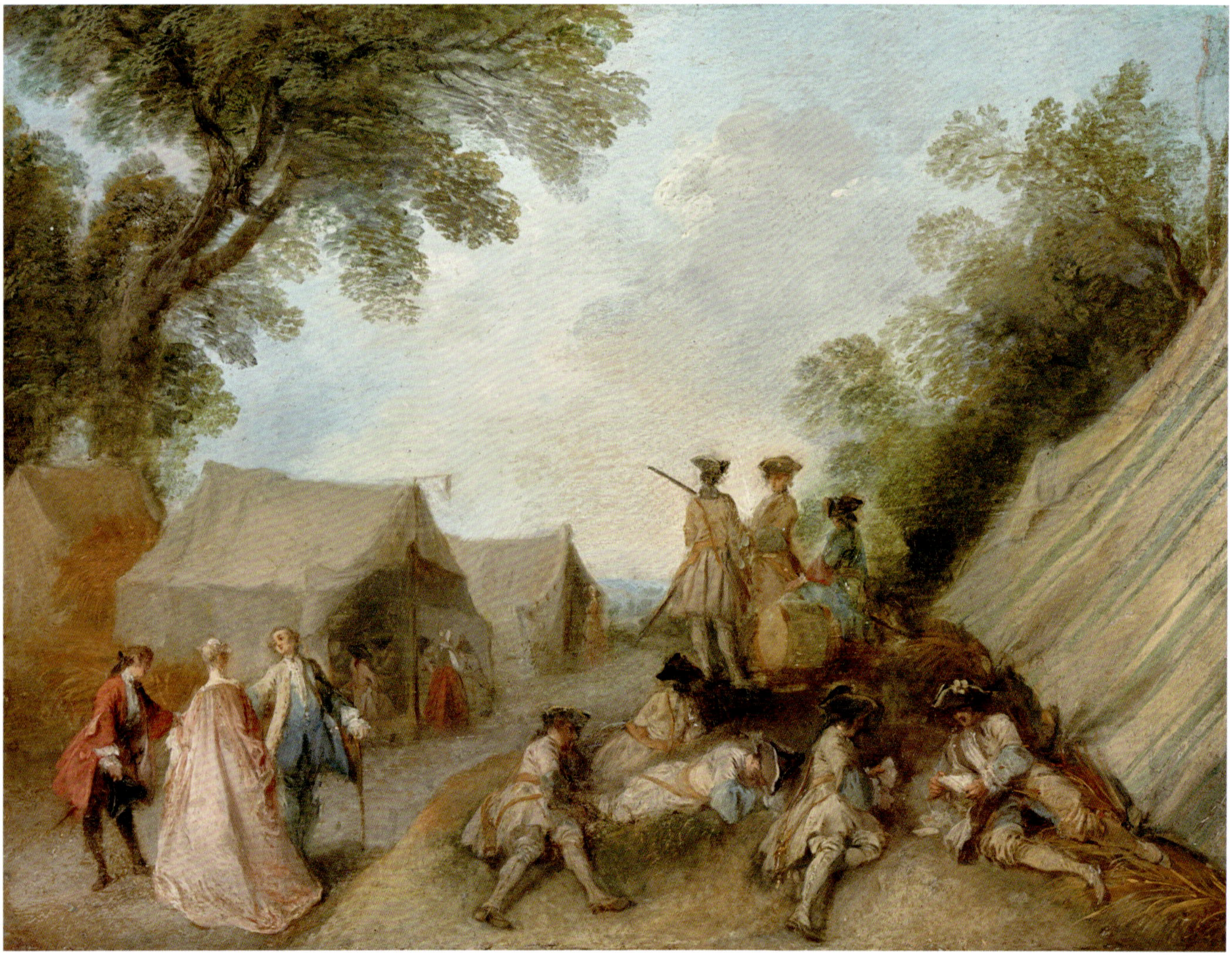

what de Piles called "enthusiasm," which "transports the mind to a state of admiration mixed with astonishment and ravishes the mind with such violence that it does not have time to reflect."[72]

Watteau's canvases offer a different kind of experience. If de Piles staked the satisfaction of the eye and the raptures of enthusiasm on fixing the spectator's gaze in the center of the canvas, Watteau mobilizes every means at his disposal to disturb the eye's repose. To return again to *The Portal of Valenciennes* (see fig. 22), for example, the arrangement of the two soldiers gazing from the middle toward the two soldiers at the edges of the composition invites the eye to shuttle between center and periphery as it follows the paths of the soldiers' looks. The various sources of light that illuminate the soldiers further unsettle the eye, thwarting the kind of intense absorption favored by de Piles.

What Watteau offers, then, is a new mode of viewing and a new relation to the canvas. A work like Wouwerman's *Cavalry Camp* (see fig. 29) seals every seam of representation, offers a simulacrum that seduces by idealizing nature. It exemplifies de Piles's advice that "good distribution [of objects] serves marvelously to express the subject. It gives force and grace to what is invented; it pulls the figures from confusion, and makes everything represented in the picture clearer, more apparent [*sensible*], and more capable of calling to and stopping the spectator."[73] Watteau's paintings, by contrast, consistently deliver a disordered scene, making the spectator aware of the artifice of his constructions and dispelling the comforting fiction of complete identification with the painted world. In *Recruits Going to Join the Regiment* (see figs. 26 and 27), for example, the eye travels across the graceful arabesque of figures, gliding across the opaque surfaces that enclose the soldiers' interiority but never able to enter into it. Though constructed from fragments of minutely observed bodies in motion, the scene fails to cohere. Rather than engrossing viewers in illusion, the work pushes them away, triggering contemplation, even reverie.[74]

From this perspective, we must reconsider what Watteau was after in these paintings and what attracted his audience to them. The military scenes of seventeenth-century Holland that inspired him were created for the pleasure of a bourgeois audience largely removed from the miseries of military life.[75] Similarly, Watteau's own canvases were aimed at a Parisian audience—cosmopolitan, affluent, and mostly unattached to Versailles and the court.[76] But, unlike their precedents, they are haunted by the specter of the War of the Spanish Succession, the effects of which no one in France escaped. And in this light, the paintings' refusal to cohere can be said to visualize the costs of war on the individual and society: Watteau shows us community on the verge of disintegration, and the spectator's own inability to be absorbed fully into the painted world makes that vision visceral. Yet it is difficult to imagine, as some scholars have suggested, that Watteau intended to indict war, however subtly, or that the admirers of his work appreciated them as critical commentaries on Louis XIV's militancy.[77] Watteau's vision is too elusive and ambiguous to proffer any "position" on war.

Like their northern forerunners, Watteau's military paintings were created primarily for their viewers' pleasure, but this was a pleasure of a deeper sort, more in line with the cultural and intellectual currents then sweeping Europe that put a strain on the old order of political, intellectual, and cultural authority.[78] Perhaps the gentleman officers who admired the works, like Caylus and La Roque, appreciated the way they reproduced their own psychological distance from the experience of the lowly infantrymen who served under them—but the lack of connection among his soldiers holds greater significance. It serves ultimately as a meditation on what it means to be an individual in society. It dramatizes the new territory that was emerging between public and private realms, at a moment when the conflicting demands of each were becoming increasingly apparent. Too small to be viewed comfortably by more than one person, Watteau's canvases were meant for the individual, for contemplation in the sort of intimate *cabinets*, small rooms for private retreat, that were becoming fashionable.[79] Eschewing the placid, idealizing visions of Wouwerman, Watteau undoes the fiction of intersubjective transparency and perfect social cohesion to elicit a new kind of experience. Unable to lose themselves entirely in the scene or access the interiority of the figures depicted within it, viewers are left to return to their own inner experience, to retreat into themselves. Watteau takes an apparently unpleasant subject and makes it a source of a new kind of subjective pleasure.

It is worth noting that much of what we have observed in Watteau's military paintings obtains also in his more famous *fêtes galantes*—for instance, the lovers' gazes that never quite meet or the compositions that never cohere into a unified whole. The theme of military life occupied a special place in Watteau's vision of subjectivity in the way it pushed the issue of the gap between self and other to an extreme, but the content of the *fêtes galantes* also provided a point of access to the issue. In a way, the problem of the opacity of others' inner lives is even more glaring here since it is tested by the relation that promises to dissolve the boundary between self and other: love. War and love, then, are not so dissimilar in Watteau's universe, for if love joins people together, so does war—not only for companionship but, more fundamentally, for survival. In this sense, both the military works and the *fêtes galantes* offer a vision of coexistence within a community, but it is a fragile coexistence. And it is the way they capture this that gives Watteau's works their poignancy, shaped as they are by the essentially modern insight that society is held together by only the thinnest of threads, that our connections are menaced by mutual incomprehension and estrangement. Yet, as Watteau understood, the very existence of society, in the realms of military life and courtly love alike, depends on our forging ahead anyway. ⚜

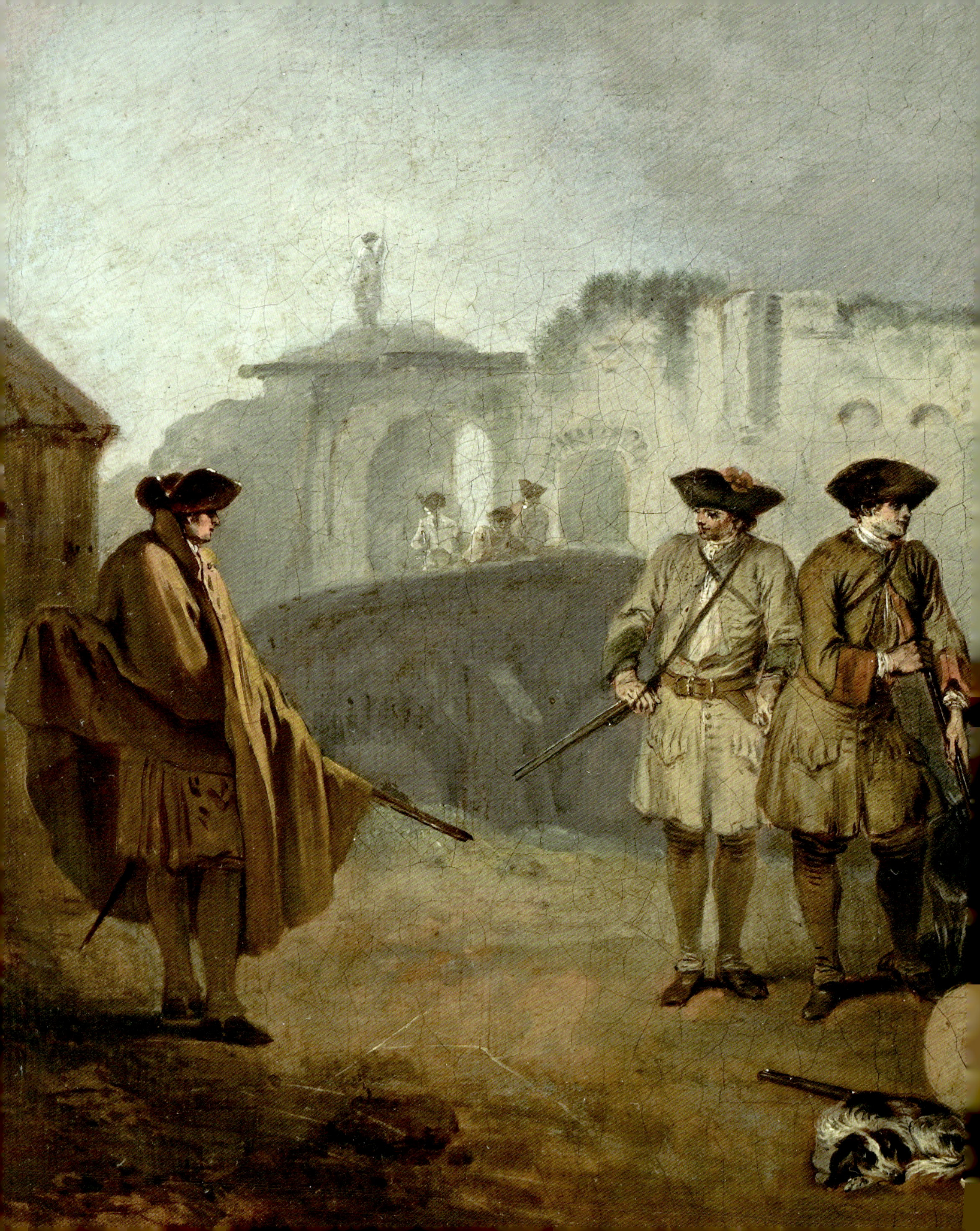

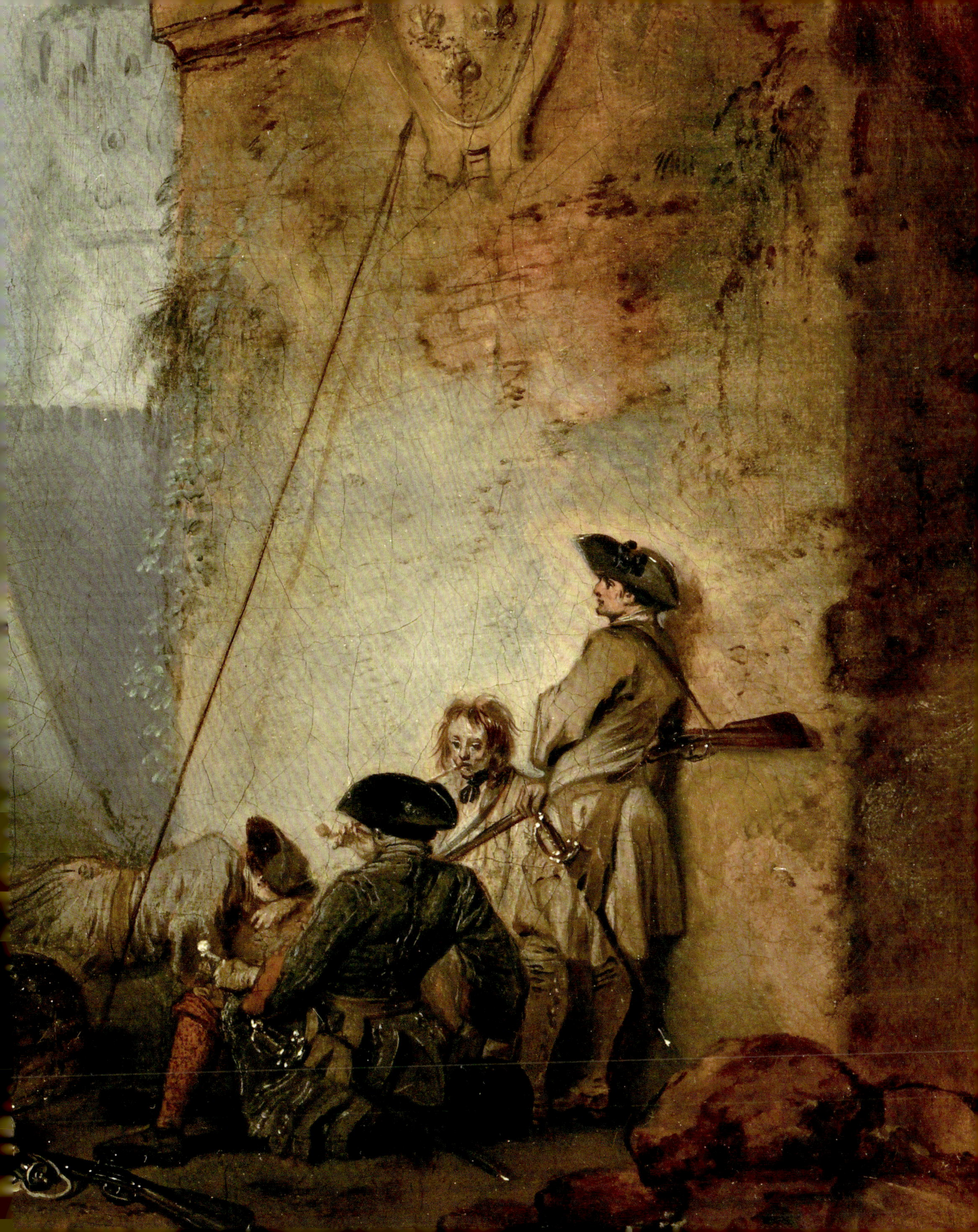

Notes

1. Gersaint 1984, 33–34. The exact painting to which Gersaint is referring has been the subject of some debate. Scholars have traditionally identified the works as *Return from the Campaign* and *Bivouac* (cat. 44), but Dacier, Vuaflart, C. Michel, and Glorieux believe that Gersaint is talking about *Recruits Going to Join the Regiment* (cat. 51) and *Halt of a Detachment* (cat. 50). See Michel 2008, 37; and Glorieux 2011, 79. The drawings related to *Recruits Going to Join the Regiment* (cats. 24–29), among Watteau's boldest and most sophisticated drawings of soldiers, suggest a later date for *Recruits Going to Join the Regiment.*

2. For a long time, scholars believed that Watteau returned home in 1709, but a recently discovered passport delivered to him in 1710 for travel to the province of Hainault confirms a later date. See Hattori 2004. Glorieux (2011, 79) speculates that one of the reasons Watteau wanted to return home when he did was that on February 22, 1710, his grandfather, Bartholomé Watteau, had died, leaving his grandmother with financial difficulties. In any case, it appears to have been a brief visit. As his friend, the collector Jean de Jullienne, writes, "he did not stay long, and after having made a few paintings, among them several studies of camps and soldiers from nature, he returned to Paris." Jullienne 1984, 14.

3. There is no firm chronology for Watteau's military works. Some scholars have argued that they all date from around 1709–12, but it has become clear that some of the drawings and paintings were executed as late as 1715. See "Complete List of Watteau's Military Works" in this publication.

4. Caylus 1984, 62.

5. Oliver Banks (1977, 143) even ventures that the popularity of the military paintings eclipsed that of all of Watteau's other work.

6. The Battle of Malplaquet took place on September 11, 1709. On the War of the Spanish Succession and the Battle of Malplaquet, see Lynn 1999, 266–360. On the French army in the age of Louis XIV, see Corvisier 1964 and Lynn 1997.

7. Plax 2000, 96–98.

8. It was Edgar Munhall (1992, 20–21) who suggested that *The Portal of Valenciennes* actually depicts the ramparts of Valenciennes, but the evidence is not conclusive (the title was not given until 1912). More recently, Guillaume Glorieux (2011, 87) has proposed that Watteau copied the background from the title page of the print series *Dessins de quelques conduites de troupes, canons et attaques de villes* by Stefano della Bella (1610–1664).

9. On the taste for Flemish and Dutch painting in early eighteenth-century France, see Banks 1977, 60–105; and Ziskin 2012. Banks also discusses the influence of these works on Watteau's military works. There was a wide variety of seventeenth-century Dutch and Flemish military scenes; Watteau seems to have drawn most from scenes of military camps, known as Legerkamp scenes. On the Legerkamp genre, see Spaans 1998, 164–81.

10. Farge 1996, 81. Similarly, Hal Opperman has written, "War disrupts the interior landscape of man, his tranquility, his most primitive and sacred right . . . Watteau depicts a state of serenity *in spite of.*" Opperman 1987, 28. Italics in the original.

11. War, as Christy Pichichero (2008a, 2–3) observes in her illuminating study of military culture in eighteenth-century France, "offer[s] itself as a privileged space or circumstance for man to discover and define his relationship to self and other."

12. Dezallier d'Argenville 1984, 47. Jullienne (1984, 17) made a similar remark in his biography of the artist.

13. Caylus 1984, 78.

14. Ibid., 79.

15. Glorieux 2011, 83.

16. Wintermute et al. 1999, 98.

17. Lajer-Burcharth 2015, 33.

18. DeJean 1997, 78–123.

19. Campe and Weber 2014, 1.

20. DeJean 1997, 78–123. For various perspectives on selfhood and interiority in the seventeenth and eighteenth centuries, see Tocanne 1978, 141–65; Muchembled 1988; Beugnot 1996; Rohou 2002; and Wahrman 2004.

21. Charles Perrault, *Parallèle des Anciens et des Modernes, en ce qui regarde les arts et les sciences*, vol. 2 (Paris 1692), 30, quoted in DeJean 1997, 110. I have altered her translation slightly.

22. Bell 2007, 44.

23. Pichichero 2008a, 11–51.

24. Puységur 1749, n.p., published posthumously. On Puységur, see Colson 1999, 145–50.

25. Opperman 1987, 23–28.

26. Pichichero 2008b.

27. "[I]t was," as Joan DeJean (1997, 123) writes, "widely accepted that, in the emotional exchange that was the essence of the affective revolution, each sensitive heart recognized simultaneously its own emotions and those of its partner heart. This was the dream of transparency, an idealized vision . . . according to which perfect self-knowledge was synonymous with perfect knowledge of the other."

28. See especially Bryson 1983, 69–88. My interpretation here is indebted to Bryson's, but where he focuses on the narrative implications of Watteau's divergences from Le Brun, I focus on their affective implications.

29. See Montagu 1994.

30. On the painting, see Kirchner 2013.

31. Even though, in fact, he gets the narrative wrong, writing that Sisygambis, in yellow, bows before Alexander after mistaking Hephaestion for him when in fact she is shown in the midst of her error, bowing before Hephaestion.

32. Félibien 1704, 14. The original French edition was published in 1663. I have altered Parsons's translation.

33. On the illegibility of Watteau's bodies, see Bryson 1983, 58–88.

34. Coypel 2003, 416.

35. Bryson 1983, 39–43.

36. Coypel 2003, 494.

37. La Bruyère 1691, 246.

38. A parallel can also be found in the verses accompanying engraved portraits of the period, which emphasize that though artists can perfectly depict the faces of their sitters they cannot capture their spirit or heart. See Coquery 1997, 30.

39. Or perhaps, since his studies for his more courtly *fêtes galantes* betray the same refusal, it more generally reflects his status as an outsider to the actual court.

40. Our own inability to decipher *The Family of Darius at the Feet of Alexander* with Félibien's ease confirms Watteau's implicit stance: far from being universal, Le Brun's system of expression conforms to a culturally and historically specific code alien to us today.

Cat. 52 (detail)

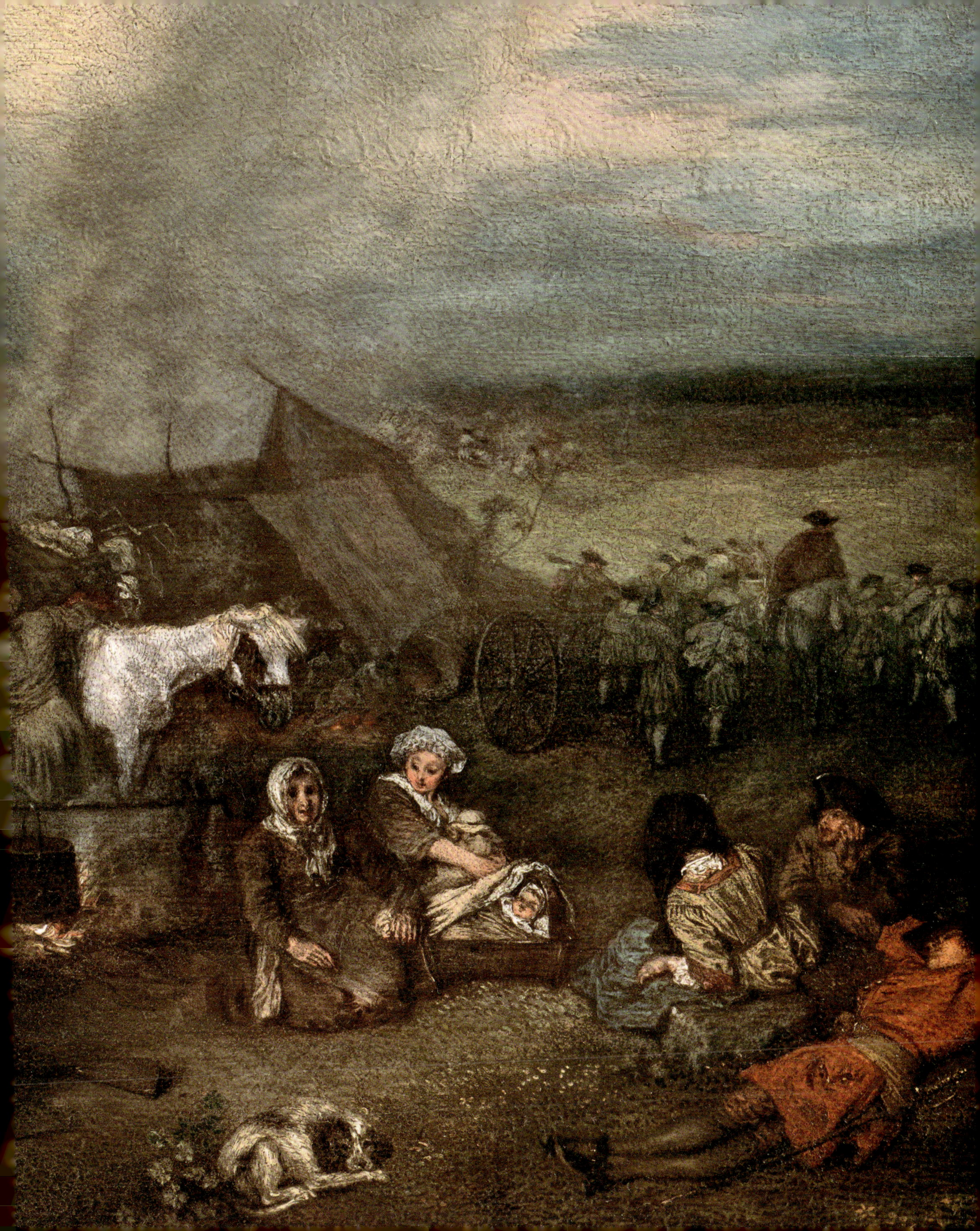

41. Lajer-Burcharth 2015, 24–30. However, I differ from Lajer-Burcharth in seeing Watteau's empiricist approach in Lockean rather than Humean terms. For Lajer-Burcharth, "Watteau's figure studies speak of an understanding of the person as an irreducible diversity of impressions that unfold in time to an observing mind" (2015, 27); that is, they reflect David Hume's view that personal identity is a fiction, that we are nothing but a series of fleeting sensory impressions. As will become clear, I am arguing for a differing view of Watteau's empiricism. Drawing from John Locke, I see in Watteau's focus on moments of private withdrawal—on moments of interiority—an acknowledgment of exactly the kind of coherent, interiorized self rejected by Hume.

42. Lajer-Burcharth (2015) explores the diverse implication of temporality for Watteau's drawing practice at length.

43. Locke 1996, 138.

44. Ibid., 146.

45. Seigel 2005, 101.

46. Tillerot 2010, 312–13.

47. On the importance of the "idea" in French art theory, see Puttfarken 2000, 229–62. On its ascent in European art theory, see Panofsky 1968.

48. For a useful overview of academic drawing practice in seventeenth- and eighteenth-century France, as well as Watteau's place within that tradition and his subsequent influence on it, see Mérot and Raux-Carpentier 1998, 25–51.

49. However, as Marianne Roland Michel (1984, 113) points out, the drawings could just as likely be the record of a scene Watteau actually observed or a drawing done from memory after the painting. Other drawings are worth mentioning, but they are not strictly related to the military paintings. One is *Soldiers Playing Cards in a Ruin* (cat. 4); for a long time, it was considered a study made from nature, possibly a scene Watteau observed while in Valenciennes or else a compositional study for a painting that was never executed, but Martin Eidelberg (2001, 31–34) has shown that it is in fact based on a painting by Henry Ferguson, *Soldiers Playing Cards in a Ruin* (whereabouts unknown). The other drawing is *Soldiers Helping Their Wounded Comrades* (Rosenberg and Prat 1996, cat. 73). Margaret Morgan Grasselli (1987, 99–100) calls it a military scene, but, though the men are armed, they do not appear to be soldiers, given their attire. Furthermore, the dramatic yet mysterious subject, with its relative unity of action, does not relate to any of the other military works and thus should not, in my opinion, be classified with them. On Watteau's compositional drawings more generally, see Eidelberg 1977, chs. 1, 3, and 4.

50. On this kind of procedure in eighteenth-century art more generally, see Pullins *forthcoming*.

51. Caylus 1984, 78–79.

52. Rosenberg and Prat 1996, 282.

53. Caylus 1984, 79.

54. Vidal 1992, 47; ibid., 45.

55. On women in military camps in early modern Europe, see Lynn 2008, 66–117. Mary Vidal (1992, 46–47) and Julie Anne Plax (2000, 84–86) offer provocative interpretations of the women in *The Halt* in their respective studies.

56. Unusually, all of the figures on these sheets were used in the painting, though they were likely cut from a larger sheet with other figures, as were most of Watteau's drawings.

57. Susanna Caviglia (2016, 40–69) has uncovered a related, though distinct, phenomenon in French history painting of the mid-eighteenth century, in which artists' use of absorbed figures drawn from life in their canvases effected a crisis of pictorial narrative. The classic study of absorption in eighteenth-century French painting is Fried 1980.

58. It should be noted, however, that the man lying down with his head buried in his arm is similar to the sleeping soldier in the sheet of the *Three Studies of a Soldier and a Kneeling Man* (cat. 15) discussed above, though he does not match the sketch exactly. The figure could therefore be adopted from the drawing or from a now-lost study. Also interesting, although a direct relation to the painting is unlikely, is that Watteau has reprised the drawing's combination of a sitting, standing, and sleeping soldier, now showing the sitting man from behind, the standing man completely upright, and the sleeping one at a more horizontal angle, as well as adding the sallow-faced soldier slumped against the wall.

59. Félibien 1704, 14. I have altered Parsons's translation.

60. For an analogous chain of emotions in seventeenth-century French theater, see Guyot and Thouret 2009.

61. André Félibien, "Mémoires . . . ," in Blunt 1964, 196–97.

62. Jullienne 1726, vol. 1, preface, no page number.

63. Adhémar and Huyghe 1950, 99; Camesasca and Sunderland 1971, 99; quoted in Opperman 1987, 24.

64. See Puttfarken 1985, 38–124; and Puttfarken 2000, 263–78.

65. De Piles 1766, 100.

66. Wouwerman likely followed the standard procedure used in the French Royal Academy, beginning with compositional studies and then making individual studies. Schumacher 2006, 56.

67. Edgar Munhall (1992, 16) makes a similar observation.

68. De Piles 1766, 285.

69. Ibid., 285–88.

70. On the use of de Piles's *tout ensemble* as an ordering device, see Démoris 1997, 47–50.

71. De Piles 1766, 76; and De Piles 1699, 60.

72. De Piles 1766, 107.

73. Ibid., 76.

74. I have explored Watteau's subversions of de Piles's theories and his invitation to reverie in greater depth in Wile 2014, 319–37.

75. Rosen 2006, 170–71.

76. On Watteau's audience, see Michel 2008, 123–63.

77. Opperman 1987 and Plax 2000, 53–107.

78. See Hazard 2013 and DeJean 1997.

79. On the rise of private space and its relation to selfhood, see Ranum 1989, 207–64.

Cat. 19 (detail)

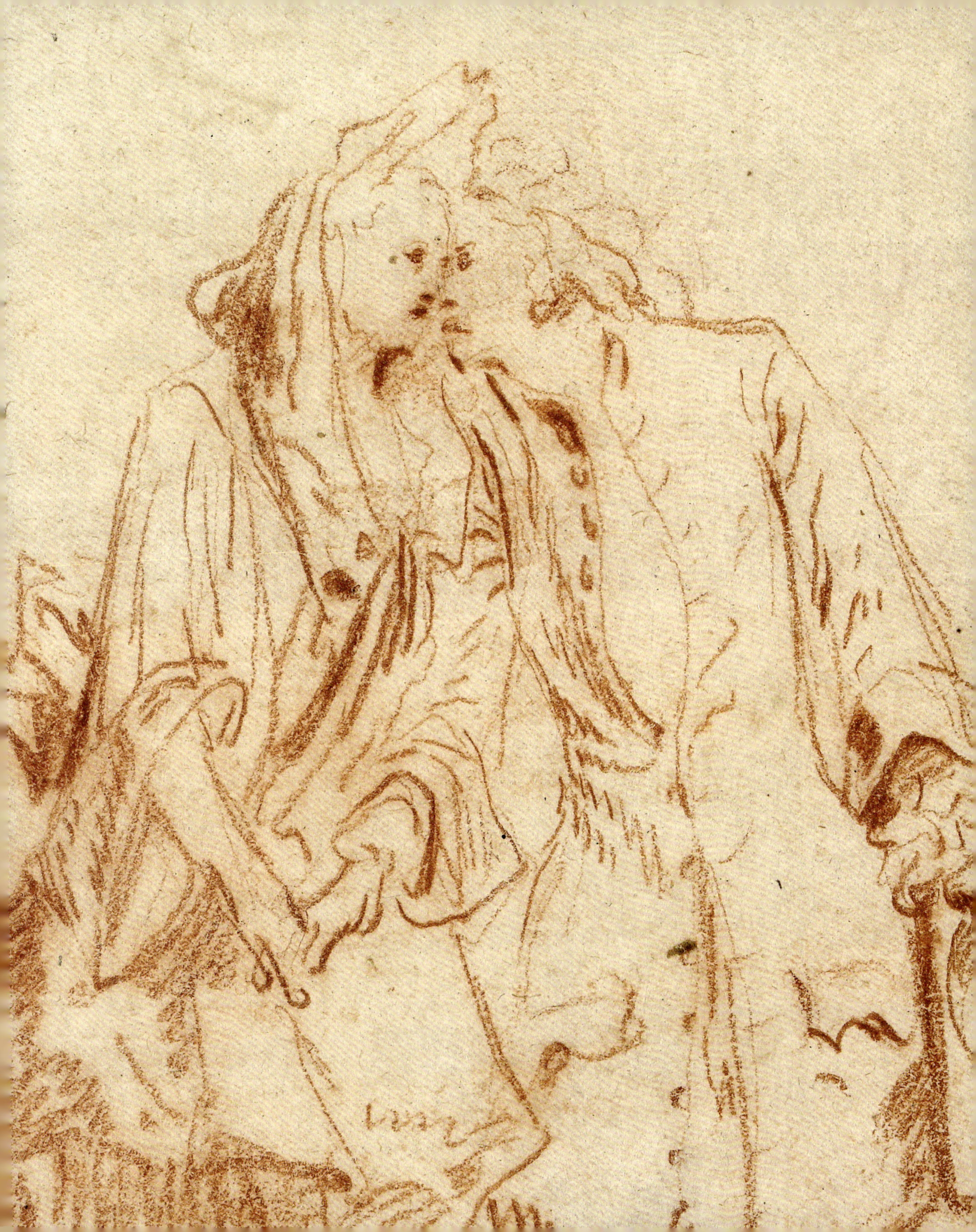

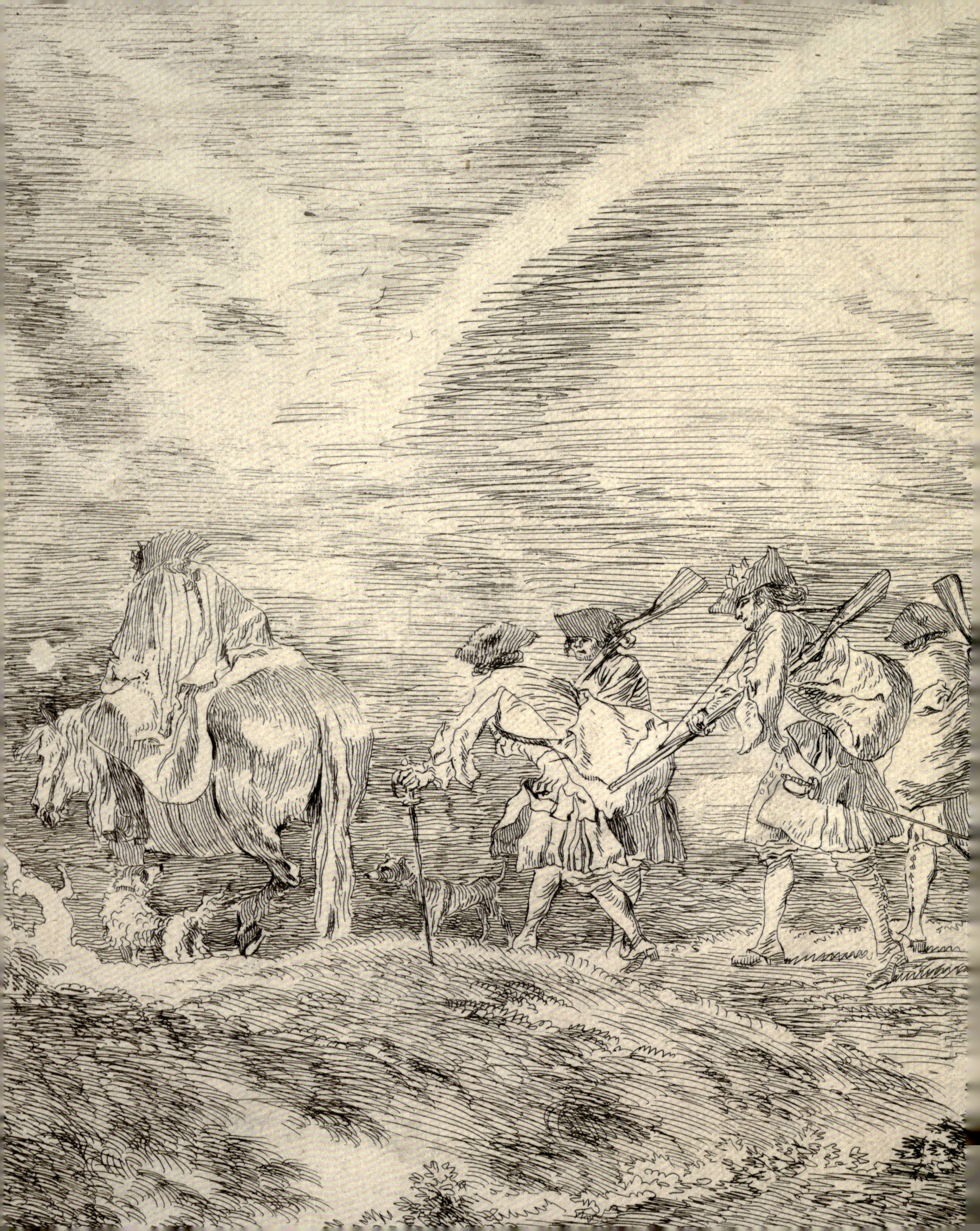

COMPLETE LIST OF WATTEAU'S MILITARY WORKS

This list represents the first complete catalogue of Watteau's military work: drawing, painting, and print. Its compilation presented certain difficulties. Copies and pastiches after Watteau's military works (which space limitations prevent me from including here) proliferated in the eighteenth century, and the number of drawings and paintings accepted as by Watteau has varied considerably over the last century and beyond. What follows, therefore, represents a conservative compilation of what most scholars today attribute to Watteau. I have left out works not strictly related to the military works, including the military men in *Figures de modes*, but I have included drawings that Watteau used in his military paintings even if they themselves do not depict military subjects, such as cats. 20 and 31. Since many of Watteau's drawings and paintings are now lost, I have also listed prints after Watteau's work in Jean de Jullienne's extraordinary effort to engrave the artist's entire oeuvre, known collectively as the *Recueil Jullienne*—the two volumes of the *Figures de différents caractères* for the drawings (the first volume appearing in 1726 and the second in 1728) and the two volumes of *Œuvre gravé* for the paintings (published in 1735, with prints released individually beforehand). These collections are in no small part responsible for the fame of Watteau's military works in the eighteenth century. I have, finally, listed the proofs for the *Figures de différents caractères*, compiled in the collection known as the *Recueil de Valenciennes*.

My intention is to show the range of Watteau's representation of military subjects and document the connections between his drawings and paintings; as a result, my entries are not meant to be exhaustive. Bibliographic entries represent only a selection of the literature on each work. In the case of drawings and engravings after lost drawings, I give only catalogue numbers from Pierre Rosenberg and Louis-Antoine Prat's *Antoine Watteau, 1684–1721: Catalogue raisonné des dessins*, the definitive catalogue of Watteau's drawings, and significant work that has appeared after its publication. For earlier work, including Martin Eidelberg and Margaret Morgan Grasselli's important discussions, I refer readers to Rosenberg and Prat's bibliography. Catalogue numbers for drawings refer to volumes 1 and 3 for engravings after lost drawings. Unfortunately, no catalogue raisonné of comparable quality to Rosenberg and Prat's yet exists for Watteau's paintings, so I have listed catalogue numbers for some (but not all) of the catalogues raisonnés we do have, in addition to other significant references. Rather than repeat references to books and articles that discuss the military works as a group in each entry, I refer readers here to the following works: Banks 1977, 143–50; Michel 1984, 167–70; Posner 1984, 31–40; Opperman 1987, 23–28; Vidal 1992, 43–49; Farge 1996; Plax 2000, 53–107; Michel 2008, 174–75; and Glorieux 2011, 78–96.

For most of Watteau's military work, dating with certainty is impossible; even the two paintings to which Edme-François Gersaint refers in his biography (1984, 33–34) are a matter of debate. Generally, Watteau's military paintings are dated from about 1708 to 1715, and within that timespan a stylistic progression seems discernible, from the stiff early studies to the freer, bolder final studies. Nonetheless, Watteau shifted styles often, and scholars do not agree on where all of the studies fall within that range. The chronology I propose here will certainly not be accepted by all, and I do not claim it is definitive. The recent rediscovery of Watteau's passport (Hattori 2004), however, does give at least one firm date from which to work and compels us to date many of the drawings a bit later than they have been by Rosenberg and Prat and others—assuming, as I do, that Watteau did not begin depicting military subjects in earnest until his return to Valenciennes, which his passport confirms was in September 1710 rather than sometime in 1709, as had often been presumed. The dates proposed here reflect this revision. In the interest of space, I explain my dating only if it diverges significantly from the opinions of most scholars or if scholarly opinion is already sharply at odds.

Those works with an asterisk (*) are in the exhibition that this catalogue accompanies.

Abbreviations

AH: Adhémar and Huyghe 1950
C: Camesasca 1982
DVH: Dacier, Vuaflart, and Hérold 1921–29
F: Ferré 1972
G: Goncourt 1875
RP: Rosenberg and Prat 1996

Cat. 51 (detail)

Drawings

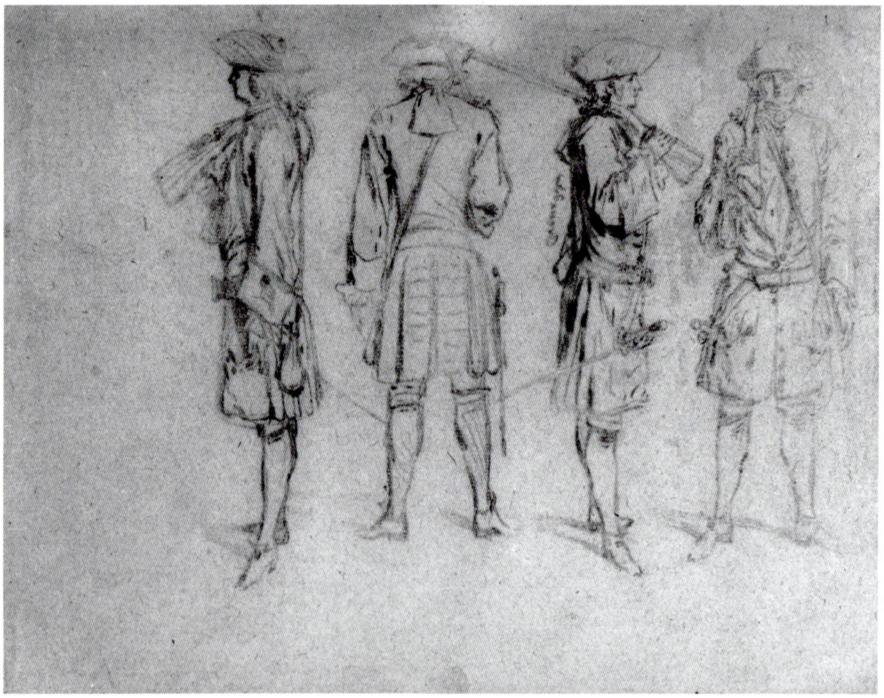

1

Four Studies of a Soldier with a Musket, ca. 1709
Counterproof in red chalk, laid down (original lost), 6 ½ × 8 ⅝ in. (16.5 × 21.8 cm)
Nationalmuseum, Stockholm (NM H 217: 157/1866)

Inscription: Vertically between the figures in red chalk: *Grenadier* (in counterproof).
Provenance: Acquired from Watteau by Count Carl Gustav Tessin; entered into the collection of the Royal Library in Stockholm, then into the Royal Museum, Stockholm.
Selected literature: RP cat. 25.
Prints after: Four figures etched in reverse after the drawing by Jean Audran in *Figures de différents caractères*, nos. 233–36.

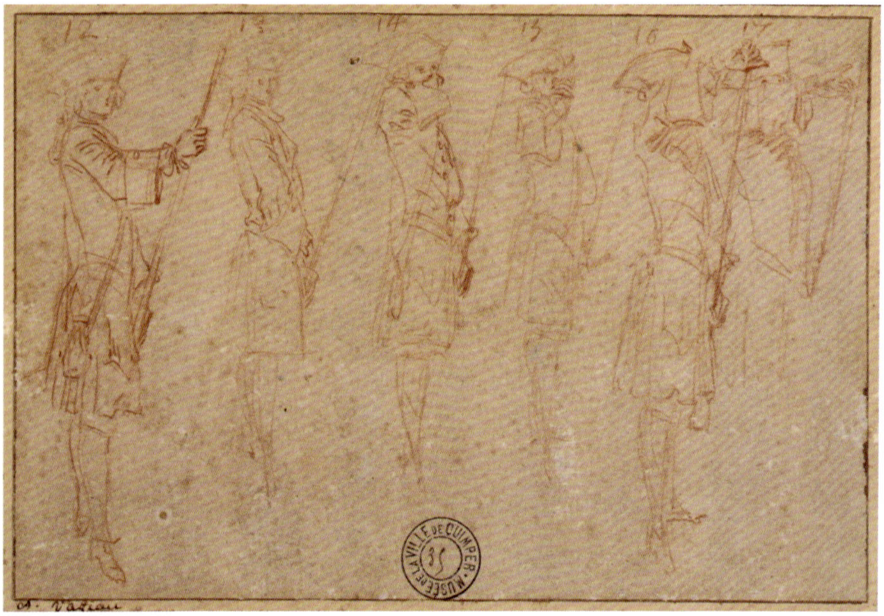

2

Six Studies of a Soldier Charging His Musket, ca. 1709
Red chalk, within brown ink framing lines, 5 ⅛ × 7 ½ in. (13 × 19.2 cm)
Musée des Beaux-Arts, Quimper (Q.14) (Fig. 6)

Inscription: From left to right: *12, 13, 14, 15, 16, 17*; on the mount board, in brown ink: *A. Vatiau*.
Provenance: Count Jean-Marie de Silguy (1785–1864); left to the Musée des Beaux-Art, Quimper, 1864.
Selected literature: RP cat. 26.

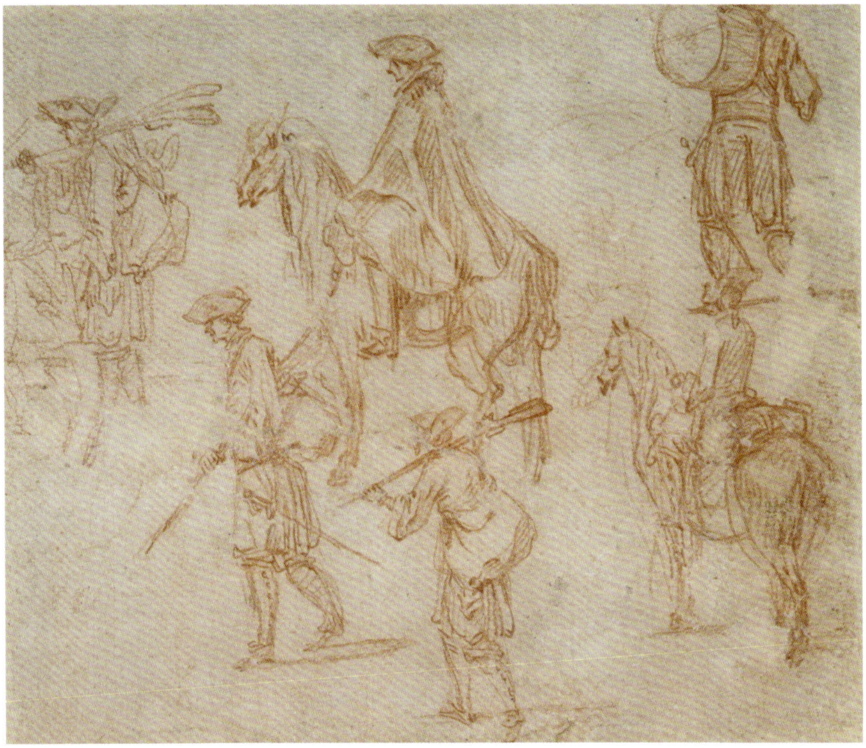

3*

Studies of Foot Soldiers, a Drummer, and Two Cavaliers (verso), ca. 1709–10
Recto: *Two Men Standing, a Seated Woman and the Head of a Woman*
Red chalk, 6 ¼ × 7 ⅝ in. (16 × 19.5 cm)
National Gallery of Scotland, Edinburgh (D 5631)

Provenance: Jean Denis Lempereur (1701–1779); Collection Villeboeuf, Paris, 1935. Stolen during World War II and found in 1945 in Germany. Colnaghi, London, 1951; Mrs. Eliot Hodgkin, London; accepted by HM Government in lieu of Inheritance Tax and allocated to the National Gallery of Scotland, 2010.
Selected literature: RP cat. 94; Clarke 2010, 126–27.
Counterproof: A counterproof is at the Nationalmuseum in Stockholm (NM 216: 157/1866). Part of a lot acquired by Count Carl Gustav Tessin from Watteau in 1715.
Related paintings: Many of the figures are similar to those in *Return from the Campaign* (cat. 45), but none match exactly. Michael Clarke suggests that the figures are related to *Recruits Going to Join the Regiment* (cat. 51), but the connection is not convincing.

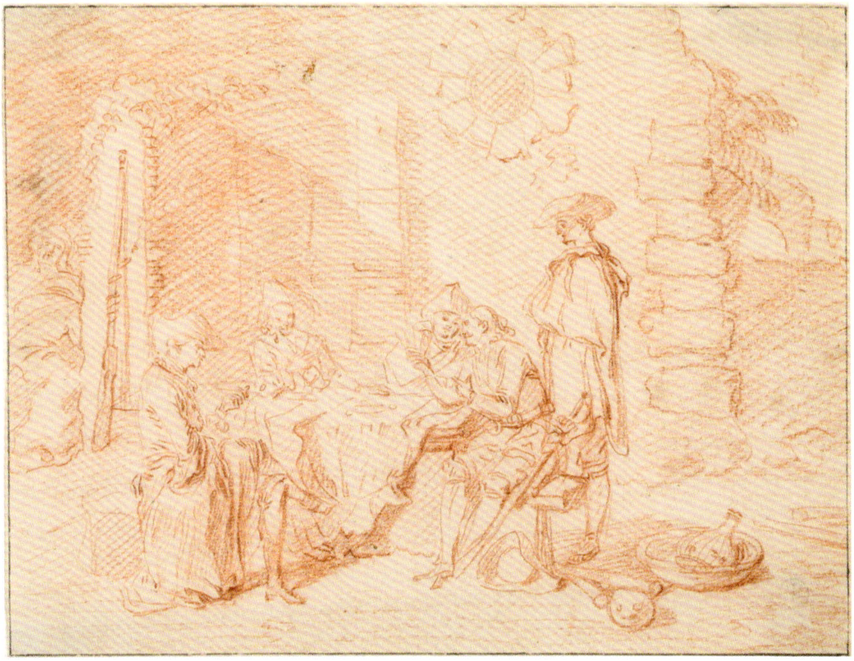

4

Soldiers Playing Cards in a Ruin, ca. 1710.
Red chalk, within brown ink framing lines, 6 ½ × 8 ⅜ in. (16.4 × 21.4 cm)
Graphische Sammlung im Städelsches Kunstinstitut, Frankfurt (1065)

Provenance: Städelsches Kunstinstitut since at least 1862.
Selected literature: RP cat. 124; Eidelberg 2001, 31–34.
Related paintings: Although the sketch was long thought to be drawn after nature, Martin Eidelberg has shown it to be drawn after a painting of the same name by Henry Ferguson.

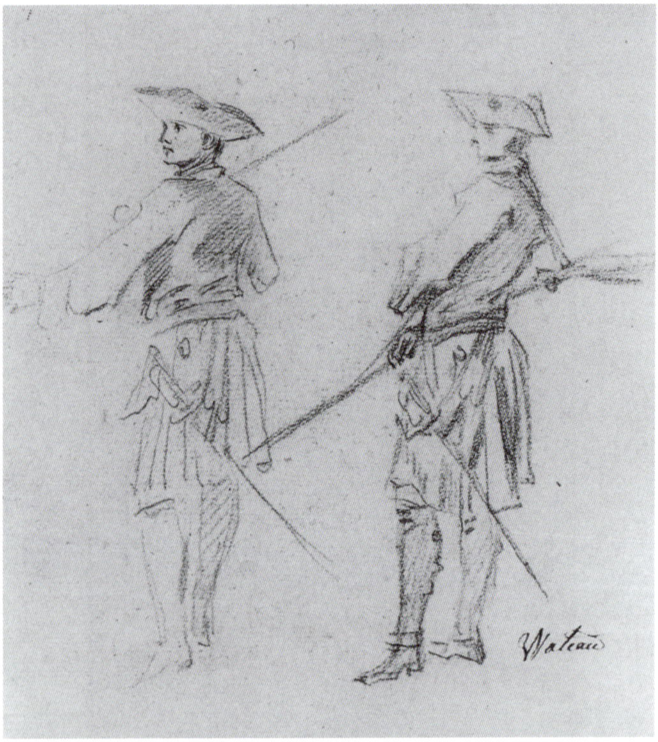

5

Two Studies of a Soldier Holding a Musket (recto), ca. 1710
Verso: *Group of Figures in Landscape*, counterproof in red chalk
Red chalk, 6 ⅛ × 5 ⅝ in. (15.5 × 14.2 cm)
Location unknown
(Fig. 24)

Inscription: In brown ink, bottom right: *Watteau.*
Provenance: Sale, Paris, Hôtel Drouot, December 15, 1986, lot 23; sale, Paris, Hôtel Drouot, July 16, 1987, lot 8; sale, Paris, Hôtel Drouot, November 29, 1991, lot 310; Paris, art market; sale, Paris, Hôtel Drouot, December 1, 1992, lot 70.
Selected literature: RP cat. 60.
Related paintings: The figure on the right is used in *The Portal of Valenciennes* (cat. 46).

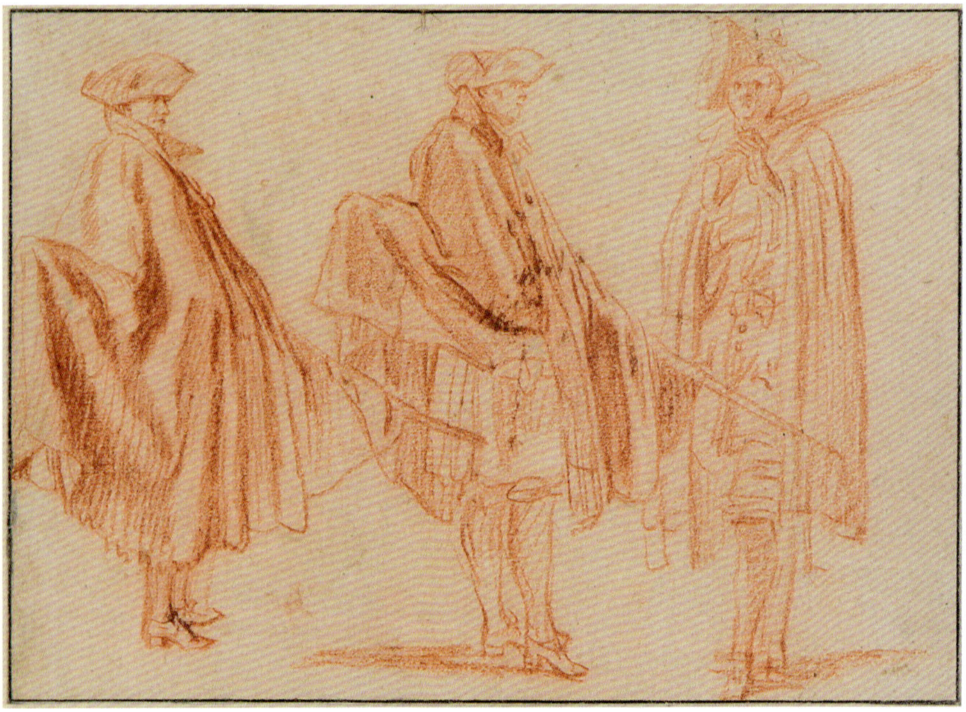

6*

Three Studies of Soldiers Holding Muskets and Wearing Capes, ca. 1710
Red chalk and stump on cream paper, within black ink framing lines, 5 ¾ × 8 in. (14.5 × 20.4 cm)
The Courtauld Institute Galleries, London (PG 217)
(Fig. 25)

Provenance: Contat-Desfontaines collection, Paris, in 1931. London, Colnaghi, 1950; acquired by Count Antoine Seilern (1901–1978); left to the Courtauld Institute of Art, 1978.
Selected literature: RP cat. 59.
Prints after: Three figures in reverse by J. Audran in *Figures de différents caractères*: nos. 241, 95, and 127; a proof of plate no. 127 appears, with added landscape, in the *Recueil de Valenciennes*.
Related paintings: The figure on the left appears in *The Portal of Valenciennes* (cat. 46).

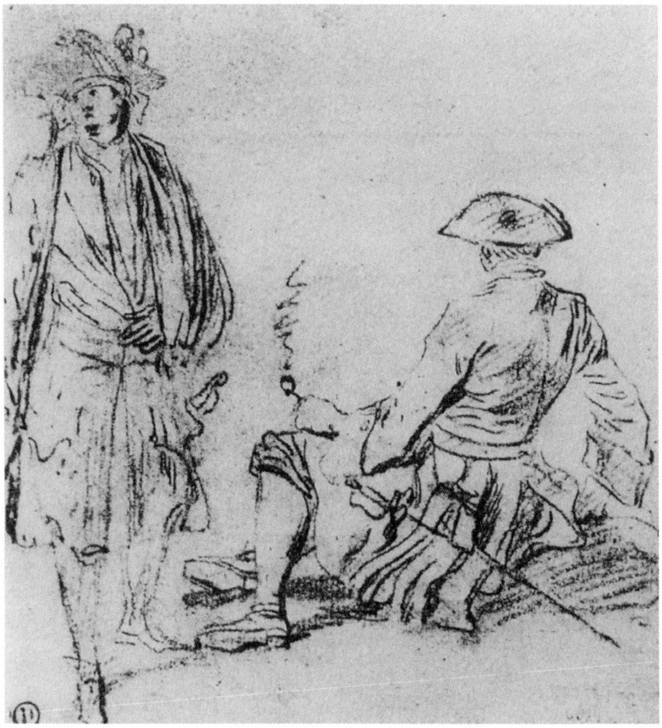

7

Two Studies of a Soldier, One Standing, the Other Seated and Holding a Pipe, ca. 1710
Red chalk, 5 ⅛ × 4 ¾ in. (13 × 12.2 cm)
Location unknown
(Fig. 23)

Provenance: A. Mouriau, first half of nineteenth century; his sale, Paris, Hôtel Drouot, March 11–12, 1858, lot 325 (with cat. 8). George Danyau, second half of nineteenth century. "Madame L. du C." in Paris, 1957.
Selected literature: RP cat. 57.
Related paintings: The soldier on the right appears, with some variations, in *The Portal of Valenciennes* (cat. 46).
Related drawings: Originally, the drawing was probably part of a single sheet with cat. 8.

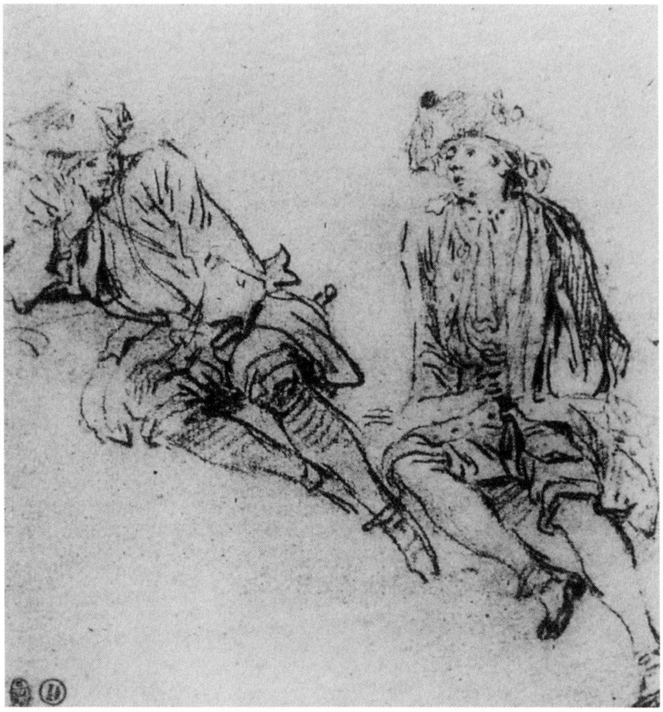

8

Two Studies of a Seated Soldier, ca. 1710
Red chalk, 5 ⅛ × 4 ¾ in. (13 × 12.2 cm)
Location unknown
(Fig. 21)

Provenance: See preceding entry.
Selected literature: RP cat. 58.
Related paintings: Both figures appear in *The Halt* (cat. 43).
Related drawings: Originally, the drawing was probably part of a single sheet with cat. 7.

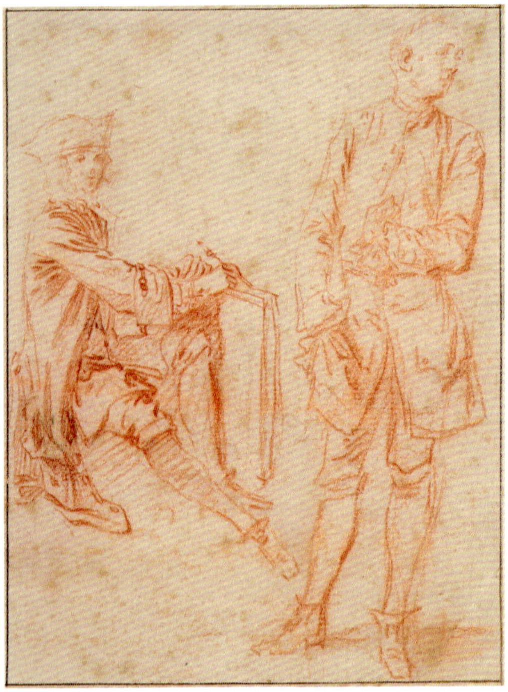

9*

Studies of a Seated Man with Drawing Portfolio and Standing Man, ca. 1710
Red chalk, within brown ink framing lines, 4 ⅞ × 3 ⅝ in. (12.4 × 9.2 cm)
Private collection

Provenance: Camille Groult (1837–1908); her son Jean Groult (1868–1951); sale, Paris, Hôtel Drouot, November 20, 1941; Agnew, London. Mrs. John Dewar, London, 1957; W. B. Henderson, 1968; sale, New York, Sotheby's, January 24, 2007, lot 70.
Selected literature: RP cat. 65.
Counterproof: A counterproof, which also features cat. 10, is at the Nationalmuseum in Stockholm (NM 2821/1863). Part of a lot acquired by Count Carl Gustav Tessin from Watteau in 1715.
Related paintings: The figure on the right, now with tricorne hat, appears in *Bivouac* (cat. 44).
Related drawings: Originally, the fragment was part of a sheet with cat. 10.

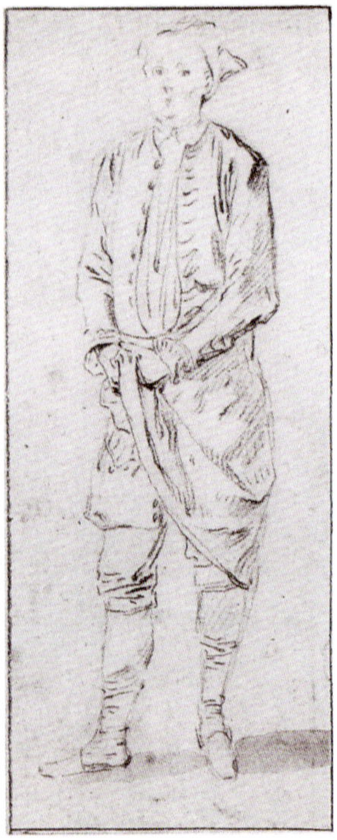

10

Study of a Cook, ca. 1710
Red chalk, within framing lines, touches of wash on the bottom, probably from another hand, 4 ¾ × 2 in. (12 × 5 cm)
Private collection

Provenance: Camille Groult (1837–1908); her son Jean Groult (1868–1951); sale, Paris, Hôtel Drouot, November 20, 1941, part of lot 17; Agnew, London. Mrs. John Dewar, London, 1957; Paris, Galerie Cailleux, in 1968; Paris.
Selected literature: RP cat. 64.
Counterproof: See preceding entry.
Related paintings: The figure appears in *Bivouac* (cat. 44).
Related drawings: See preceding entry.

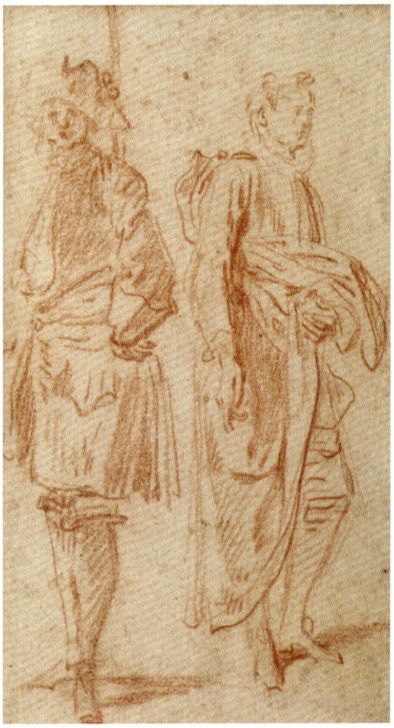

11*

Two Studies of Standing Soldiers, ca. 1710
Red chalk on aged-toned paper, within black ink framing lines, 5 ⅝ × 3 ⅛ in. (14.3 × 8 cm)
Collection Professor Donald Stone, New York; promised gift to the National Gallery of Art, Washington

Inscription: On verso, in black chalk: *Mon, de Lope.*
Provenance: Basel, art market, 1987; sale, Paris, Hôtel Drouot, November 29–30, 1989; Paris, Galerie Cailleux; sale, New York, Christie's, January 28, 1999, lot 115.
Selected literature: RP cat. 61.
Related paintings: The figure on the left is used for the central figure in *Halt of a Detachment* (cat. 50).

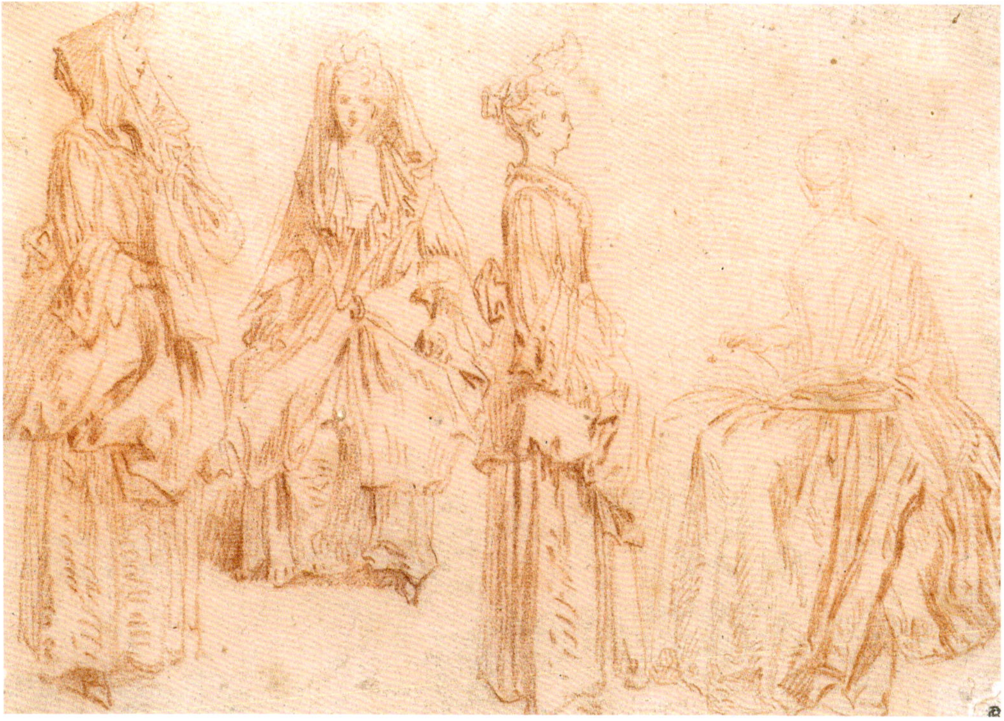

12*

Four Studies of Women, Alternately Standing and Seated, ca. 1710
Red chalk, 5 ¼ × 8 in. (13.4 × 20.3 cm)
Indianapolis Museum of Art; The Clowes Collection (2010.43)
(Fig. 20)

Provenance: Eugène Rodrigues (1853–1928). Dr. George Henry Alexander Clowes (1877–1958), Indianapolis, from 1955; part of Clowes Fund, Indianapolis, after 1958; Indianapolis Museum of Art since 1972.
Selected literature: RP cat. 68.
Counterproof: A counterproof is at the Nationalmuseum in Stockholm (NM THC 4050). Perhaps part of the collection of Count Carl Gustav Tessin (1695–1770).
Related paintings: The seated woman with a veil appears in *The Halt* (cat. 43).

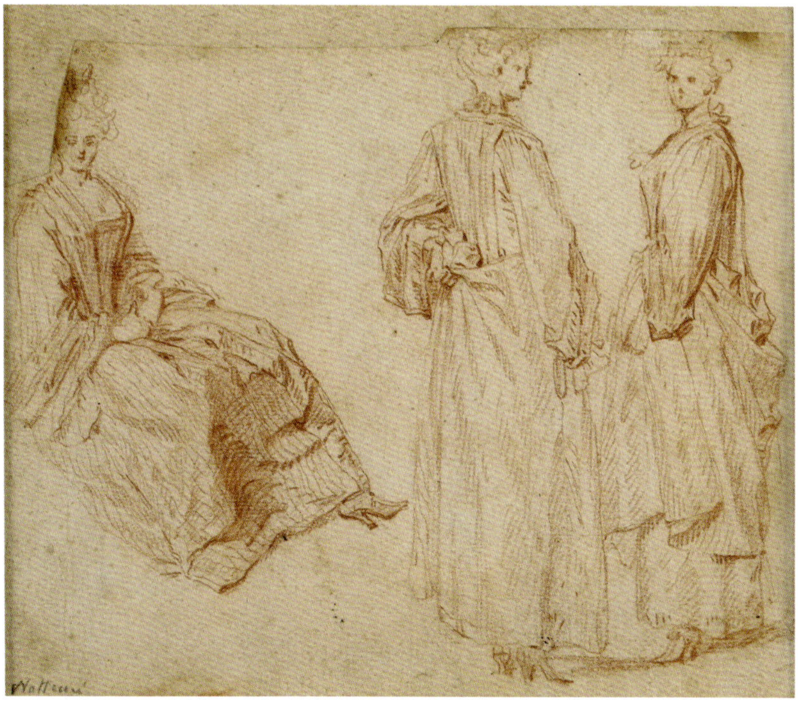

13

Three Studies of Women, ca. 1710
Red chalk, cut irregularly on the upper part, traces of burning, 6 ½ × 7 ½ in. (16.4 × 19 cm)
Musée Carnavalet, Paris (D. 7077)
(Fig. 19)

Inscription: In graphite, bottom left: *Watteau*
Provenance: Gift of Charles Macier (1846–1911) to Musée Carnavalet, Paris, 1903.
Selected literature: RP cat. 104.
Related prints: The middle figure is etched by Benoît Audran, as it appears in *The Halt* (see cat. 43)
Related paintings: The middle figure appears in *The Halt* (cat. 43). The figure on the right can be related to three non-military paintings by Watteau: *La mariée de village*, *La musette*, and *Le bal champêtre*.

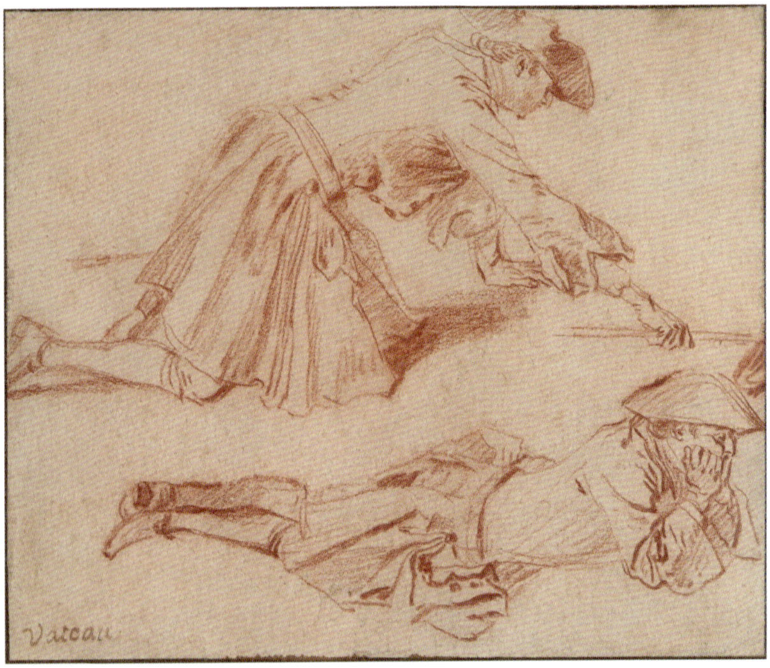

14*

Two Studies of a Soldier, One Kneeling, the Other Lying Down, ca. 1710
Red chalk, within black ink framing lines, 5 ⅛ × 6 in. (13 × 15.3 cm)
Private collection
(Fig. 5)

Inscription: Lower left: *Vateau.*
Provenance: Sale of "Monsieur F," Paris, Hôtel Drouot, March 16, 1863, lot 127; Jean Gigoux (1806–1894), his sale, Paris, Hôtel Drouot, January 21–23, 1873, lot 293; Camille Groult (1837–1908), Paris, by descent to his son, Jean Groult (1868–1951); his grandson, Pierre Bordeaux-Groult (1916–2007); from whom acquired by private collector in 1983; sale, New York, Sotheby's, lot 85, January 28, 2015; private collector, New York.
Selected literature: RP cat. 66; Wintermute et al. 1999, 100, no. 4.
Counterproof: Private collection, Paris.
Prints after: Figures are etched in reverse by J. Audran in *Figures de différents caractères*: kneeling man (no. 76); man lying down (no. 75).
Related paintings: Both figures appear in *Bivouac* (cat. 44).

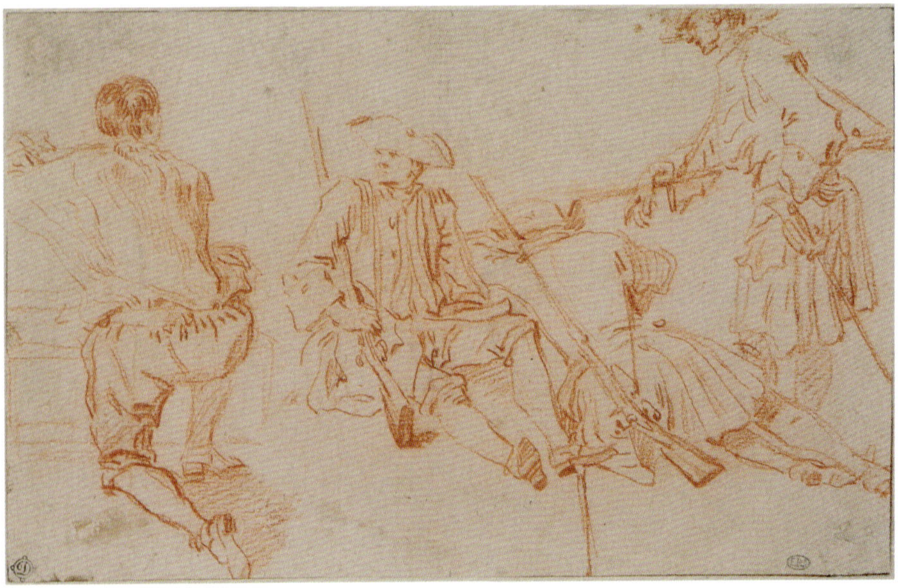

15*

Three Studies of a Soldier and a Kneeling Man, ca. 1710
Red chalk, within brown ink framing lines, 4 ¾ × 7 ⅝ in. (12.2 × 19.5 cm)
École nationale supérieure des Beaux-Arts, Paris (1605)
(Fig. 4)

Provenance: Édouard Desperer (1804–1865); his sale, Paris, Hôtel Drouot, June 7–10, 1865, part of lot 531; Alfred Armand (1805–1888); his nephew, Prosper Valton (d. 1907); left by his widow to the École nationale supérieure des Beaux-Arts de Paris, 1908.
Selected literature: RP cat. 67.
Related paintings: Two central figures appear, in reverse order, in *Halt of a Detachment* (cat. 50). All four figures appear in *The Halt* (cat. 43).

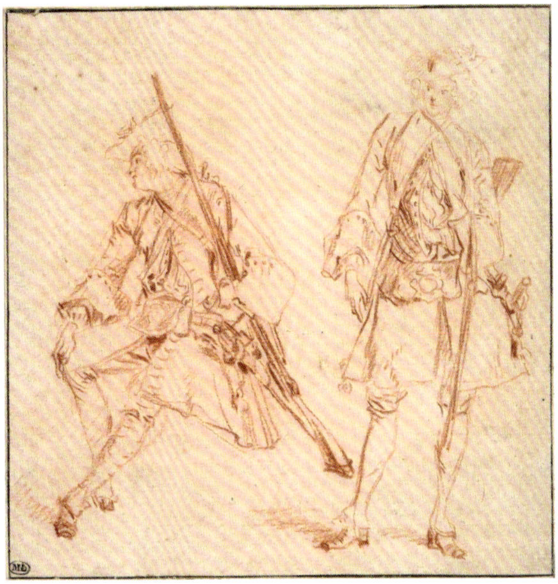

16*

Two Studies of a Soldier, One Seated, the Other Standing, ca. 1712
Red chalk, within brown ink framing lines, 5 ⅝ × 5 ⅜ in. (14.2 × 13.8 cm)
Musée du Louvre, Paris (27544)

Provenance: Charles Paul Jean Baptiste Bourgevin Vialart de Saint-Morys (1743–1795); seized from émigrés in 1793; Paris, Musée du Louvre, Département des Arts graphiques.
Selected literature: RP cat. 152; Grasselli 2001, 314.
Prints after: Etched in *Figures de différents caractères*: seated man by Edme Jeaurat (no. 126); standing man by J. Audran (no. 289).
Related paintings: The seated figure appears in *Departure of a Garrison* (cat. 49).
Related drawings: Grasselli suggests—rightly, I believe—that cats. 16–18 depict the same model and may have been executed during a single session.

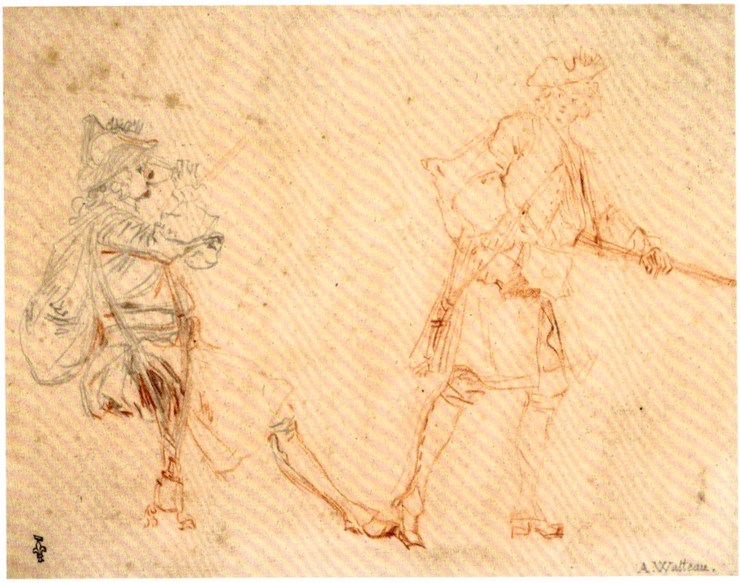

17

Two Studies of a Soldier, One Seated, the Other Marching toward the Right, ca. 1712
Red chalk and graphite, 5 ¾ × 7 ½ in. (14.6 × 19 cm)
Musée Condé, Chantilly (DE448)

Inscription: Bottom right, in graphite: *A. Watteau*.
Provenance: Andrew James (d. before 1857); his daughter Sarah Ann James, London; her sale, London, Christie's, June 22–23, 1891, lot 355; duc d'Aumale (1822–1897); donated to the Institut de France in 1866 and entered into the collection of the Musée Condé, Chantilly, upon his death.
Selected literature: RP cat. 153.
Prints after: The seated man is etched in *Figures de différents caractères* by J. Audran (no. 14); a proof with added landscape appears in the *Recueil de Valenciennes*.
Related paintings: Both figures appear in *Departure of a Garrison* (cat. 49).
Related drawings: See previous entry.

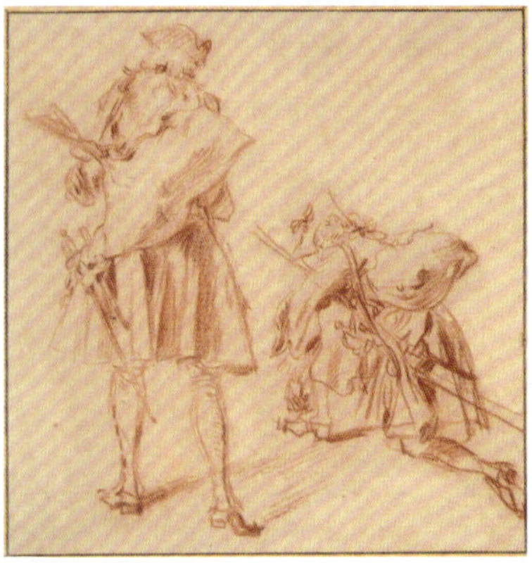

18*

Two Studies of a Soldier Viewed from Behind, ca. 1712
Red chalk, within brown ink framing lines, 6 ⅜ × 6 ⅛ in. (16.1 × 15.6 cm)
Yale University Art Gallery, New Haven; Everett V. Meeks, B.A. 1901, Fund (1961.9.39)
(Fig. 8)

Provenance: Jean-Pierre Norblin de la Gourdaine (1745–1830); Martin Norblin de la Gourdaine (1781–1854); baronne de Conantré; her daughter, baronne de Rublé; her daughter, Mme de Witte; her daughter, marquise de Bryas (Orange). Paris, Galerie Cailleux, in 1958; acquired by Yale University Art Gallery in 1958 with Everett V. Meeks, B.A. 1901, Fund.
Selected literature: RP cat. 277; Wintermute et al. 1999, 112, cat. 11; Grasselli 2001, 314; Boorsch and Marciari et al. 2006, 187–89, cat. 62; Lajer-Burcharth 2015, 33.
Prints after: The figure on the right is etched in *Figures de différents caractères* by J. Audran (no. 242).
Related drawings: See entry for cat. 16.

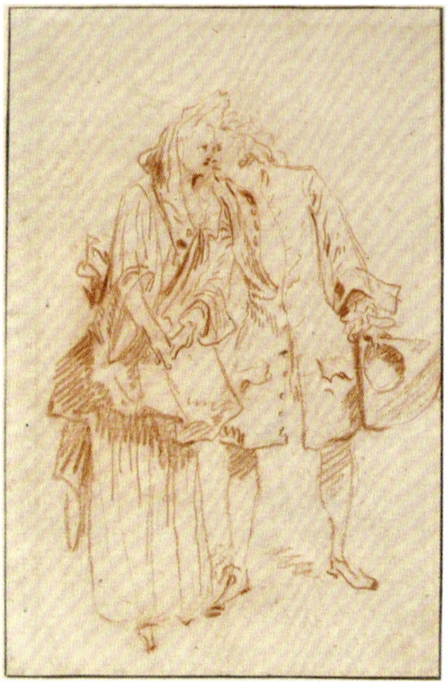

19

Study of a Man Kissing a Woman (recto), ca. 1712
Verso: *Two Studies of a Man Viewed from the Back*
Red chalk, within brown ink framing lines, 6 ⅜ × 4 ¼ in. (16.3 × 10.8 cm)
Ashmolean Museum, Oxford (WA 1934. 277)

Provenance: Georges Mühlbacher (d. 1906); his sale, Paris, Galerie Georges Petit, May 15–18, 1899, lot 311. Acquired by Ashmolean Museum, 1934.
Selected literature: RP cat. 129.
Prints after: Etched by Louis Desplaces in *Figures de différents caractères* (no. 190).
Related paintings: The two figures appear in *Departure of a Garrison* (cat. 49), but the woman no longer wears a *fontage*.

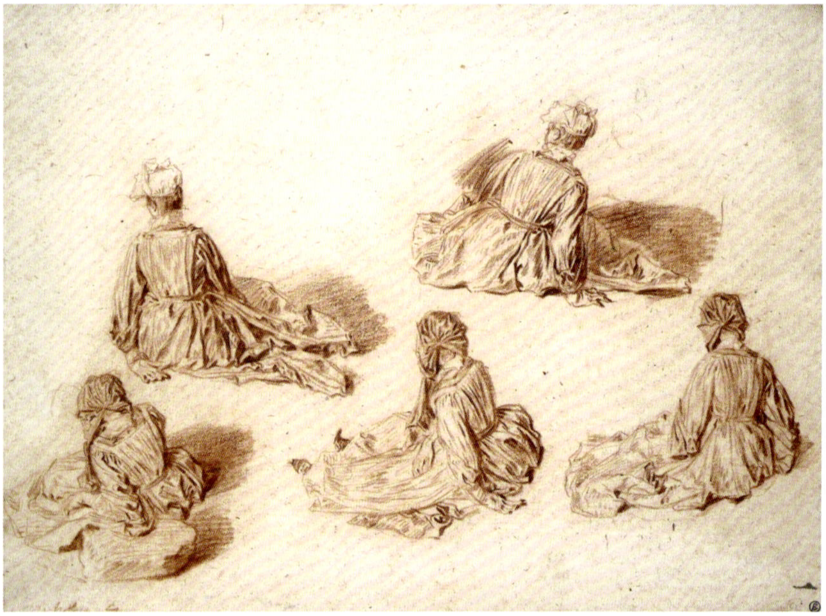

20

Five Studies of Women Seated on the Ground, ca. 1713
Red chalk, within brown ink framing lines, 7 ¼ × 9 ⅞ in. (18.3 × 25.2 cm)
The British Museum, London (1895,0915.944)

Provenance: Possibly Gabriel Huquier (1695–1772); possibly his sale, Paris, November 9, 1772, part of lot 443 or 444. Possibly the Morelle sale, Paris, April 19, 1786, lot 350. Thomas Dimsdale (1758–1823); Edward Vernon Utterson (1775/76–1856), London; his sale, London, Christie's, February 24–27, 1857, lot 648; Sir Charles Robinson (1824–1913); John Malcolm of Poltalloch (1805–1893) around 1860; acquired from his son, John Wingfield Malcolm, by the British Museum, 1895.
Selected literature: RP cat. 181.
Related paintings: The woman on the bottom left appears in *The Supply Train* (cat. 52).

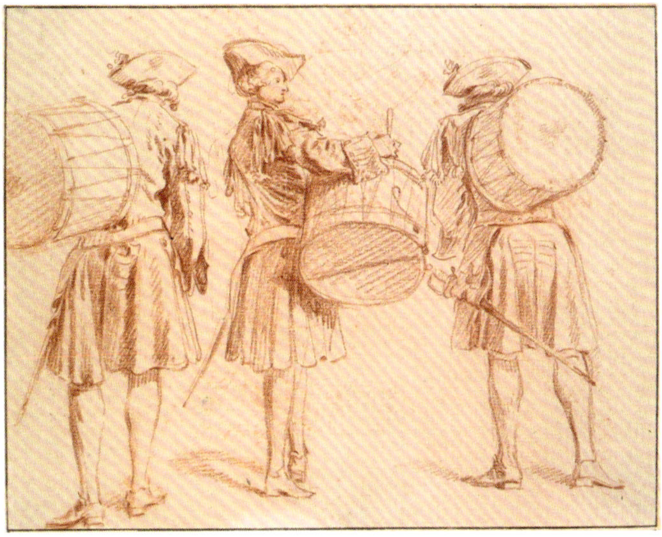

21*

Three Studies of a Military Drummer, ca. 1713
Red chalk on cream paper, within brown ink framing lines, laid down on off-white card, 6 ⅛ × 7 ¾ in. (15.5 × 19.6 cm)
Fogg Museum, Harvard Art Museums; Gift of John S. Newberry (1964.14)
(Fig. 9)

Provenance: Jean-Pierre Norblin de la Gourdaine (1745–1830); Martin Norblin de la Gourdaine (1781–1854); baronne de Conantré; her daughter, baronne de Rublé; her daughter, Mme de Witte; her daughter, marquise de Bryas (Orange). Paris, Galerie Cailleux, in 1958; acquired by John S. Newberry (1914–1964), 1958; gift to the Fogg Museum, 1964.
Selected literature: RP cat. 210; Lajer-Burcharth 2015, 13–14.
Prints after: All three figures are etched in *Figures de différents caractères* by J. Audran (nos. 240, 60, and 111).
Related paintings: The figure on the left appears in *The Respite from War* (cat. 47). The other two figures appear in *Departure of a Garrison* (cat. 49).

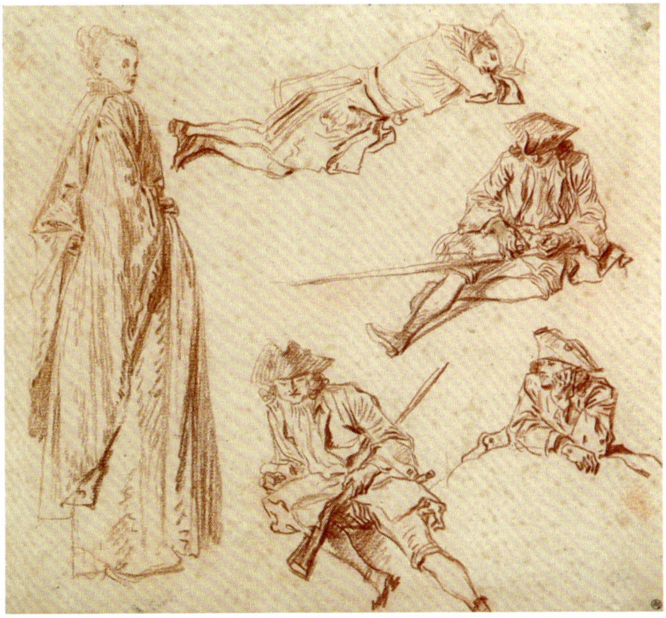

22

Four Studies of Soldiers at Rest and a Standing Woman, ca. 1713–14
Verso: The figure resting his head on his hand is traced in red chalk.
Red chalk on beige paper, 7 × 7 ¾ in. (17.9 × 19.8 cm)
Museum Boijmans Van Beuningen, Rotterdam (F.I. 150)
(Fig. 2)

Provenance: Pierre Jean Mariette (1694–1774); sale of his collection, Paris, November 15, 1775–January 30, 1776, part of lot 1389; to J.-D. Lempereur. Sale, Paris, Hôtel Drouot, April 27, 1885, lot 59. Acquired in 1927 by Franz Koenigs (1881–1941), Rotterdam-Haarlem; acquired in 1940 by Daniel George and given to the Museum Boijmans Van Beuningen.
Selected literature: RP cat. 180; Grasselli 2001, 314; Lajer-Burcharth 2015, 33.
Related paintings: All four soldiers appear in *The Respite from War* (cat. 47); the man resting his chin on his hand appears again in *The Supply Train* (cat. 52).

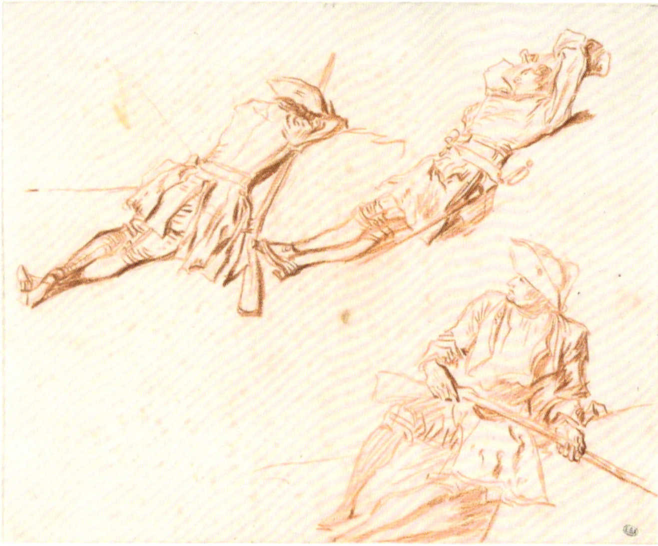

23*

Three Studies of Resting Soldiers (recto), ca. 1713–14
Verso: *A Group of Actors*
Red chalk, 6 ⅞ × 8 ½ in. (17.5 × 21.7 cm)
École nationale supérieure des Beaux-Arts, Paris (1608)
(Fig. 3)

Provenance: Édouard Guichardot; his sale, Paris, Hôtel Drouot, July 7–20, 1875, lot 406; Alfred Armand (1805–1888); his nephew, Prosper Valton (d. 1907); bequest of his widow to the École nationale supérieure des Beaux-Arts, Paris, 1908.

Selected literature: RP cat. 179; Grasselli 2001, 314; Lajer-Burcharth 2015, 27.
Related paintings: The figure on the left appears, with his musket in a different position, in *Halt of a Detachment* (cat. 50). The middle figure appears in *The Supply Train* (cat. 52).
Related drawings: Rosenberg and Prat point out that this drawing seems to depict the same model as cat. 22 and suggest that the two drawings could have been executed on the same day.

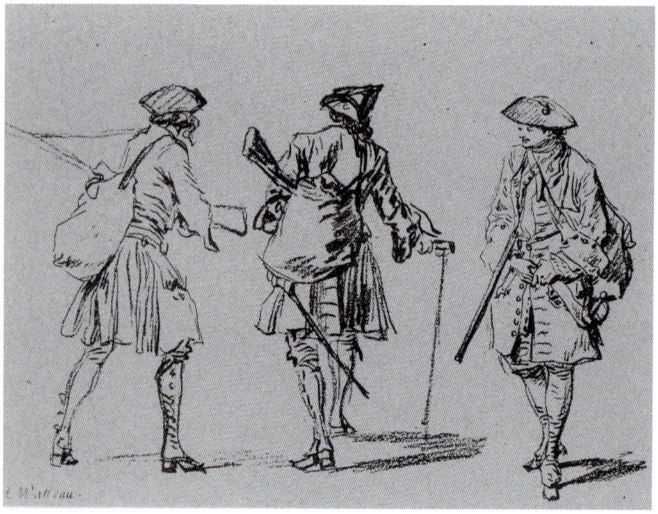

24

Three Studies of a Soldier, Two from Behind, ca. 1713–15
Red chalk, 6 ⅛ × 8 in. (15.5 × 20.2 cm)
Location unknown

Inscription: Bottom left, in ink: *A Watteau.*
Provenance: Adrien Fauchier-Magnan (1873–1965), Paris; his sale, London, Sotheby's, December 4, 1935, lot 69.
Selected literature: RP cat. 176; Grasselli 2001, 314.
Prints after: All three figures are etched in *Figures de différents caractères* by J. Audran (nos. 174, 243, 175); a proof of no. 243 appears, with added landscape, in the *Recueil de Valenciennes*.
Paintings after: The middle figure appears in *Recruits Going to Join the Regiment* (cat. 51).

Related drawings: Grasselli suggests convincingly that cats. 24–29 might have been drawn during the same session. The dating of these drawings diverges widely.
Remarks: Rosenberg and Prat, who do not view them as a cohesive group, date them variously between 1712 and 1715, while Grasselli suggests 1714–15 as a more accurate date for the entire group. The bold lines, rhythmic poses, and sheer dynamism of these drawings do suggest a later date.

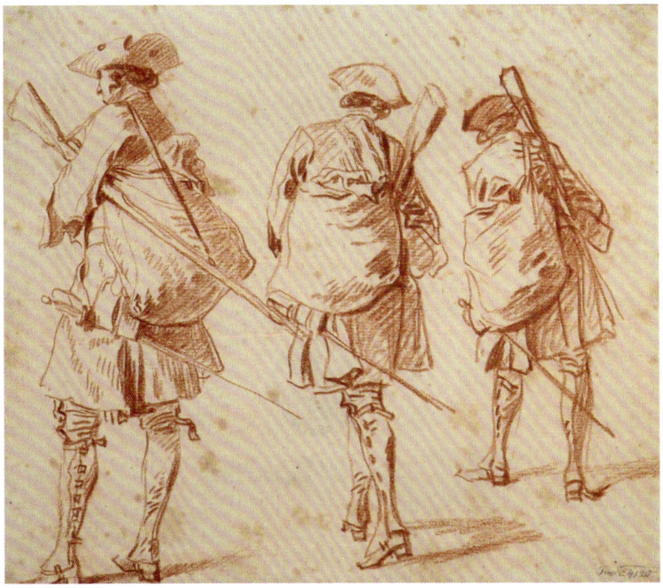

25

Three Studies of a Soldier from Behind, ca. 1713–15
Red chalk on cream paper, 6 ¾ × 7 ⅞ in. (17.3 × 19.9 cm)
Staatliche Museen zu Berlin, Kupferstichkabinett, Sammlung der Zeichnungen und Druckgraphik (KdZ 1771)

Inscription: Bottom right, in graphite: *Inv. 4120*; verso, in ink: *Watteau*.
Provenance: Daniel Saint (1778–1847); his sale, Paris, May 4–7, 1846; Barthold Suermondt (1818–1887), Aix-la-Chapelle; acquired, with the rest of his collection, by the Museen zu Berlin, Kupferstichkabinett, Sammlung der Zeichnungen und Druckgraphik, 1874.
Selected literature: RP cat. 177; Grasselli 2001, 314.
Prints after: The figures in the middle and right were etched in reverse in *Figures de différents caractères* by J. Audran (nos. 257* and 189); a proof of no. 257 appears, with added landscape, in the *Recueil de Valenciennes*.
Related paintings: The figure on the right appears, with some variations, in *Recruits Going to Join the Regiment* (cat. 51). The figure in the center is in the background of *The Supply Train* (cat. 52). Some have related this figure to *Departure of a Garrison* (cat. 49), but none of the soldiers in the painting corresponds exactly.
Related drawings: See preceding entry.

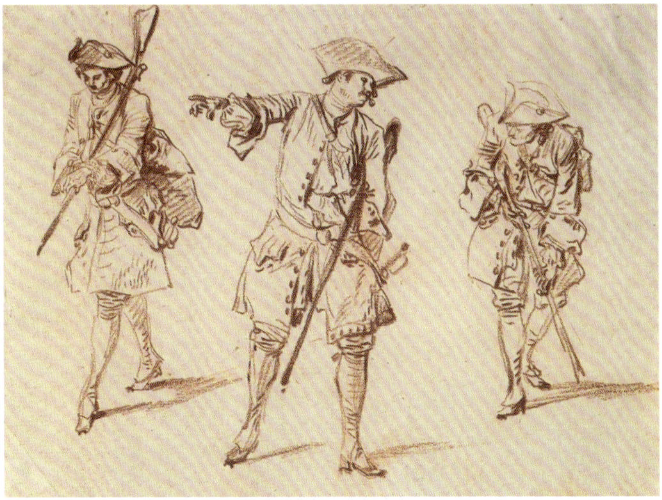

26

Three Studies of a Soldier Marching, ca. 1713–15
Red chalk on cream paper, 5 ¾ × 7 ⅞ in. (14.5 × 20 cm)
Location unknown

Provenance: Possibly Jean Antoine Vassal de Saint-Hubert; possibly his sale, March 29, 1779, lot 92; John Postle Heseltine (1843–1929); Baron Élie de Rothschild (1917–2007) in 1957.
Selected literature: RP cat. 178; Grasselli 2001, 314; Lajer-Burcharth 2015, 34–35.
Counterproof: A counterproof is in a private collection in Paris.
Related paintings: The figure on the right appears in *Recruits Going to Join the Regiment* (cat. 51) with a shorter musket.
Related drawings: See entry for cat. 24.

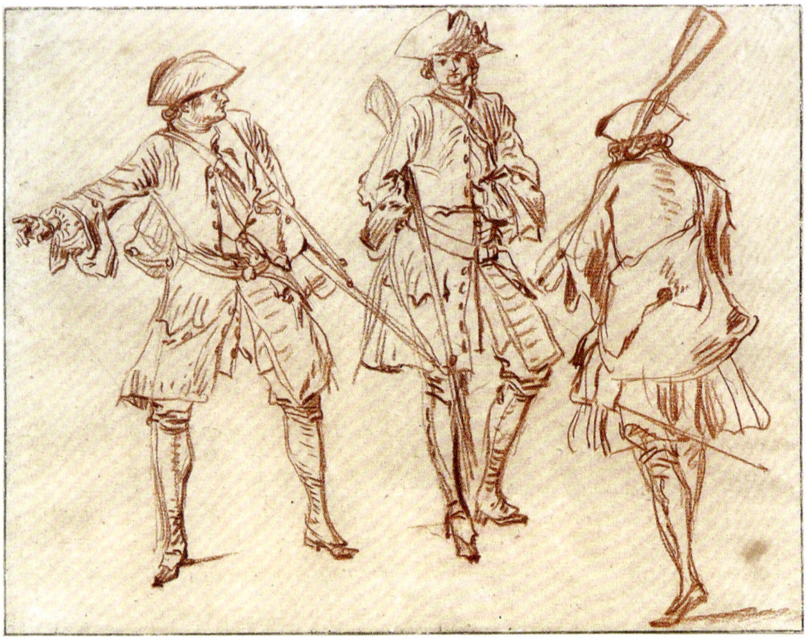

27*

Three Studies of a Soldier, One from Behind, ca. 1713–15
Red chalk, within black ink framing lines, 6 × 7 ¾ in. (15.1 × 19.9 cm)
Fondation Custodia, Collection Frits Lugt, Paris (7208)
(Fig. 7)

Provenance: Jean-Pierre Norblin de la Gourdaine (1745–1830); Martin Norblin de la Gourdaine (1781–1854); baronne de Conantré; her daughter, baronne de Rublé; her daughter, Mme de Witte; her daughter, marquise de Bryas (Orange). Paris, Galerie Cailleux, in 1958; acquired by Frits Lugt (1884–1970), 1958.
Selected literature: RP cat. 209; Grasselli 2001, 314; Bailey et al. 2009, 27–29, 185–86, cat. 1; Lajer-Burcharth 2015, 34–35.
Prints after: All the figures are etched by L. Desplaces in *Figures de différents caractères* (nos. 59, 13, and 290); a proof of no. 290, with landscape added, appears in the *Recueil de Valenciennes*.
Related paintings: The figure on the far right appears in *Recruits Going to Join the Regiment* (cat. 51).
Related drawings: See entry for cat. 24.

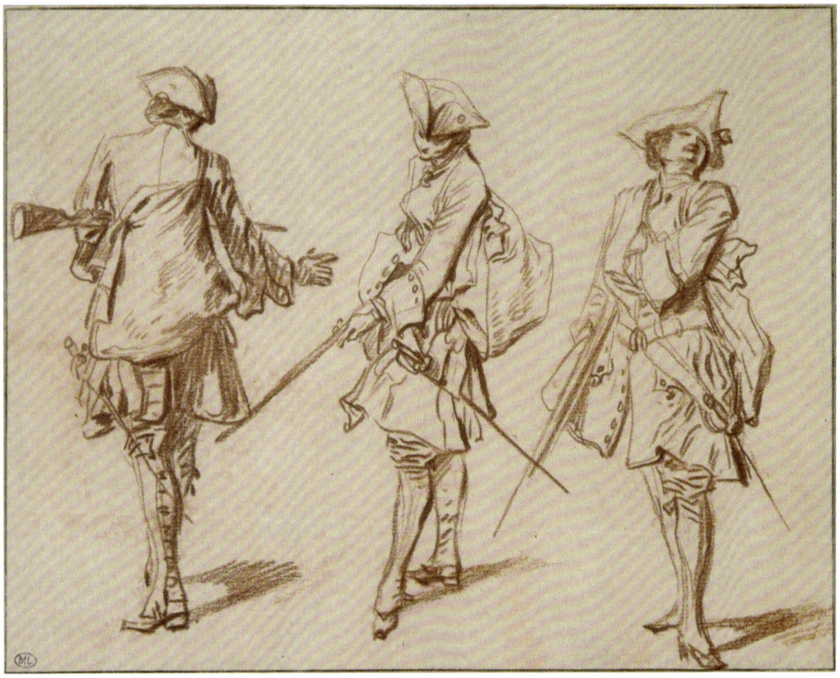

28*

Three Views of a Soldier, One from Behind, ca. 1713–15
Red chalk, within black ink framing lines, 6 ¾ × 8 ⅝ in. (17 × 21.9 cm)
Musée du Louvre, Paris (RF 51752)

Provenance: Jean-Pierre Norblin de la Gourdaine (1745–1830); Martin Norblin de la Gourdaine (1781–1854); baronne de Conantré; her daughter, baronne de Rublé; her daughter, Mme de Witte; her daughter, marquise de Bryas (Orange). Paris, Galerie Cailleux, 1958; Raoul Dastrac (1891–1969), Paris; Madame Roland Lacroix, née Hélène Ryaux. Gift of Roland Lacroix, in memory of Raoul Dastrac, to the Musée du Louvre, 1997.
Selected literature: RP cat. 278.
Prints after: All three figures are etched in reverse in *Figures de différents caractères* by J. Audran (nos. 258*, 113, and 43); a proof of no. 43 appears, with added landscape, in the *Recueil de Valenciennes*.
Related drawings: See entry for cat. 24.

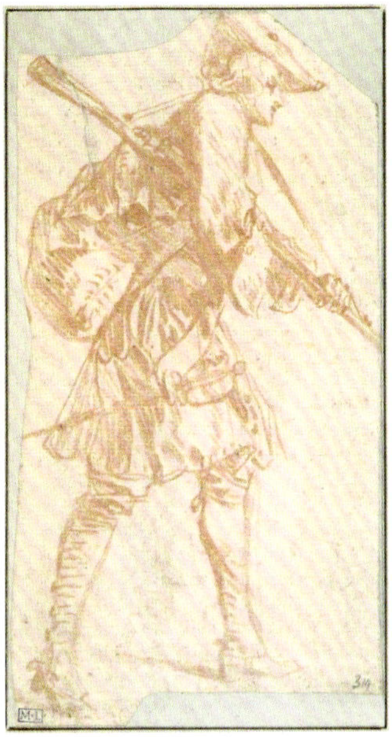

29

Study of a Marching Soldier, ca. 1713–15
Counterproof in red chalk, cut irregularly, 6 × 3 ⅜ in. (15.4 × 8.5 cm)
Musée du Louvre, Paris (RF 51805)

Inscription: Bottom right, in brown ink: *314*.
Provenance: "Cabinet de M.L," his sale, Paris, Hôtel Drouot, March 16, 1863, lot 127; Jean Gigoux; his sale, Paris, Hôtel Drouot, January 20–22, 1873, lot 293; Camille Groult (1837–1908); Jean Groult (1868–1951); public sale, Paris, December 19, 1941; Léon Lepeltier (1877–1960); Robert Lepeltier (1913–1996); gift of Odette Lepeltier, in honor of her husband, Robert Lepeltier, to the Musée du Louvre, 1998.
Selected literature: RP cat. 151; Louvre 2015.
Related paintings: The figure appears in *Recruits Going to Join the Regiment* (cat. 51).

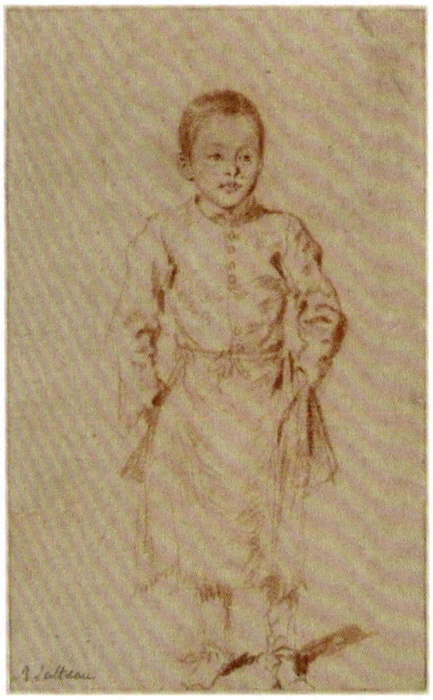

30

Study of Kitchen Boy, ca. 1715
Red chalk on cream paper, laid down, 7 ⅜ × 4 ⅝ in. (18.7 × 11.7 cm)
The British Museum, London (1895,0915.937)

Inscription: Bottom left, in brown ink: *Watteau*.
Provenance: Acquired after 1896 by John Malcolm of Poltalloch (1805–1893); acquired from his son, Colonel John Winfield Malcolm, with the rest of his collection, in 1895.
Selected literature: RP cat. 302.
Related paintings: The figure appears in *The Supply Train* (cat. 52).
Prints after: The figure appears in *Figures de différents caractères*, etched by F. Boucher (no. 193).

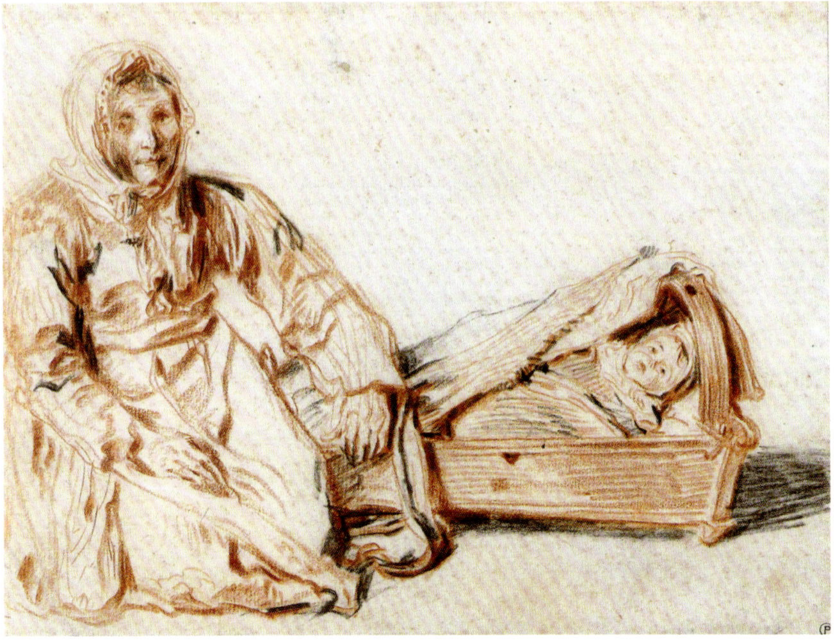

31

Study of an Old Savoyarde and Infant, ca. 1715
Trois crayons, 6 ½ × 8 ½ in. (16.4 × 21.5 cm)
Collection Louis-Antoine Prat

Provenance: Camille Groult (1837–1908); her son Jean Groult (1865–1951); his son, Pierre Bordeaux-Groult; New York, Wildenstein Gallery; Paris, art market; Prat Collection since 1990.
Selected literature: RP cat. 301.
Counterproof: A counterproof was sold in 1961; its current location is unknown.
Related paintings: Both figures appear in *The Supply Train* (cat. 52).

Drawings Known Only through Prints

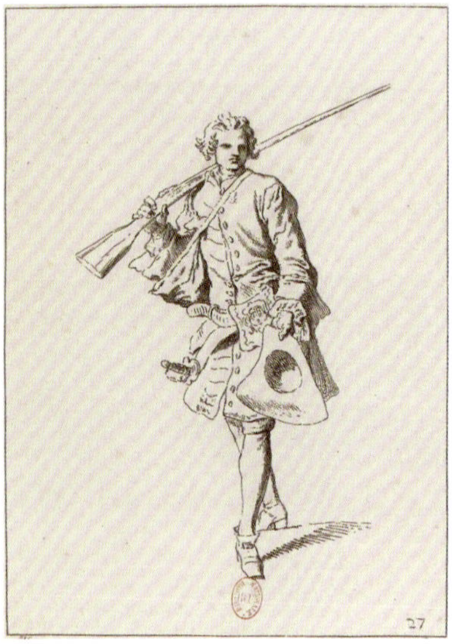

32

View of Soldier Holding a Tricorne Hat
Etching
No. 27 in *Figures de différents caractères*, etched by J. Audran, ca. 1726–28
Bibliothèque nationale de France

Selected literature: RP cat. G8.
Related paintings: Used in *Departure of a Garrison* (cat. 49).

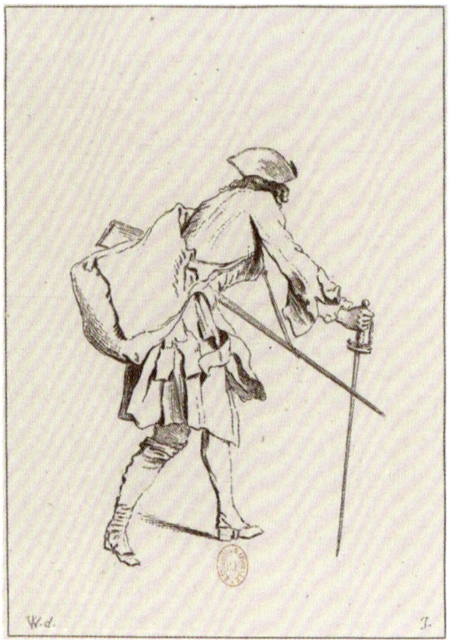

33

Soldier Leaning on a Sword
Etching
No. 42 in *Figures de différents caractères*, etched by J. Audran, ca. 1726–28
Bibliothèque nationale de France

Selected literature: RP cat. G14.
Related paintings: Used in *Recruits Going to Join the Regiment* (cat. 51).

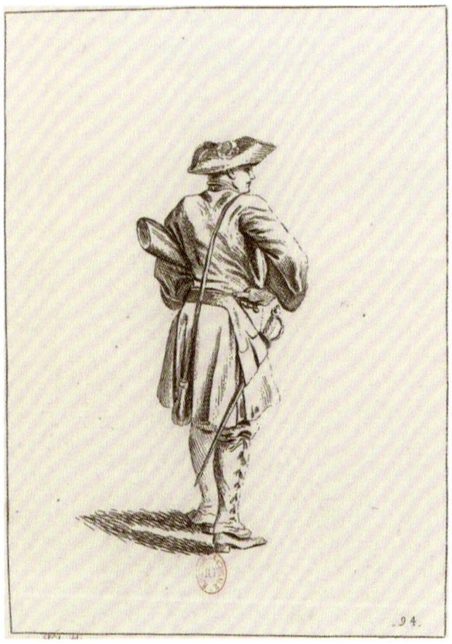

34

Three-Quarter View of a Soldier
Etching
No. 94 in *Figures de différents caractères*, etched by F. Boucher, ca. 1726–28; proof, with added landscape, in the *Recueil de Valenciennes*
Bibliothèque nationale de France

Selected literature: RP cat. G35.
Related paintings: Used in *The Line of March* (cat. 42).

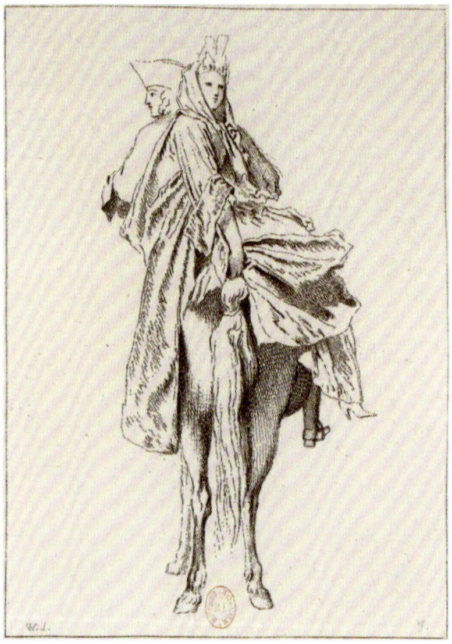

35

Cavalier and a Woman on a Horse
Etching
No. 112 in *Figures de différents caractères*, etched by J. Audran, ca. 1726–28
Bibliothèque nationale de France

Selected literature: RP cat. G44.
Related paintings: Used in *Departure of a Garrison* (cat. 49).

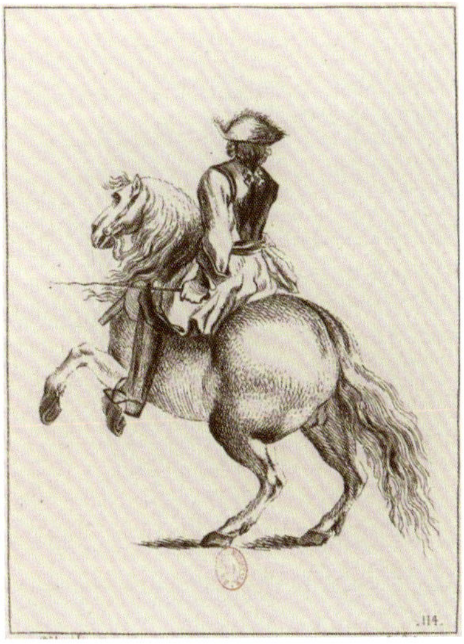

36

Three-Quarter View of a Cavalier on a Horse, Seen from the Back
Etching
No. 114 in *Figures de différents caractères*, etched by F. Boucher, ca. 1726–28; proof, with added landscape, in the *Recueil de Valenciennes*
Bibliothèque nationale de France

Selected literature: RP cat. G45.
Related paintings: Used in *The Line of March* (cat. 42).

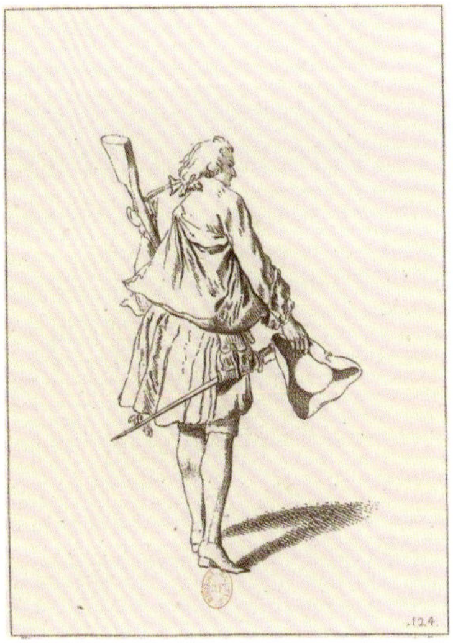

37

View of a Soldier Holding a Tricorne Hat from Behind
Etching
No. 128 in *Figures de différents caractères*, etched by J. Audran, ca. 1726–28
Bibliothèque nationale de France

Selected literature: RP cat. G47.
Related paintings: Used in *Departure of a Garrison* (cat. 49).

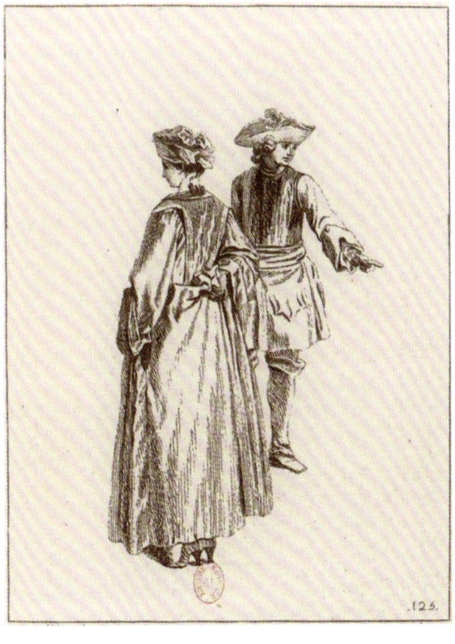

38

A Woman and an Officer
Etching
No. 125 in *Figures de différents caractères*, etched by B. Audran, ca. 1726–28
Bibliothèque nationale de France

Selected literature: RP cat. G48; Eidelberg 2014.
Related paintings: Group appears in *The Halt* (cat. 43). The woman appears alone in *Three Studies of Women* (cat. 13). Rosenberg and Prat suggest that this group was copied from the painting rather than a drawing. Eidelberg suggests that the engraving was copied after an oil counterproof taken directly from the painting.

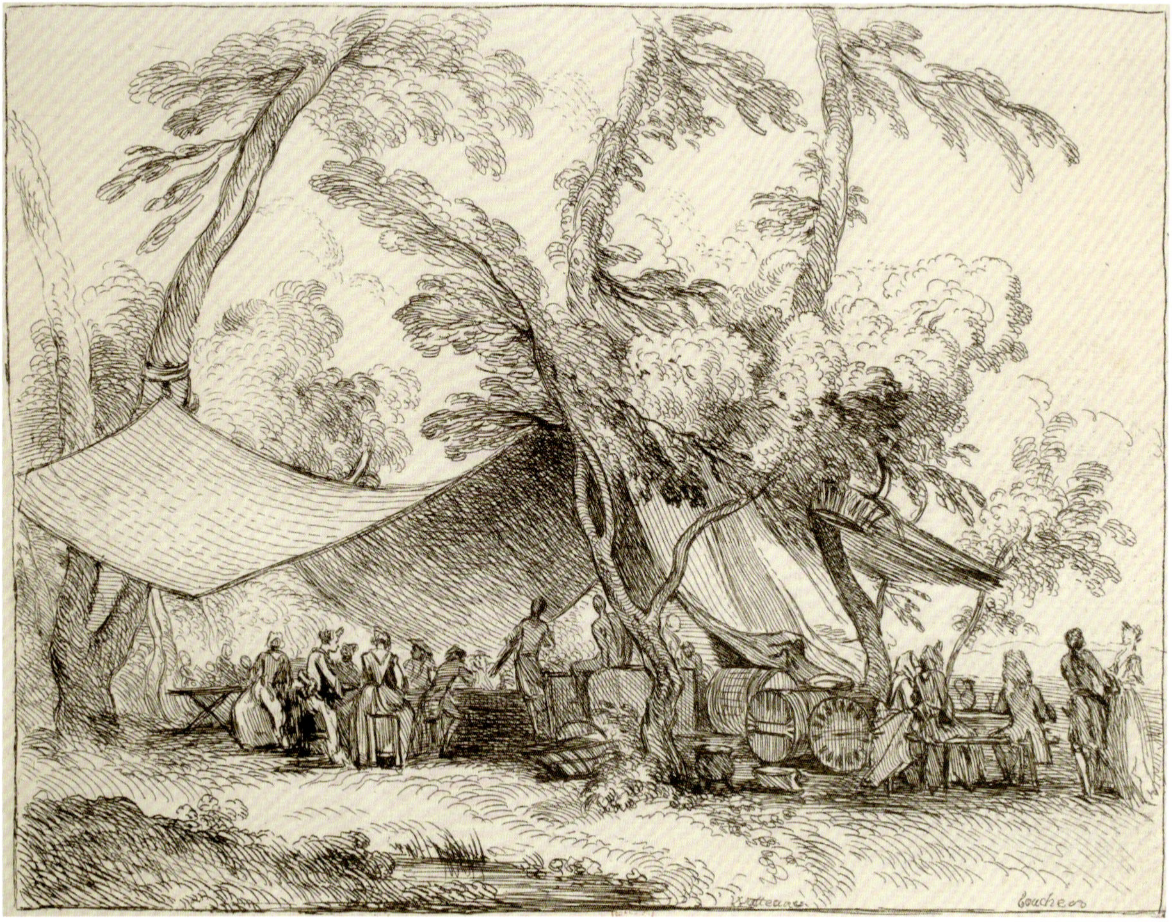

39

Scene under a Tent
Etching
No. 270 in *Figures de différents caractères*, etched by F. Boucher, ca. 1726–28
Bibliothèque nationale de France
(Fig. 14)

Selected literature: RP cat. G97.
Related paintings: Similar to *The Respite from War* (cat. 47).

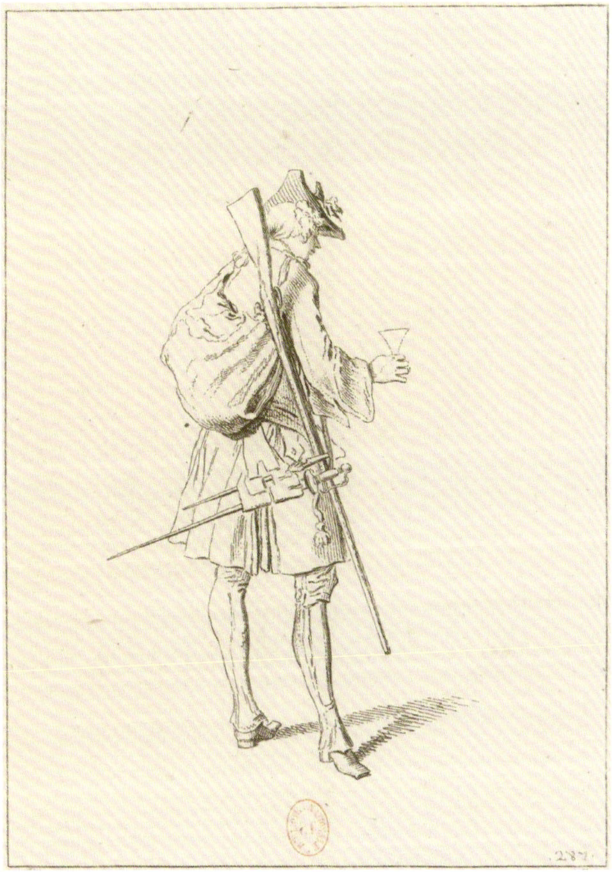

40

Three-Quarter View of a Soldier from Behind Holding a Glass
Etching
No. 287 in *Figures de différents caractères*, etched by E. Jeaurat, ca. 1726–28; proof, with added landscape, in the *Recueil de Valenciennes*
Bibliothèque nationale de France

Selected literature: RP cat. G102.
Related paintings: Used, with variations, in *Departure of a Garrison* (cat. 49).

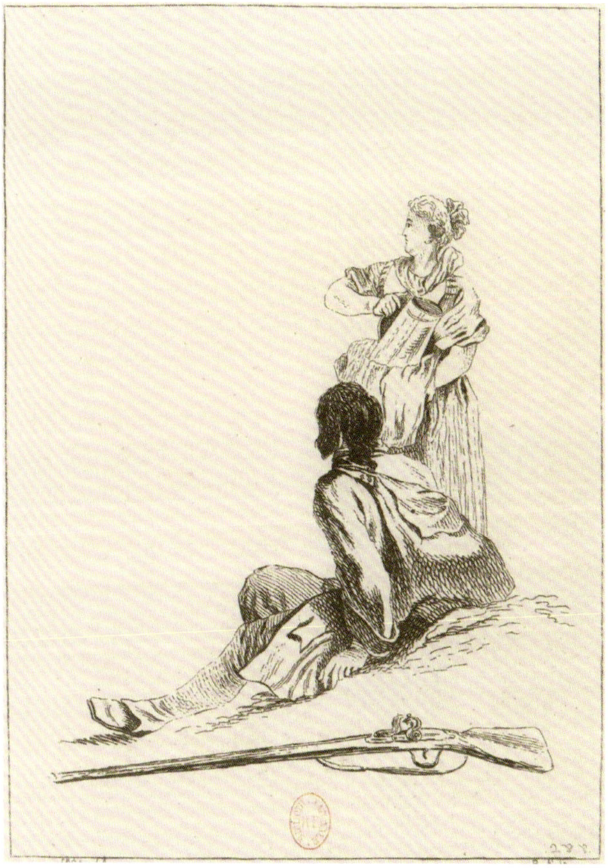

41

Soldier Seated on the Ground and a Woman Holding a Pitcher
Etching
No. 288 in *Figures de différents caractères*, etched by F. Boucher, ca. 1726–28
Bibliothèque nationale de France

Selected literature: RP cat. G103.
Related paintings: Used, with variation in the placement of the musket, in *The Line of March* (cat. 42) or copied from painting.

Paintings

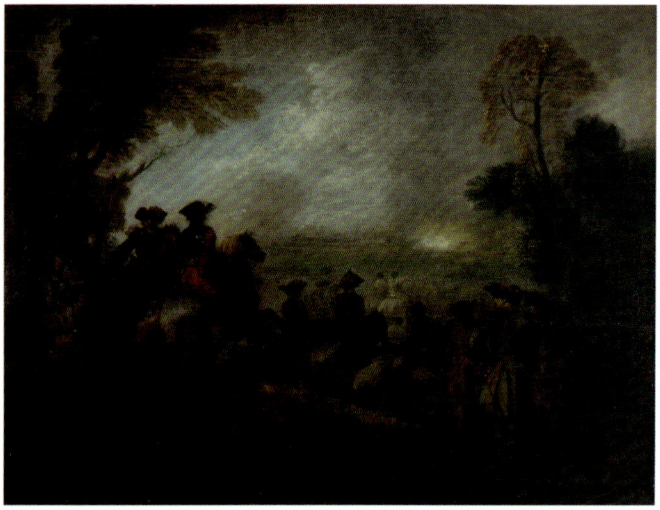

42*

The Line of March (*Défilé*), ca. 1710
Oil on canvas, 15 ⅜ × 19 ⁵⁄₁₆ in. (39 × 49 cm)
(originally in oval frame and later extended)
York Museums Trust (York Art Gallery), York (YORAG 762)
(Fig. 1)

Provenance: Jean de Jullienne (1686–1766), Paris, by 1730; no longer in his collection by ca. 1756. Louis François Joseph de Bourbon, Prince of Conti (1717–1776); Paris, April 8, 1777, lot 665 (with pendant); Augustin Ménageot, Paris, March 17, 1778, lot 107 (with pendant); M. Dubois, Paris, March 31, 1784, no. 78 (with pendant); anonymous sale of Dubois collection, Paris, March 20, 1785, lot 79 (with pendant). Acquired from Spiller in June 1927 by F. D. Licett Green; offered through the Art Fund to the York Art Gallery by F. D. Licett Green in 1955.
Selected literature: G cat. 58; DVH cat. 223; AH cat. 38; C cat. 41; F cat. B5; Rosenbaum 1979, 142–44; Grasselli and Rosenberg 1984, 250–52, cat. 4; Munhall 1992, 18; Glorieux 2011, 87; Vogtherr 2011, 33–37.
Prints after: The engraving was made in the same direction as the painting, with the original oval format extended to a rectangle, by Jean Moyreau before June 1730, when it was announced in the *Mercure de France*. It is unclear when the edges of the painting were expanded and whether they were extended to match the print or vice versa.
Related drawings: Cats. 34, 36, 41.
Related paintings: Since 1729, *The Halt* (cat. 43) and *The Line of March* have been considered pendants. Rosenberg, however, believes that they were not intended as such and were put together artificially. In the absence of documentary evidence, the visual evidence yields no definitive answer either way. Since then, Glorieux has suggested that *The Halt*, along with *The Line of March* and *The Portal of Valenciennes* (cat. 46), formed a series of paintings inserted into a boiserie panel, since all were originally oval shaped and roughly the same size—an idea already rejected by Munhall on the basis of the identical early provenance of *The Halt* and *The Line of March* and the lack of provenance for *The Portal of Valenciennes*. Oval paintings were common in the eighteenth century, and there is no compelling reason to believe that the works would have been inserted into paneling as part of a decorative scheme.

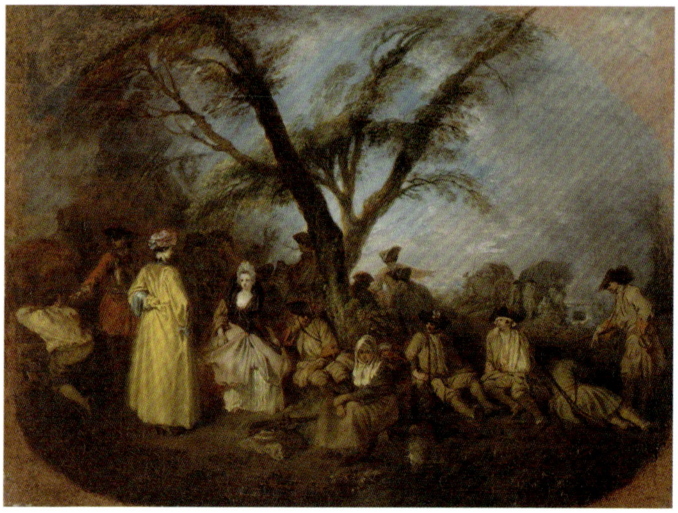

43*

The Halt (*Alte*), ca. 1710
Oil on canvas, 12 ⅝ × 16 ¾ in. (32 × 42.5 cm)
(originally in oval frame and later extended)
Museo Thyssen-Bornemisza, Madrid (431 [1975.51])
(Fig. 16)

Provenance: Jean de Jullienne, Paris, by 1729; no longer in his collection by 1756. Louis François Joseph de Bourbon, Prince of Conti (1717–1776); his sale, Paris, April 8, 1777, lot 665 (with pendant); sold to Augustin Ménageot (1700–1784); his sale, Paris, March 17, 1778, lot 107 (with pendant); M. Dubois, Paris, March 31–April 5, 1784, lot 78 (with pendant), unsold; anonymous sale of Dubois collection, Paris, March 20, 1785, lot 79 (with pendant); Chevalier Lambert sale, Paris, March 27, 1787, lot 185. Earl of Egremont, Petworth House, by 1834; sold by Hugh, 4th Lord Leconfield, Petworth House, 1930, to Agnew, London; New York, Wildenstein and Co., 1943; Charles E. Dunlap (1888–1966) and Phyllis I. Dunlap (1902–1975), 1946; her sale, New York, Parke-Bernet, December 4, 1975, lot 380; Lugano, collection of Baron Hans Heinrich Thyssen-Bornemisza (1921–2002, industrialist); transferred to the Museo Thyssen-Bornemisza, Madrid, 1992.
Selected literature: G cat. 57; DVH cat. 222; AH cat. 35; C cat. 40; F cat. B2; Rosenbaum 1979, 142–44; Grasselli and Rosenberg 1984, 252–54, cat. 5; Eidelberg 2014.
Prints after: The painting was engraved in reverse, with the original oval format extended to a rectangle, by Jean Moyreau before June 1730, when it was announced in the *Mercure de France*. It is unclear when the actual painting's edges were expanded and whether they were extended to match the print or vice versa.
Related drawings: Cats. 8, 12, 13, 15, 38.
Related paintings: See entry for cat. 42.

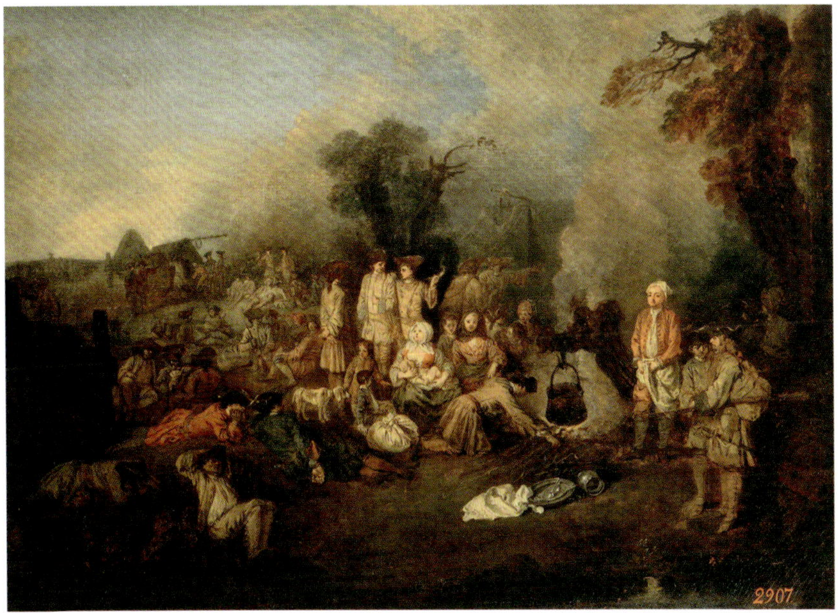

44

Bivouac (Camp volant), ca. 1710
Oil on canvas, 12 ⅞ × 17 ⅝ in.
(32.8 × 44.9 cm)
Pushkin Museum of Fine Arts,
Moscow (Ж-1226)
(Fig. 32)

Inscription: Old inventory number 2907 at lower right.
Provenance: On early provenance, see note 1 in essay in this publication. Seems to have entered the Russian collections before the ascension of Nicholas II (1868–1919) in 1894; transferred from the Hermitage to the Pushkin Museum, Moscow, 1928.
Selected literature: G cat. 52; DVH cat. 148; AH cat. 37; C cat. 44; F cat. A1; Grasselli and Rosenberg 1984, 254–56, cat. 6.
Prints after: Engraved in reverse by Charles-Nicolas Cochin (1686–1754) for the *Recueil Jullienne*; announced in the *Mercure de France* in 1727.
Related drawings: Cats. 9, 10, 14.
Related paintings: Possible pendant to *Return from the Campaign* (cat. 45).

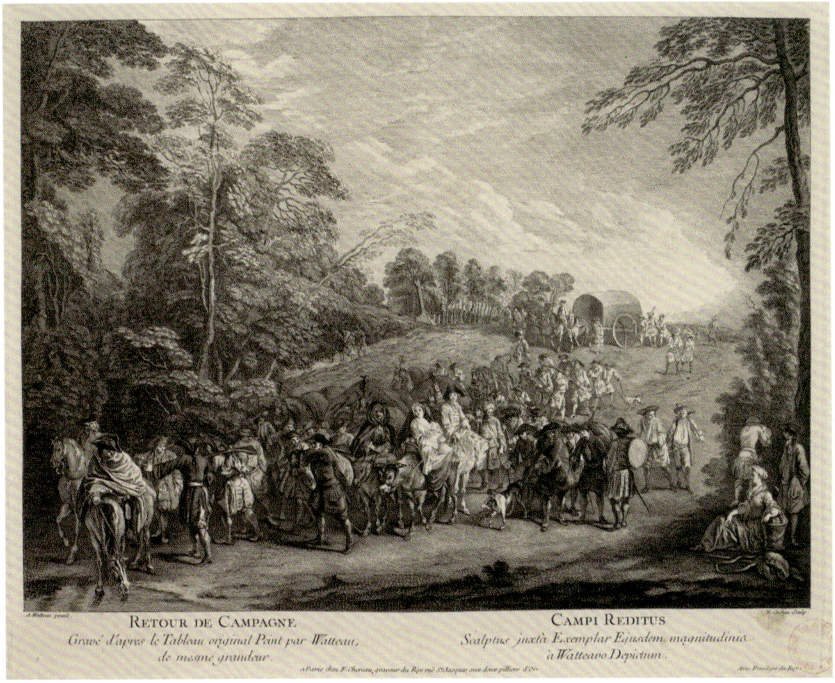

45

Return from the Campaign
(*Retour de campagne*), ca. 1710
Oil on canvas, 12 ½ × 17 ⅛ in.
(31.8 × 43.4 cm) (probable)
Lost

Provenance: For early provenance, see note 1 in essay. May have once belonged to Edme-François Gersaint.
Selected literature: G cat. 53; DVH cat. 147; AH cat. 36; C cat. 43.
Prints after: Engraved by Charles-Nicolas Cochin for the *Recueil Jullienne*; announced in the *Mercure de France* in 1727. "Of the same size" as the painting—12 ½ × 17 ⅛ in. (31.8 × 43.4 cm).
Related drawings: Cat. 3.
Related paintings: Possible pendant to *Bivouac* (cat. 44).

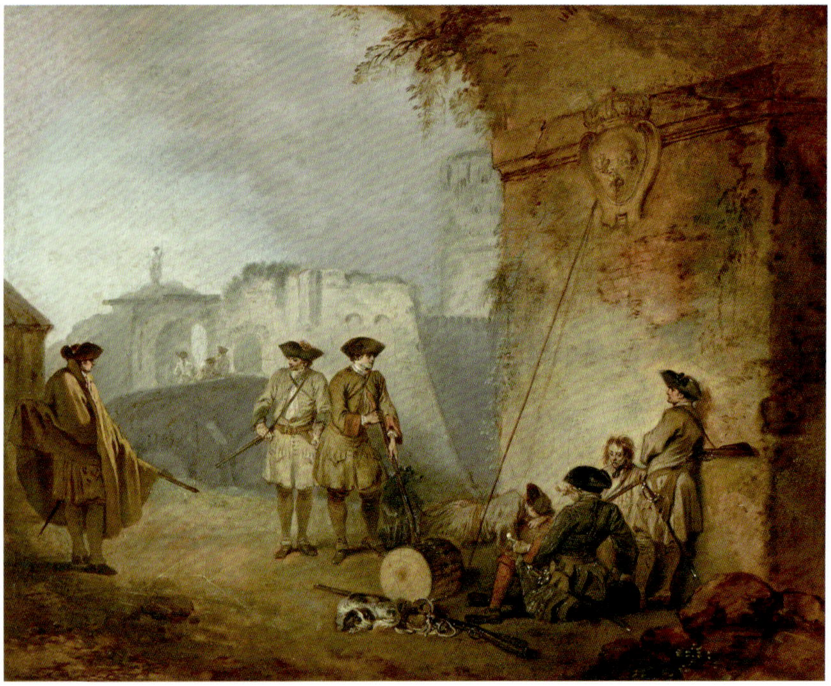

46*

The Portal of Valenciennes (*La Porte de Valenciennes*), ca. 1710–11
Oil on canvas, 12 ¾ × 16 in. (32.5 × 40.5 cm) (originally in oval frame and later extended)
The Frick Collection, New York; purchased with funds from the bequest of Arthemise Redpath, 1991 (91.1.173)
(Fig. 22)

Provenance: Théophile-Étienne-Joseph Thoré (1807–1869); sale, Paris, December 5, 1892, lot 39, as by Jean-Baptiste Pater; Jacques Doucet (1853–1929), Paris; his sale, Paris, June 6, 1912, lot 192, as by Watteau; Albert Lehmann, Paris; sale, Paris, June 8, 1925, lot 222, as by Watteau; Otto Bemberg, Paris, as of 1961; Luis Bemberg and by descent; sale, Sotheby's, London, December 12, 1990, lot 7, as by Watteau; Colnaghi USA, Ltd., New York; purchased by The Frick Collection, 1991.
Selected literature: Munhall 1992; Bailey et al. 2003, 122, 355, cat. 1.
Related drawings: Cats. 5, 6, 7.
Related paintings: See entry for cat. 42.

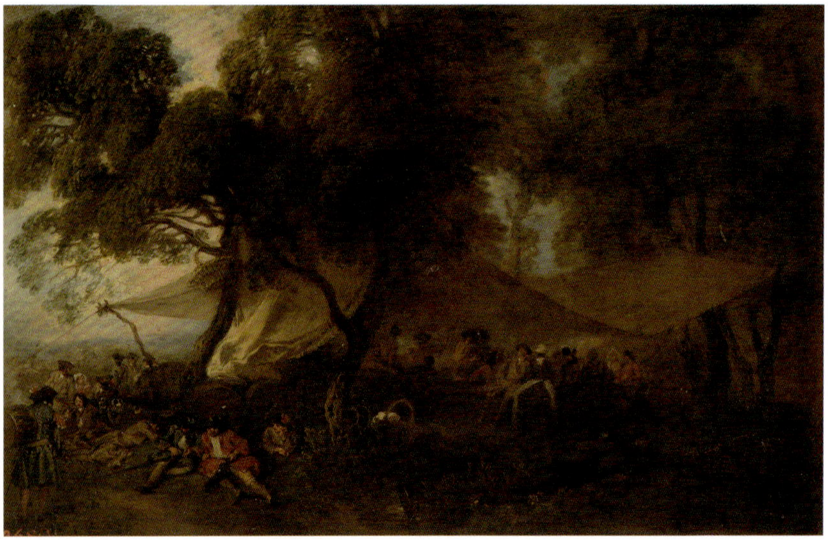

47

The Respite from War (*Les délassements de la guerre*), ca. 1713–14
Oil on copper, 8 ½ × 13 ⅛ in. (21.5 × 33.5 cm)
The State Hermitage Museum, Saint Petersburg (ГЭ-1162)
(Figs. 15, 17)

Provenance: Belonged, with its pendant, to Antoine de La Roque (1672–1744); his sale, May 1745, lot 44; sold to Edme-François Gersaint(?); by 1755 in the collection of Louis-Antoine Crozat, baron de Thiers (1699–1770); acquired by Catherine the Great of Russia, 1772.
Selected literature: G cat. 55; DVH cat. 216; AH cat. 95; C cat. 96; F cat. A5; Grasselli and Rosenberg 1984, 282–83, cat. 16.
Prints after: Engraved in reverse by Gérard Scotin (1698–?) for the *Recueil Jullienne* and announced, with its pendant, in the *Mercure de France* in June 1731. Almost exactly the same dimensions as the painting.
Related paintings: Pendant to *The Burdens of War* (cat. 48), also in the Hermitage.
Related drawings: Cats. 21, 22, 39.

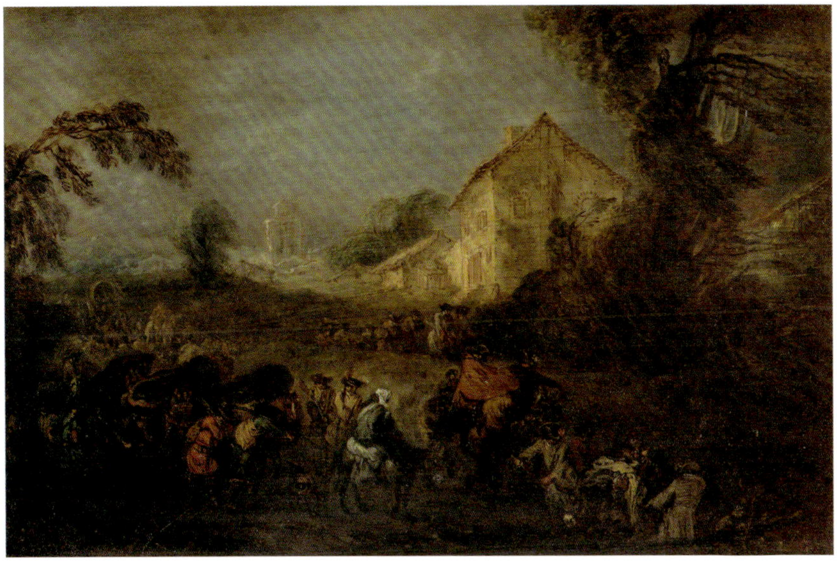

48

The Burdens of War (*Les fatigues de la guerre*), ca. 1713–14
Oil on copper, 8 ½ × 13 ⅛ in. (21.5 × 33.5 cm)
The State Hermitage Museum, Saint Petersburg (ГЭ-1159)
(Fig. 31)

Provenance: See preceding entry.
Selected literature: G cat. 54; DVH cat. 138; AH cat. 96; C cat. 97; F cat. A6; Grasselli and Rosenberg 1984, 280–82, cat. 15.
Prints after: See preceding entry.
Related paintings: Pendant to *The Respite from War* (cat. 47), also in the Hermitage.

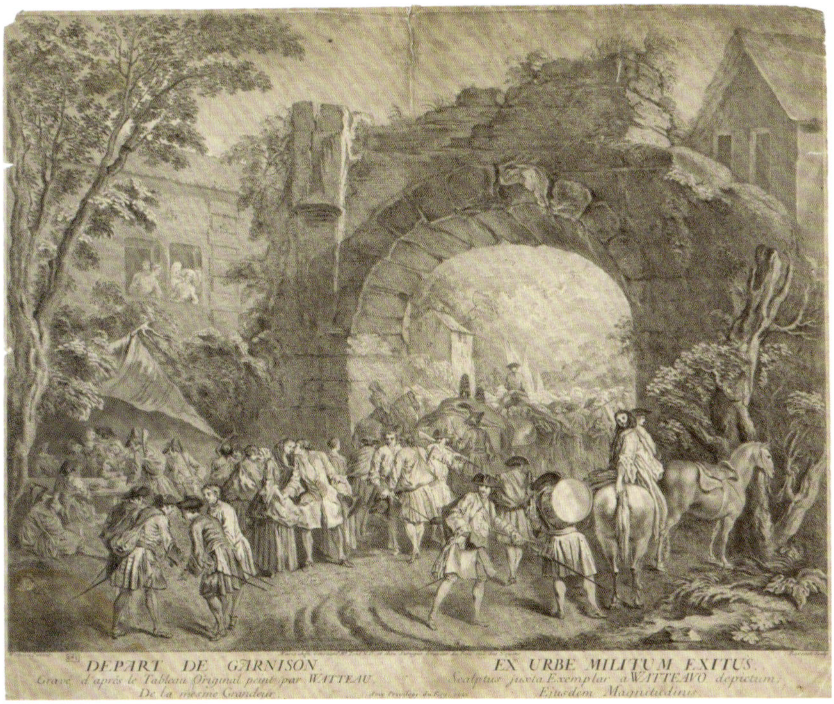

49

Departure of a Garrison (*Départ de garnison*), ca. 1714
Oil on canvas, dimensions unknown
Lost

Provenance: La Haye Sale, Paris 1754; lost.
Selected literature: G cat. 59; DVH cat. 276; AH cat. 50; C cat. 59; F cat. B3.
Prints after: Engraved by S. F. Ravenet, announced in June 1737 and again in June 1738. The original painting is the same size as the engraving (42.7 × 56.3 cm) according to the print, but 55 by 70 cm according to the auction catalogue for La Haye Sale. Engraved too late to be included in the *Recueil Jullienne*.
Related drawings: Cats. 16, 17, 19, 21, 32, 35, 37, 40.

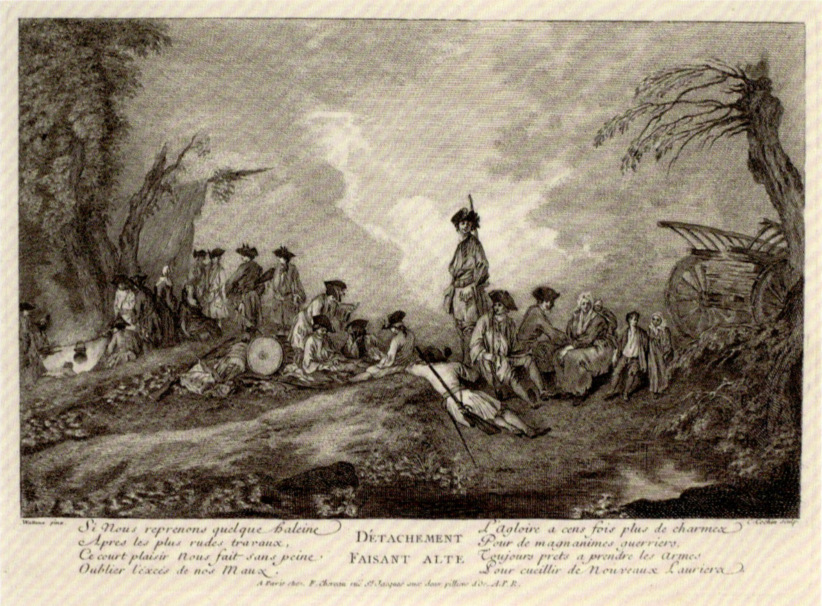

50*

Halt of a Detachment (*Détachement faisant halte*), ca. 1715
Oil on canvas, dimensions unknown
Lost
(Fig. 30)

Provenance: On early provenance: see Remarks for cat. 51 and n. 1, p. 72, in this publication.
Selected literature: G cat. 51; DVH cat. 179; AH cat. 70; C cat. 55; F cat. B4.
Prints after: Engraved by Charles-Nicolas Cochin by 1729. Dimensions of engraving: 8 ⅜ × 13 ⅜ in. (21.2 × 33.9 cm)
Related drawings: Cats. 11, 15, 23.
Related paintings: Possible pendant to *Recruits Going to Join the Regiment* (cat. 51).

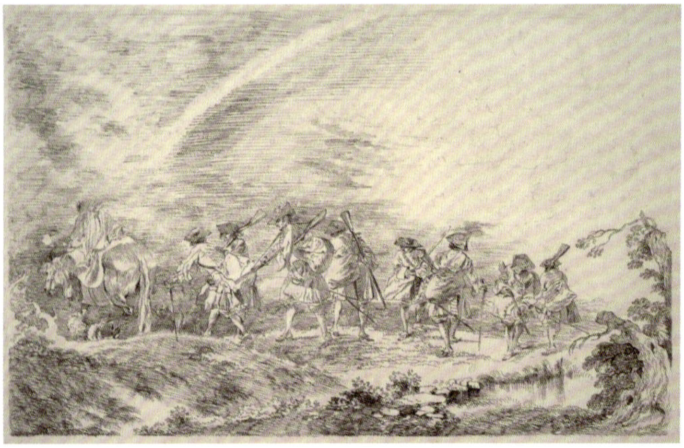

51

Recruits Going to Join the Regiment (*Recrue allant joindre le régiment*), ca. 1715
Oil on canvas, dimensions unknown
Lost
(Fig. 26)

Prints after: *First state, Watteau. Etching with dry point, ca. 1716. Second state (fig. 27) retouched by Henri-Simon Thomassin for the *Recueil Jullienne*. Two other states are known. Etching, dry point, and engraving, ca. 1716–26. Dimensions of engraving: 8 ⅞ × 13 ½ in. (22.6 × 34.2 cm).
Provenance of painting: On early provenance: see "Remarks" below and note 1 in essay.
Selected literature: G cat. 2; DVH cat. 178; AH cat. 34; C cat. 42; F cat. B1; Grasselli and Rosenberg 1984, 236–37, cat. 7; Sahut et al. 2010, 22–24; Stein et al. 2013, 21–22, 186, no. 2.
Related drawings: Cats. 24–27, 29, 33. The figures in cat. 28 are similar to those in *Recruits Going to Join the Regiment*, but none match exactly.
Related paintings: Possible pendant to *Halt of a Detachment* (cat. 50).
Remarks: The etching is one of only two Watteau made after his own paintings (the other is *Les habits sont italiens*). Among the changes Thomassin made when he retouched the etching—shortly after Watteau completed it—was to move the rainbow. It has been suggested that this was the painting referred to by Edme-François Gersaint that Watteau sold to Pierre Sirois before he left for Valenciennes in 1710, but given the sophistication of the composition and the figures' poses, as well as the later date for the related drawings proposed by Grasselli, this seems unlikely.

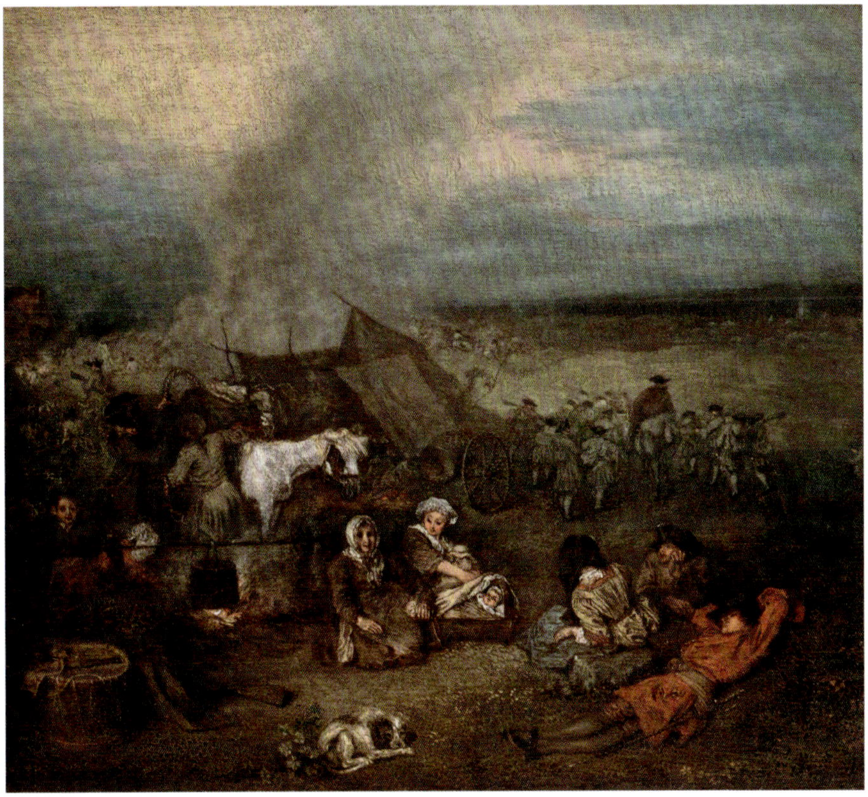

52*

The Supply Train (*Escorte d'équipages*), ca. 1715
Oil on panel, 11 ⅛ × 12 ⅜ in. (28.2 × 31.4 cm);
about 2 ½ in. (6 cm) of landscape cut off right side of original by 1756
Collection Lionel and Ariane Sauvage
(Fig. 18)

Provenance: Jean de Jullienne (1686–1766), Paris, by 1731 (sold before 1756); Cardinal Silvio Valenti Gonzaga (1690–1756), Mantua and Rome; bequeathed to his nephews, Marques Carlo Valenti Gonzaga (d. 1783) and Cardinal Luigi Valenti Gonzaga (1725–1808); Pietro Camuccini (1761–1833), Rome, who purchased it in 1818 with other works from the estate of Cardinal Luigi Valenti Gonzaga; by descent to his nephew, Giovanni Battista, Baron Camuccini (1819–1904), Rome and by descent; sale, New York, Christie's, January 29, 2009, lot 89, to a private collector.
Selected literature: G cat. 56; DVH cat. 125; AH cat. 39; C cat. 57; Christie's 2009, 228–31, lot 89.
Related drawings: Cats. 20, 22, 23, 25, 30, 31.

Prints after: Engraved (in reverse) by Laurent Cars (see below) by April 1731, when it was announced in the *Mercure de France.*

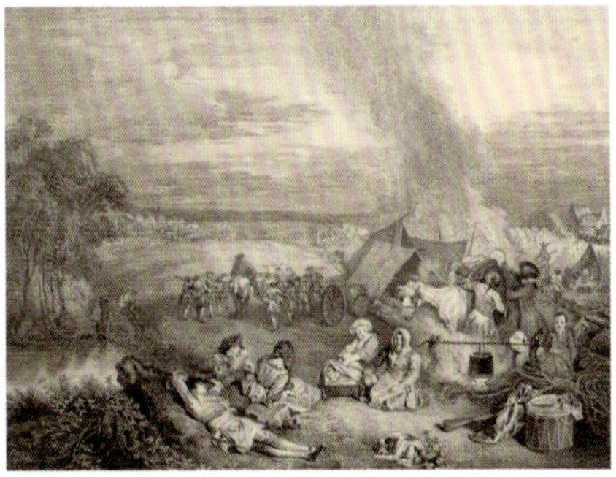

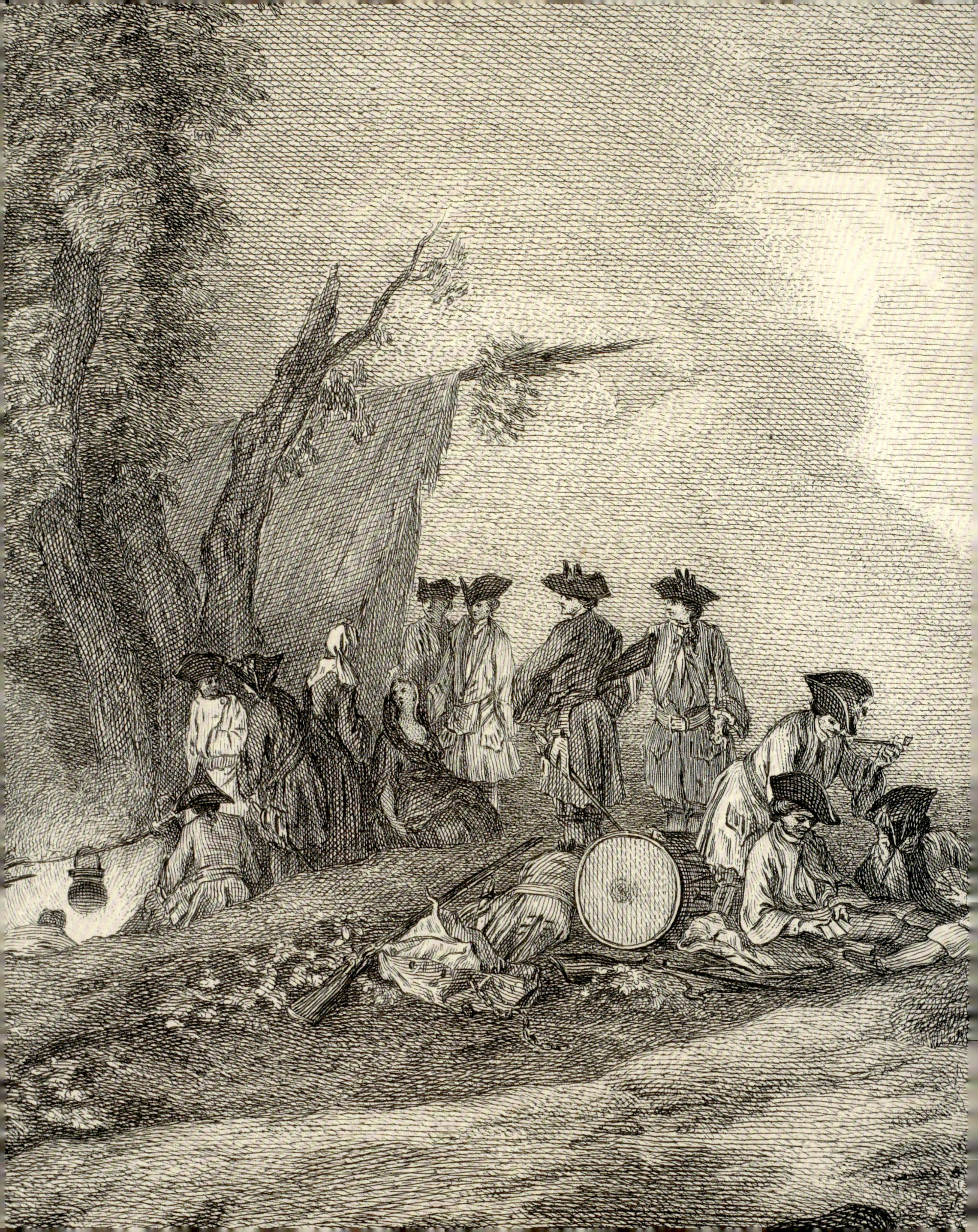

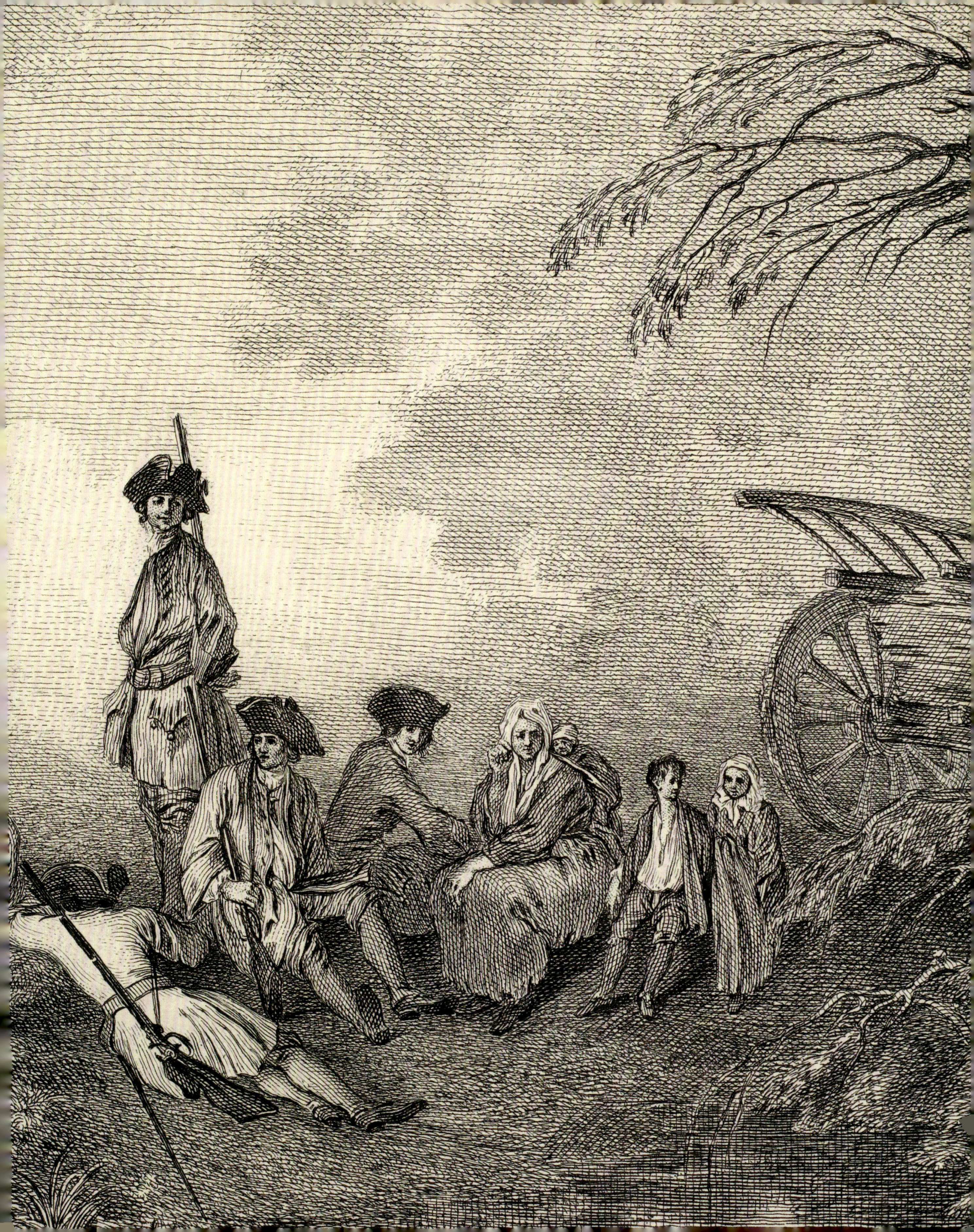

Selected Bibliography

ADHÉMAR AND HUYGHE 1950

Adhémar, Hélène, and René Huyghe. *Watteau; sa vie, son oeuvre. Précédé de l'univers de Watteau, par René Huyghe; catalogue des peintures et illustration par Hélène Adhémar.* Paris: Pierre Tisné, 1950.

BAILEY ET AL. 2003

Bailey, Colin, et. al. *The Age of Watteau, Chardin, and Fragonard: Masterpieces of French Genre Painting.* Exh. cat. New Haven: Yale University Press in association with the National Gallery of Canada, Ottawa, 2003.

BAILEY ET AL. 2009

Bailey, Colin, et al. *Watteau to Degas: French Drawings from the Frits Lugt Collection.* Exh. cat. New York: The Frick Collection in association with the Fondation Custodia, Paris, 2009.

BANKS 1977

Banks, Oliver T. *Watteau and the North: Studies in the Dutch and Flemish Baroque Influence on French Rococo Painting.* New York: Garland, 1977.

BELL 2007

Bell, David A. *The First Total War: Napoleon's Europe and the Birth of Warfare as We Know It.* Boston and New York: Mariner Books, 2007.

BEUGNOT 1996

Beugnot, Bernard. "Loisir, retraite, solitude: de l'espace privé à la littérature." In *Le Loisir lettré à l'âge classique.* Edited by Marc Fumaroli, Philippe-Joseph Salazar, and Emmanuel Bury. Geneva: Droz, 1996.

BLUNT 1964

Blunt, Anthony, ed. *Nicolas Poussin: lettres et propos sur l' art.* Paris: Hermann, 1964.

BOORSCH AND MARCIARI ET AL. 2006

Boorsch, Suzanne, and John Marciari et al. *Master Drawings from the Yale University Art Gallery.* New Haven and London: Yale University Art Gallery in association with Yale University Press, 2006.

BRYSON 1983

Bryson, Norman. *Word and Image: French Painting of the Ancien Régime.* Cambridge: Cambridge University Press, 1983.

CAMESASCA 1982

Camesasca, Ettore. *Tout l'œuvre peint de Watteau.* Introduction by Pierre Rosenberg. Paris: Flammarion, 1982.

CAMESASCA AND SUNDERLAND 1971

Camesasca, Ettore, and John Sunderland. *The Complete Paintings of Watteau.* London: Weidenfeld & Nicolson, 1971.

CAMPE AND WEBER 2014

Campe, Rüdiger, and Julia Weber, eds. *Rethinking Emotion: Interiority and Exteriority in Premodern, Modern, and Contemporary Thought.* Berlin and Boston: Walter de Gruyter GmbH, 2014.

CAVIGLIA 2016

Caviglia, Susanna. "Life Drawing and the Crisis of *Historia* in French Eighteenth-Century Painting." *Art History* 39, no. 1 (Feb. 2016): 40–69.

CAYLUS 1984

Caylus, comte de, Anne-Claude-Philippe de Tubières. "La Vie d'Antoine Watteau, peintre de figures et de paysages, sujets gallants et modernes, lue à l'Académie le 3 février 1748" (1748). In Rosenberg 1984, 53–91.

CHRISTIE'S 2009

Important Old Master Paintings and Sculpture, Part I. Sale cat., Christie's, New York, January 28, 2009.

CLARKE 2010

Clarke, Michael. *Poussin to Seurat: French Drawings from the National Gallery of Scotland.* Exh. cat. Edinburgh: National Galleries of Scotland, 2010.

COLSON 1999

Colson, Bruno. *L'Art de la guerre de Machiavel à Clausewitz.* Namur: Presses universitaires de Namur, 1999.

COQUERY 1997

Coquery, Jean de. "Le Portrait vu du Grand Siècle." In *Visages du Grand Siècle: le portrait français sous le règne de Louis XIV,* 15–34. Exh. cat. Paris: Somogy, 1997.

CORVISIER 1964

Corvisier, André. *L'Armée française de la fin du XVIIe siècle au ministère de Choiseul. Le soldat.* Paris: Presses universitaires de France, 1964.

COYPEL 2003

Coypel, Antoine. "Sur l'ésthétique du peintre" (1712–21). In *Les Conférences de l'Académie royale de peinture et de sculpture au XVIIe,* 411–521. 2nd ed. Edited by Alain Mérot. Paris: École nationale supérieure des Beaux-Arts, 2003.

DACIER, VUAFLART, AND HÉROLD 1921–29

Dacier, Émile, Albert Vuaflart, and Jacques Hérold. *Jean de Jullienne et les graveurs de Watteau au XVIIIe siècle.* 3 vols. Paris: Pour les membres de la Société, 1921–29.

DEZALLIER D'ARGENVILLE 1984

Dezallier d'Argenville, Antoine-Joseph. "Autre *abrégé* de la vie d'Antoine Watteau" (1745). In Rosenberg 1984, 46–52.

DEJEAN 1997

DeJean, Joan. *Ancients against Moderns: Culture Wars and the Making of a Fin de Siècle.* Chicago and London: University of Chicago Press, 1997.

DÉMORIS 1997

Démoris, René. "De la vérité en peinture chez Félibien et Roger de Piles: imitation, représentation, illusion." In "La Naissance de la théorie de l'art en France, 1640–1720." Edited by Stefan Germer and Christian Michel. Special issue, *Revue d'Esthétique* 31–32 (1997): 37–50.

DE PILES 1699
De Piles, Roger. *Dialogue sur le coloris*. Paris: Chez Nicolas Langlois, 1699.

DE PILES 1766
De Piles, Roger. *Cours de peinture par principe* (1708). New ed. Paris: Chez Charles-Antoine Jombert, 1766.

EIDELBERG 1977
Eidelberg, Martin. *Watteau's Drawings: Their Use and Significance*. New York: Garland, 1977.

EIDELBERG 2001
Eidelberg, Martin. "The Case of the Vanishing Watteau." *Gazette des Beaux-Arts* (July/August 2001): 15–40.

EIDELBERG 2014
Eidelberg, Martin. "*L'Alte*." *A Watteau Abecedario*. Last modified August 2014. http://watteau-abecedario.org/alte000.htm.

FARGE 1996
Farge, Arlette. *Les Fatigues de la guerre*. Paris: Gallimard, 1996.

FÉLIBIEN 1704
Félibien, André. *The Tent of Darius Explain'd: or The Queens of Persia at The Feet of Alexander*. Bilingual ed. translated by Colonel Parsons. London: André Félibien, 1704.

FERRÉ 1972
Ferré, Jean. *Watteau*. Madrid: Arthena, 1972.

FRIED 1980
Fried, Michael. *Absorption and Theatricality: Painting and Beholder in the Age of Diderot*. Chicago: University of Chicago Press, 1980.

GERSAINT 1984
Gersaint, E.-F. "Abrégé de la vie d'Antoine Watteau" (1744). In Rosenberg 1984.

GLORIEUX 2011
Glorieux, Guillaume. *Watteau*. Paris: Citadelles & Mazenod, 2011.

GONCOURT 1875
Goncourt, Edmond de. *Catalogue raisonné de l'oeuvre peint, dessiné et gravé d'Antoine Watteau*. Paris: Rapilly, 1875.

GRASSELLI 1987
Grasselli, Margaret Morgan. *The Drawings of Antoine Watteau: Stylistic Development and Problems of Chronology*. 2 vols. New York: Garland, 1987.

GRASSELLI 2001
Grasselli, Margaret Morgan. Review of Rosenberg and Prat 1996. *Master Drawings* 39, no. 3 (Fall 2001): 310–34.

GRASSELLI AND ROSENBERG 1984
Grasselli, Margaret Morgan, and Pierre Rosenberg. *Watteau 1684–1721*. Exh. cat. Washington, D.C.: National Gallery of Art, 1984.

GUYOT AND THOURET 2009
Guyot, Sylvaine, and Clotilde Thouret. "Des émotions en chaîne: représentation théâtrale et circulation publique des affects au XVIIe siècle." *Littératures Classiques* 1, no. 68 (2009): 225–41.

HATTORI 2004
Hattori, Cordélia. "Passeports délivrés à des artistes au XVIIIe siècle: à Watteau, à Oudry et à quelques autres." *Les Cahiers d'Histoire de l'Art* 2 (2004): 23–32.

HAZARD 2013
Hazard, Paul. *The Crisis of the European Mind, 1680–1715* (1935). Translated by J. Lewis May. New York: New York Review Books, 2013.

JULLIENNE 1726
Jullienne, Jean de, ed. *Figures de différents caractères, de paysages et d'études dessinées d'après nature par Antoine Watteau*. 3 vols. Paris: Chez Audran/Chez F. Chéreau 1726.

JULLIENNE 1984
Jullienne, Jean de. "Abrégé de la vie d'Antoine Watteau, Peintre du Roy en son Académie Royale de Peinture et de Sculpture" (1726). In Rosenberg 1984, 11–17.

KIRCHNER 2013
Kirchner, Thomas. *Les Reines de Perse aux pieds d'Alexandre de Charles Le Brun. Tableau-manifeste de l'art français du XVIIe siècle*. Paris: Éditions de la maison des sciences de l'homme, 2013.

LA BRUYÈRE 1691
La Bruyère, Jean de. *Les Caractères de Théophraste traduits du grec avec les caractères ou les mœurs de ce siècle*. 6th ed. Paris, 1691.

LAJER-BURCHARTH 2015
Lajer-Burcharth, Ewa. "Drawing Time." *October* 151 (Winter 2015): 3–42.

LOCKE 1996
Locke, John. *An Essay Concerning Human Understanding* (1689). Edited by Kenneth Winkler. Indianapolis and Cambridge: Hackett, 1996.

LOUVRE 2015
Musée de Louvre, département des Arts graphiques. "Watteau Antoine, *Soldat armé d'un fusil et d'un epée marchant vers la droite*." Last modified April 18, 2015. http://arts-graphiques.louvre.fr/detail/oeuvres/12/507521-Soldat-arme-dun-fusil-et-dune-epee-marchant-vers-la-droite.

LYNN 1997
Lynn, John A. *Giant of the Grand Siècle: The French Army, 1610–1715*. Cambridge: Cambridge University Press, 1997.

LYNN 1999
Lynn, John A. *The Wars of Louis XIV, 1667–1714*. Modern Wars in Perspective. London and New York: Routledge, 1999.

LYNN 2008
Lynn, John A. *Women, Armies and Warfare in Early Modern Europe.* Cambridge: Cambridge University Press, 2008.

MÉROT AND RAUX-CARPENTIER 1998
Mérot, Alain, and Sophie Raux-Carpentier. "Academicism & Anti-Academicism: Drawing in France in the Seventeenth and Eighteen Centuries." In *Mastery & Elegance: Two Centuries of French Drawings from the Collection of Jeffrey E. Horvitz*, 25–51. Exh. cat. Edited by Alvin L. Clark, Jr. Cambridge: Harvard University Art Museums, 1998.

MICHEL 1984
Michel, Marianne Roland. *Watteau: An Artist of the Eighteenth Century.* Secaucus, NJ: Chartwell Books, 1984.

MICHEL 2008
Michel, Christian. *Le "Célèbre Watteau."* Geneva: Droz, 2008.

MONTAGU 1994
Montagu, Jennifer. *The Expression of the Passions: The Origin and Influence of Charles Le Brun's "Conférence sur l'expression générale et particulière."* New Haven and London: Yale University Press, 1994.

MUCHEMBLED 1988
Muchembled, Robert. *L'Invention de l'homme moderne: sensibilités, mœurs et comportements collectifs sous l'Ancien Régime.* Paris: Fayard, 1988.

MUNHALL 1992
Munhall, Edgar. *Little Notes Concerning Watteau's "Portal of Valenciennes."* New York: The Frick Collection, 1992.

OPPERMAN 1987
Opperman, Hal. "The Theme of Peace in Watteau." In *Antoine Watteau: The Painter, His Age and His Legend*, 23–28. Edited by François Moureau and Margaret Morgan Grasselli. Paris and Geneva: Champion-Slatkine, 1987.

PANOFSKY 1968
Panofsky, Erwin. *Idea: A Concept in Art Theory.* Translated by Joseph J. S. Peake. New York: Harper & Row, 1968.

PERRAULT 1688–97
Perrault, Charles. *Parallèle des Anciens et des Modernes, en ce qui regarde les arts et les sciences.* 4 vols. Paris: Chez Jean Baptiste Coignard, 1688–97.

PICHICHERO 2008a
Pichichero, Christy. "Battles of the Self: War and Subjectivity in Early Modern France." Ph.D. diss., Stanford University, 2008.

PICHICHERO 2008b
Pichichero, Christy. "Le Soldat Sensible: Military Psychology and Social Egalitarianism in the Enlightenment French Army." *French Historical Studies* 31, no. 4 (Fall 2008): 553–80.

PLAX 2000
Plax, Julie Anne. *Watteau and the Cultural Politics of Eighteenth-Century France.* Cambridge: Cambridge University Press, 2000.

POSNER 1984
Posner, Donald. *Antoine Watteau.* Ithaca: Cornell University Press, 1984.

PULLINS *FORTHCOMING*
Pullins, David. "Images as Objects: The Problem of Figural Ornament in Eighteenth-Century France." In *Histories of Ornament: From Global to Local.* Edited by Gülru Necipoglu and Alina Payne. Princeton: Princeton University Press. Forthcoming.

PUTTFARKEN 1985
Puttfarken, Thomas. *Roger de Piles' Theory of Art.* New Haven and London: Yale University Press, 1985.

PUTTFARKEN 2000
Puttfarken, Thomas. *The Discovery of Pictorial Composition: Theories of Visual Order in Painting, 1400–1800.* New Haven and London: Yale University Press, 2000.

PUYSÉGUR 1749
Puységur, Jean-François de Chastenet de. *Art de la guerre par principes et par règles.* 2 vols. Paris: Chez Jombert, 1749.

RANUM 1989
Ranum, Orsest. "The Refuges of Intimacy." In *A History of Private Life*. Vol. 3. *Passions of the Renaissance*, 207–64. Translated by Arthur Goldhammer. Edited by Roger Chartier. Cambridge: Harvard University Press, Belknap Press, 1989.

ROHOU 2002
Rohou, Jean. *Le XVIIe siècle, une révolution de la conscience humaine.* Paris: Éditions du Seuil, 2002.

ROSEN 2006
Rosen, Jochai. "The Dutch Guardroom Scene of the Golden Age: A Definition." *Artibus et Historiae* 27, no. 53 (2006): 151–74.

ROSENBAUM 1979
Rosenbaum, Allen. *Old Master Paintings from the Collection of Baron Thyssen-Bornemisza.* Washington, D.C.: International Exhibitions Foundation, 1979.

ROSENBERG 1984
Rosenberg, Pierre, ed. *Vies anciennes de Watteau.* Paris: Hermann, 1984.

ROSENBERG AND PRAT 1996
Rosenberg, Pierre, and Louis-Antoine Prat. *Antoine Watteau, 1684–1721: Catalogue raisonné des dessins.* 3 vols. Milan: Leonardo Arte, 1996.

SAHUT et al. 2010
Sahut, Marie-Catherine, et al. *Antoine Watteau et l'art de l'estampe.* Exh. cat. Paris: Musée du Louvre, 2010.

SCHUMACHER 2006
Schumacher, Birgit. *Philips Wouwerman: The Horse Painter of the Golden Age.* 2 vols. Doornspijk: Davaco Publishers, 2006.

SEIGEL 2005

Seigel, Jerrold. *The Idea of the Self: Thought and Experience in Western Europe Since the Seventeenth Century.* Cambridge: Cambridge University Press, 2005.

SPAANS 1998

Spaans, Erik. "Legerkampen op zeventiende-eeuwse schilderijen: beeld en werkelijkheid." In *Beelden van een Strijd, Oorlog en Kunst voor de Vrede van Munster 1621–1648*, 164–81. Exh. cat. Delft: Stedelijk Museum Het Prinsenhof, 1998.

STEIN ET AL. 2013

Stein, Perrin, et al. *Artists and Amateurs: Etching in 18th-Century France.* Exh. cat. New Haven and London: Yale University Press, 2013.

TILLEROT 2010

Tillerot, Isabelle. *Jean de Jullienne et les collectionneurs de son temps: un regard singulier sur le tableau.* Paris: Éditions de la Maison des sciences de l'homme, 2010.

TOCANNE 1978

Tocanne, Bernard. *L'Idée de la nature en France dans la seconde moitié du XVIIe siècle.* Paris: Klincksieck, 1978.

VIDAL 1992

Vidal, Mary. *Watteau's Painted Conversations: Art, Literature, and Talk in Seventeenth- and Eighteenth-Century France.* New Haven and London: Yale University Press, 1992.

VOGTHERR 2011

Vogtherr, Christoph. *Watteau at the Wallace Collection.* Exh. cat. London: The Wallace Collection, 2011.

WAHRMAN 2004

Wahrman, Dror. *The Making of the Modern Self: Identity and Culture in Eighteenth-Century England.* New Haven: Yale University Press, 2004.

WILE 2014

Wile, Aaron. "Watteau, Reverie, and Selfhood." *The Art Bulletin* 96, no. 3 (Sept. 2014): 319–37.

WINTERMUTE et al. 1999

Wintermute, Alan, et al. *Watteau and His World: French Drawing from 1700 to 1750.* Exh. cat. London and New York: Merrell Holberton and the American Federation of Arts, 1999.

ZISKIN 2012

Ziskin, Rochelle. *Sheltering Art: Collecting and Social Identity in Early Eighteenth-Century Paris.* University Park: Pennsylvania State University Press, 2012.

Photo Credits

Photographs in this book have been provided by the owners or custodians of the work. The following list applies to those photographs for which a separate credit is due.

Fig. 2	Studio Tromp, Rotterdam
Fig. 3/cat. 23	© Beaux-Arts de Paris, Dist. RMN-Grand Palais / Art Resource, NY
Fig. 4/cat. 15	© Beaux-Arts de Paris, Dist. RMN-Grand Palais / Art Resource, NY
Fig. 5/cat. 14	Michael Bodycomb
Fig. 6/cat. 2	© Musée des beaux-arts de Quimper
Fig. 9/cat. 21	Imaging Department © President and Fellows of Harvard College
Fig. 10	© RMN-Grand Palais / Art Resource, NY
Fig 11	Photo Gérard Blot. © RMN-Grand Palais / Art Resource, NY
Fig. 12	Thierry Le Mage. © RMN-Grand Palais / Art Resource, NY
Fig. 13	© The Metropolitan Museum of Art / Art Resource, NY
Fig. 15/cat. 47	Pavel Demidov. © The State Hermitage Museum
Fig. 19/cat. 13	© Musée Carnavalet / Roger-Viollet
Fig. 22/cat. 46	Michael Bodycomb
Fig. 25/cat. 6	The Samuel Courtauld Trust, The Courtauld Gallery, London
Fig. 26/cat. 51	© The Metropolitan Museum of Art / Art Resource, NY
Fig. 27	Angele Dequier. © RMN-Grand Palais / Art Resource, NY
Fig. 29	Michael Bodycomb
Fig. 30/cat. 50	© RMN-Grand Palais / Art Resource, NY
Fig. 31/cat. 48	Pavel Demidov. © The State Hermitage Museum
Fig. 32/cat. 44	© Scala / Art Resource, NY
Fig. 33	Michael Bodycomb
Cat. 4	© Städel Museum, Frankfurt am Main
Cat. 9	Michael Bodycomb
Cat. 11	Michael Bodycomb
Cat. 16	© RMN-Grand Palais / Art Resource, NY
Cat. 17	© RMN-Grand Palais / Art Resource, NY
Cat. 19	© Ashmolean Museum, University of Oxford
Cat. 20	© The Trustees of the British Museum / Art Resource, NY
Cat. 25	bpk, Berlin / Kupferstichkabinett, Staatliche Museen / Volker-H. Schneider / Art Resource, NY
Cat. 28	© RMN-Grand Palais / Art Resource, NY
Cat. 29	Gerard Blot. © RMN-Grand Palais / Art Resource, NY
Cat. 30	© The Trustees of the British Museum / Art Resource, NY
Cat. 45	Angele Dequier. Musée du Louvre. © RMN-Grand Palais / Art Resource, NY

Cat. 21 (detail)

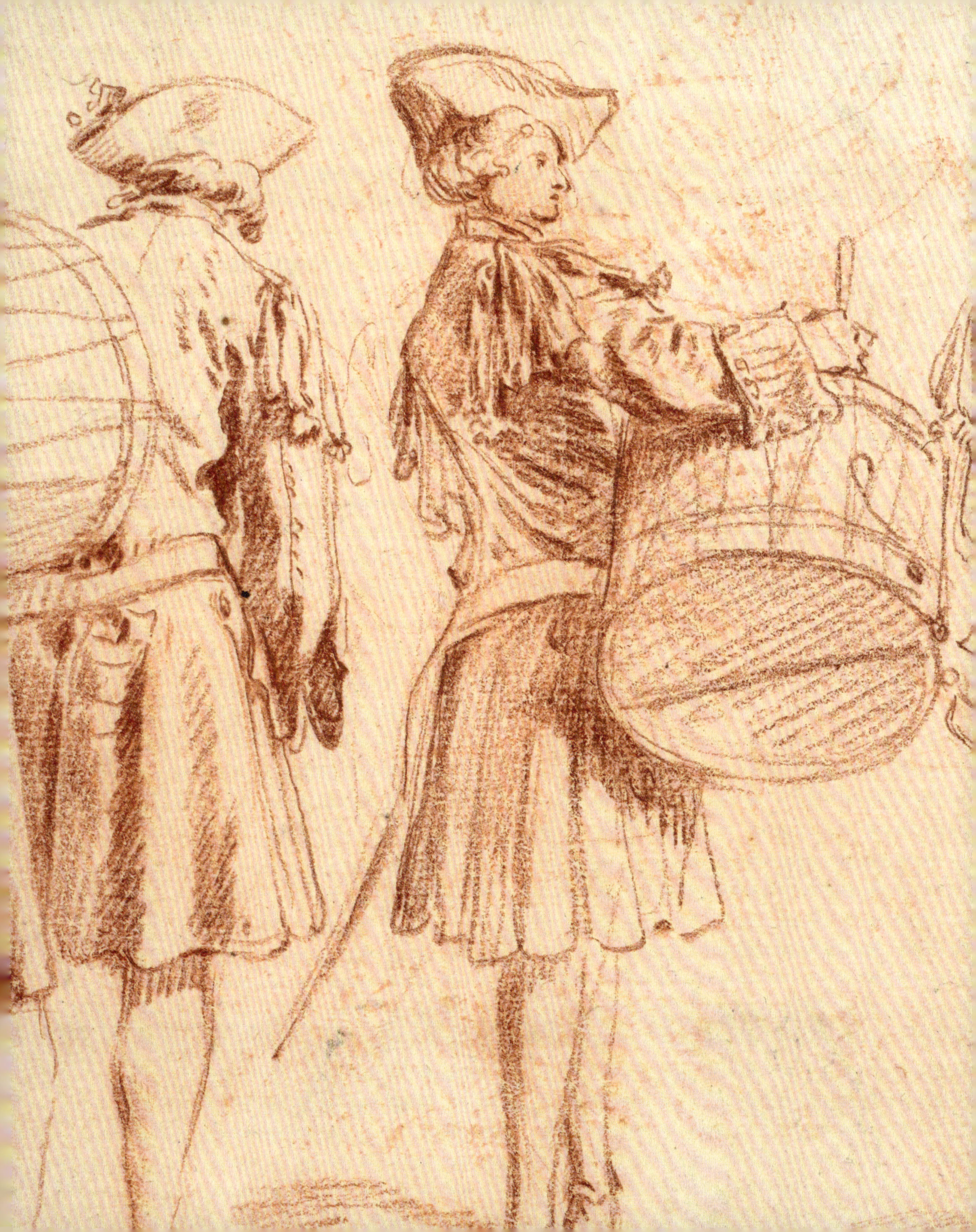

Index

Page numbers in *italics* refer to illustrations. All artworks are by Watteau unless otherwise stated.